An Introduction to Religion and Literature

Mark Knight

continuum

Continuum International Publishing Group

The Tower Building   80 Maiden Lane, Suite 704
11 York Road   New York
London SE1 7NX   NY 10038

www.continuumbooks.com

© Mark Knight 2009

British Library Cataloguing-in-Publication Data
A catalogue record for this book is available from the British Library.

ISBN 10: HB: 0-8264-9701-2
          PB: 0-8264-9702-0
ISBN 13: HB: 978-0-8264-9701-7
          PB: 978-0-8264-9702-4

Library of Congress Cataloging-in-Publication Data
Knight, Mark, 1972-
An introduction to religion and literature/Mark Knight.
    p. cm. Includes bibliographical references and index.
    ISBN 978-0-8264-9701-7 -- ISBN 978-0-8264-9702-4
    1. Religion and literature. I. Title.
    PN49.K623 2009
261.5´8--dc22   2008025540

Typeset by Newgen Imaging Systems Pvt Ltd, Chennai, India
Printed and bound in Great Britain by Cromwell Press Ltd, Trowbridge, Wiltshire

Contents

Acknowledgements

Roehampton University awarded me research leave for the second half of 2007 to work on this book and I am grateful for the time and space that this provided. I am also grateful to the staff at Continuum for their enthusiasm, helpfulness and efficiency.

All literary critics know that identifying fully the sources that influence a piece of writing is an impossible task. Aware of this, I nevertheless want to try and acknowledge those who made a positive contribution to the writing of this book. A number of people were kind enough to read one or more chapters and share their considerable wisdom with me. My thanks go to Jo Carruthers, Brian Horne, Jane Kingsley-Smith, Louise Lee, Emma Mason, Clare McManus, John Schad, and Andrew Tate. There is no doubt that this book is considerably better as a result of their input. Other individuals and interpretive communities have shaped this book in different ways, and I wish to thank the following: the Erasmus Institute 2003 summer seminar on hermeneutics, students in my undergraduate Literature and the Bible class, students on Roehampton's MA in Religion and Literature, Raynes Park Community Church, Geoffrey Hartman, Laura Peters and Russell Rook.

Writing this book has coincided with two important life events that remind me that the world of words is never too distant from the world of action. The chapter on creation was written while my wife, Jo, was pregnant with my son, Samuel. Both Jo and Samuel are living testaments to the wonderful possibilities that creation brings. The chapter on eschatology was written around the time that my friend and church leader, Nicola Garnham, passed away. Nicola taught me more than I can express here about life, death and the resurrection hope that we share. This book is dedicated to her.

Introduction

At the beginning of John Milton's *Paradise Lost* (1667) the narrator sets himself a task of considerable magnitude – an epic account of the fall of man, 'unattempted yet in prose or rhyme'; a theological justification of God's 'eternal providence'; and a detailed description of, among other things, God, the Heavenly Order and Satan.[1] It is hardly surprising that the narrator experiences increasing difficulties as the text unfolds, despite invoking the aid of the Heavenly Muse for his 'adventurous song' from the start.[2] Some of these difficulties, such as the attraction that many readers feel for Satan, are peculiar to *Paradise Lost*, as the history of Milton scholarship has shown us; others, such as the relationship between literature and the sacred material upon which it draws, are applicable to a vast array of other texts in the English literary tradition.[3] It is inevitable that the intellectual ambition and complexity of religious thought should pose challenges for literature at the same as it brings with it opportunities for new insight and understanding. One might say something similar about the effect of literature on religion: Bunyan's preface to *Pilgrim's Progress* (1678, 1684) may feel the need to anticipate the charge that 'metaphors make us blind' but, as Bunyan goes on to acknowledge, much religious dogma, at least in the Christian tradition, is mediated (rather than just illustrated) through literary forms.

The task of introducing the relationship between religion and literature is a daunting one for many reasons: all interdisciplinary study encounters difficulty as it seeks to satisfy the sometimes competing disciplinary demands of the subjects it conjoins; the boundaries of both religion and literature are notoriously wide-ranging in scope and elastic in nature; since Matthew Arnold and the emergence of English Literature as a professional subject, much has been written about the relation between religion and literature, too much to survey adequately in a book like this; and the political dimensions of belief post-9/11 render any discussion of religion as fraught as it is necessary.

The temptation to try and resolve these problems at the start of this book is considerable, yet succumbing to this temptation would obviate the possibility of considering much religion or literature before the work comes to an end.

An introduction can mean many things. In this particular case, it signals a point of entry into the study of religion and literature. *An Introduction to Religion and Literature,* as the title suggests, makes no pretence to be exhaustive or systematic; nor does it try to provide even the briefest chronological survey of the historical relation between religion and literature. Instead, the volume provides a series of linked snapshots, underlining the belief that an introduction is a starting point for the reader rather than a concluded and encyclopaedic treatise. In offering these snapshots, I am seeking to explore the extent to which religion might provide a helpful lens for thinking about literary texts. There are, of course, other equally productive ways of thinking about the relationship between religion and literature, as the extensive critical and theoretical work on the subject makes clear.[4] Most obviously, one might switch the methodology around and use literature as a lens for reading and thinking about religion. In recent years this sort of approach has generated some important theological developments, such as the rise of narrative theology, with its insistence that theological discourse is best apprehended through narrative rather than propositional statements, and an increasing interest in the reception history of the Bible, which turns to literary works, along with other sources, to uncover different ways in which sacred texts might be interpreted.[5] The value of literature to the study of religion is something that will emerge throughout this book but it is not the main focus.

Turning to religion as a lens for reading literary texts involves more than identifying religious tropes or biblical sources in literary texts, valuable though this sort of detective work can be. Religion may manifest and construct itself though literary traces but restricting the study of religion and literature in this way is as limiting as presuming that feminist literary criticism involves nothing more than the search for noteworthy representations of women in literature. To interpret literary texts from a religious perspective is to draw upon a host of theological ideas and to allow these to shape the way one thinks about the worlds that are imagined through literature. Religious thought brings with it certain ways of apprehending the whole of reality, and although the impact of reflecting on the world in the light of God is almost impossible to isolate fully, it influences both what we look for in literary texts and how we think about what we find there. A religious reading of a text is congruent at some level with virtually every branch of literary criticism and it does not have to restrict itself to subject matter typically seen as sacred; nor does a religious reading of a text have to emphasize the realm of morality as so many people seem to presume. Yet just because the interests of religion are without limit, it does not follow that the word religion is an empty signifier. Religion may mean radically different things to different people but it does not mean whatever one wants it to. If we treat religion as entirely subjective, we collapse the category altogether and do a disservice to the long history of traditions, scholars and interpretive communities that have clearly meant something specific by the word 'religion'. While religious thought is inflected with subjectivity, as is any system of thought, individual beliefs take on communal substance as they are shared, argued over, and passed down through diverse interpretive communities over time. Thus the word 'religion' is used in this book as a useful term for restoring a dimension of belief and practice that much of the modern Academy in the West, outside the work of Theology and Religious Studies departments, has tended to neglect, for a multitude of reasons. At the same time, the coherence of the term 'religion' should not mask the fact that the major belief systems associated with it – Christianity, Judaism, Islam, Sikhism, Hinduism and Buddhism – are not the same. For a start, these major world religions view the term God quite differently; to suggest that they are all talking about the same thing is to homogenize the concept of God illegitimately and ignore the extensive examinations of the term by the bodies of belief that use it. The same could be said for many other religious terms, such as creation, salvation, spirituality and the afterlife. There are, of course, significant points of convergence between different religions. Even where they disagree on substantive issues, the disagreements often have the potential for fruitful dialogue or synthesis. Yet all religions are not the same.

Faced with the diversity that religion presents us with, it is worth taking a moment to identify the belief systems that shape this particular 'introduction'. Much of the discussion in the pages that follow is shaped by Christian theology, a set of beliefs that, itself, involves considerable plurality and difference. Given that the literary material I am dealing with is from the Western tradition, there is some historical justification for the religious bias present in this book. To make too much of this, however, would be misleading – the book's focus on certain aspects of Christianity has more to do with my own areas of interest and knowledge. While this indicates a subjective approach to the explorations that follow, the concept of religious neutrality, or, for that matter, complete scholarly objectivity, is one that I reject. All critics have a religious and ideological bias, even if that bias takes the form of an agnostic attitude to the question of belief, and all critics are shaped by their environments and the material they engage with. Subjectivity does not have to preclude criticism or self-critique, nor does it have to militate against engagement with other belief systems. Parts of this book will engage closely with Jewish writers and thinkers, a decision reflecting the historic relationship between Christianity and its older sibling as well as the importance of Judaism for a number of the texts under discussion. Chapter 4 of the book will also have something to say about the world's other major Abrahamic faith, Islam, though the chapter does not pretend to offer an extended engagement with the complexities and richness of this important world religion.

This book may be shaped by religious ideas from the Christian tradition but it is not intended as a polemical piece that seeks to proselytize its readers. My desire is to open up the meaning of literary texts rather than close them down. The fact that this needs mentioning at all indicates, I fear, the extent to which an erosion of trust has made religious thought in the West subject to levels of suspicion well beyond that experienced by other systems of thought. Be that as it may, I have no interest in trying to insist that the literary texts under consideration should only be read in a religious way. Nor do I wish to 'claim' the writers I examine as 'religious'. Roland Barthes saw the death of author as a something of a victory over religious belief; I, following, Paul Ricoeur and others, see the death of the author, or at least the decline of his/her influence, as a consequence of writing per se: 'writing renders the text autonomous with respect to the intention of the author. What the text signifies no longer coincides with what the author meant . . .'[6] To think that this lack of coincidence entails a major blow to religious belief is to miss the vital point that both Christianity and Judaism are religions that are intimate with written words and the interpretive challenges they bring. Over time, the two religions have developed sophisticated and extensive resources for thinking about the relation between God and the text, and they are not necessarily committed to a naïve notion of authorial intent.[7] Our reading of literary texts is not bound by the views or beliefs of authors, a point that is liberating for religious readings of literature. G. K. Chesterton insisted, rightly, that something of the author goes into all literary creations – '[w]e have a general view of existence, whether we like it or not; it alters, or, to speak more accurately, it creates and involves everything we say or do, whether we like it not' – but no-one, including the author, is in a position to recover the extent of this involvement fully, and the public orientation of literature means that an author's belief is not the final arbiter of interpretive activity.[8] In most other literary settings, comments like this are unnecessary, but I have included them here as an antidote to the common but mistaken idea that religious readings of literature are confined to the works of religious writers. Just because Ian McEwan, to take one contemporary example, does not see himself as a religious writer, it does not follow that his fiction is incapable of producing religious readings.

The chapters that follow will consider how a religious reading of literature might be pursued. Each chapter will combine close readings of literary texts with an exploration of a particular religious idea, drawing on critical, theoretical and recent theological material as it does so. The first chapter, 'Sacred Wor(l)ds: The Doctrine of Creation and the Possible Worlds of Literature', will begin by examining the doctrine of Creation and its relation to literary creation. Linking Paul Ricoeur's idea that literary creations inaugurate new possible worlds, with a series of related theological insights, the chapter will argue that *Paradise Lost* shows us how Creation makes space for others. Having established this idea, the chapter will turn to Mary Shelley's *Frankenstein* (1818; rev. ed. 1831) and Angela Carter's *The Passion of New Eve* (1977) to consider the role of mediation and myth in opening up and enabling these new worlds. Chapter 2, 'Beings in Relation: Otherness, Personhood and the Language of the Trinity', will begin with the suggestion that the Christian doctrine of God offers a framework for structuring our understanding of the way we relate to others. The chapter will then move on to consider how this suggestion helps us make sense of the use of language by three quite different poets: John Donne, Emily Dickinson and Christina Rossetti. In Chapter 3, 'Mediating the Divine: Law, Gift and Justice', the consideration of how beings relate to one another will move to another sphere and explore the social systems that structure our mutual relations. With close attention to the Jewish idea of the Law, as well as subsequent Christian interpretations of that Law, the chapter will examine Charles Dickens's *Bleak House* (1852–3) and Franz Kafka's *The Trial* (1925). The readings developed in this chapter will build upon some of the insights emerging out of recent engagement by theologians with Jacques Derrida's work on the nature of gift and the possibility of justice. In Chapter 4, 'Interpretive Communities: Scripture, Tolerance and the People of God', Stanley Fish's work on the idea of interpretive communities will be used as a starting point for exploring the problematic interaction between tolerance and a religious commitment to the 'truths' revealed in Scripture. The discussion will centre on four literary texts that express concerns about fundamentalism, its effect on the way texts are read, and its place within a pluralistic society: George Eliot's *Silas Marner* (1861), Jeanette Winterson's *Oranges Are*

Not the Only Fruit (1985), Margaret Atwood's *The Handmaid's Tale* (1985) and Salman Rushdie's *The Satanic Verses* (1988). At stake in each of these novels is the question of how religious communities relate to the modern Western world in which they find themselves. The sense that being a stranger in the modern world can sometimes be a violent experience provides a useful route into Chapter 5, 'The Stain of Sin: Tales of Transgression in the Modern World'. This chapter seeks to rethink the Judaeo-Christian concept of sin by tracing the persistence of ideas of transgression in four literary texts from different historical epochs: William Shakespeare's *Macbeth* (1606), Samuel Taylor Coleridge's 'The Rime of the Ancient Mariner' (1798), Philip Roth's *The Human Stain* (2000), and Ian McEwan's *Atonement* (2001). Having taken the time to consider the ways in which these four texts register something of what is wrong with the world, it seems fitting to end the book by thinking about the vision of hope and a future offered by the Christian faith. Chapter 6, 'A Hope and a Future: Suffering and Redemption in Eschatological Perspective', reflects upon the way in which ideas of hope are played out in three eschatological texts from the twentieth century: George Orwell's *Nineteen Eighty-Four* (1949), Samuel Beckett's *Endgame* (1958) and Douglas Coupland's *Girlfriend in a Coma* (1998).

As the selection of texts detailed above makes clear, this book is not tied to reading literature in a particular historical context. At some level history is vital to any reading of a text, and historical context will not be discarded altogether in the discussions that follow; but if literary texts really do live on and find new readers, and if literature really does want to view itself as a discipline distinct from (though still related to) history, then there must be a way of selecting texts for a study like this, and a way of interpreting those texts, other than received notions of literary periodization. To insist on detailed historical contextualization is to presuppose a certain methodological approach to the study of English Literature, with different aims than those that motivate this work. In choosing texts to write about, I have selected texts as appropriate from across the range of English Literature. Some of the writers chosen are not English and do not strictly fit under the rubric of English Literature, but they are not unfamiliar to the syllabi of many English Literature degree programmes and I include them without apology. Other writers included here may seem surprising choices given the issues being discussed. Again, I do not apologize. What follows is *an* introduction to religion and literature, reflecting my own orientation and interests as they interact with and are shaped by the texts under discussion.

Sacred Wor(l)ds: The Doctrine of Creation and the Possible Worlds of Literature

1

The title of John Milton's *Paradise Lost* (1667) appears to give us a clear indication of the poem's subject matter and trajectory, so it is a surprise to find the prologue using pregnancy as a trope to describe the world that God brings into being. Introducing the creative work of God's Spirit, the narrator declares:

> . . . thou from the first
> Wast present, and with mighty wings outspread
> Dove-like sat'st brooding on the vast abyss
> And mad'st it pregnant . . .[1]

On one level, the reference to a period of gestation here can be explained easily by acknowledging the lyrical function of time in the account of the world given in Genesis; on another level, however, and without wishing to subject the trope to an excessively literal reading, the reference to pregnancy suggests something more extended and developmental. Not only is the nine months associated with human pregnancy more elongated than the six days used to structure Genesis 1, the birth that pregnancy results in is the start of a new life.

The way that *Paradise Lost* talks about creation discourages us from presuming that God completes his creative work in six days and urges us to reconsider the significance of day seven. Colin Gunton writes: 'The biblical notion of time as that which God gives to things for their right development is further elaborated in Genesis' depiction of God's resting on the seventh day. This appears to be a naïve way of speaking until we realize that it allows the time of creation to point forward to its fulfilment according to the purposes of God.'[2] If God rests on the seventh day, then it follows that the work of creation is ongoing. This apparently small point of detail has considerable importance, providing, as it does, a framework for seeing human activity and the salvific work of Jesus as a foreseen, intended part of the world that God brings into being. Presumably this is what Adam is thinking of towards the end of *Paradise Lost* when he declares:

> O goodness infinite, goodness immense!
> That all this good of evil shall produce,
> And evil turn to good; more wonderful
> Than that which by creation first brought forth
> Light out of darkness! . . .[3]

Within the economy of Christian systematic theology, there is an obvious benefit to reading the work of Jesus in saving the world as integral to God's plan for creation rather than as a subsequent, desperate attempt to recover an already-completed world whose perfection has been terminated abruptly. In the context of this book, a reading of creation that makes room for human activity to participate in the to-be-completed work of God helps legitimize the literary creation that Milton brings into existence in *Paradise Lost*. If creation is already complete, then it is difficult to see the work of any literary writer as more than an optional extra, an unnecessary and inadequate echo of a reality that already exists in its totality; if the work of creation is ongoing, however, then the writer can be said to partake in the creative activity of God and imagine something new.

J. Hillis Miller points out that a 'literary work is not, as many people assume, an imitation in words of some pre-existing reality but, on the contrary, it is the creation of or discovery of a new supplementary world, a metaworld, a hyper-reality. This new world is an irreplaceable addition to the already existing one.'[4] Miller's desire to think about the possible worlds of literature as something other than a static imitation is shared by Paul Ricoeur. For Ricoeur, the other worlds we encounter through literary texts, even those imagined by realist fiction, are new, by definition; yet they also possess sufficient commonality with and reference to the current world for readers to comprehend them.

Describing Ricoeur's position, Kevin Vanhoozer writes: 'Instead of viewing imaginative literature as a product of mere fancy, Ricoeur insists that . . . in the work of fiction a whole world is displayed which "condenses" reality and gathers its essentials traits into a concentrated structure or work. Fictions "remake" reality by projecting a possible world which can intersect and transform the world of the reader.'[5] Ricoeur's account of literature inaugurating alternate worlds in ways that 'disturb and rearrange our relation to reality' provides a means of making sense of the work that *Paradise Lost* is involved in.[6] By speculating on the nature of the heavenly order and its consequences for the universe, *Paradise Lost* opens our minds to see the world in new ways; in doing so, it involves itself in the ongoing work of creation.

The theological consequences of a creation that is ongoing are examined in the discussion that follows, beginning with the way that space and time make possible the multivocality that we encounter in *Paradise Lost*. Multivocality is crucial to the poem's account of creation; it leads us away from the rigid view of a despotic Creator that Stanley Fish and others have outlined in their reading of Milton's epic, and invites us to think differently about God's relationship with the world. Gunton insists that God's creative work is mediated through the world: 'Mediation denotes the way we understand one form of action – God's action – to take shape in and in relation to that which is not God; the way, that is, by which the actions of one who is creator take form in a world that is of an entirely different order from God because he made it to be so.'[7] The destructive consequences of a view of creation that fails to pay sufficient attention to this concept of mediation is the subject of the second section of this chapter, which focuses on Mary Shelley's *Frankenstein* (1818; rev. edn 1831). Although Frankenstein's account of his creative activity claims to provide an objective scientific narrative, it ignores the role that language plays in mediating our engagement with the world and fails to acknowledge the extent of its own manipulation. The result is a dark, tragic tale that leads us to reconsider the role of human interpretation in the ongoing work of creation. Recognizing the need for literary forms that convey an adequate sense of the mediated nature of creation, the final section of this chapter explores the reading of myth in Angela Carter's *The Passion of New Eve* (1977). With the help of Ricoeur, I challenge the idea that myth can only be viewed with suspicion, as a closed form of narrative that distorts our view of the world. Ricoeur shows us that myth can be the bearer of new possible worlds, a possibility that Carter's novel demonstrates clearly, despite the sceptical gloss of its author.

Creating space and time for multivocality

To find room for the new possibilities that creation bodies forth requires the boundaries and distinctions established through spatial categories. Without such vocabulary, there would be no way of talking about the division between Creator and created that is so important for Theism, nor any possibility of registering differences within creation. The importance of space in *Paradise Lost* is something that Mary Fenton is alert to in *Milton's Places of Hope: Spiritual and Political Connections of Hope with Land* (2006), where she argues that the hope expressed throughout the poem is associated with place. Even Adam's prayers, though initially described by the narrator as 'Dimensionless', are said to pass 'through heavenly doors', a reference that epitomizes the need for spatial categories when talking about religious activity.[8] Fenton's interest in geography finds support from virtually every part of the poem. It is easy to forget that the Fall takes place in a particular location, Eden, and at a certain spot within Eden, the Forbidden Tree; similarly, it is easy to miss the way in which the hope that Adam and Eve leave Paradise with is marked by spatial vocabulary:

> The world was all before them, where to choose
> Their place of rest, and providence their guide:
> They hand in hand their wandering steps and slow,
> Through Eden took their solitary way.[9]

The poem's attention to spatial language is important for two reasons: first, it allows Milton to make room for others so that they are not simply an extension of God; second, it affirms the poem's commitment to material creation, avoiding the Platonic tendency to try and escape the earthly at every opportunity.

Paradise Lost is not immune to the influence of Plato in the world it discloses. According to Plato, the Divine exists as a perfect, immaterial and unchanging Ideal, outside time and space. The influence of Neo-Platonic philosophy on the development of much early Christian theology meant that in many circles, including those to which Milton's Puritan theology can be traced, the idea of a Divine Being outside time and space became synonymous with the biblical idea of a God who brings time and space into being.[10] In *Paradise Lost* this conflation becomes deeply problematic on occasion and threatens to overwhelm the poem's sense that material beings might possess a freedom that is a vital component of the created universe. As numerous readers have observed, many of the direct references in the poem to God the Father depict a rigid and unbending being whose absolute authority precludes the possibility of divine love for the world. Reflecting on the limits of God's concern for others in the poem, Stanley Fish is adamant that 'Paradise Lost is full of moments . . . that reassert the power of omnipotence, moments that slam the door shut on those differences that would, if they were allowed a genuine existence, threaten the homogeneity of a monistic universe'. Fish goes on to insist how overwhelming the effect of Milton's monistic view of God can be: 'The entire poem on every level – stylistic, thematic, narrative – is an act of vigilance in which any effort, large or small, to escape its totalizing sway is detected and then contained.'[11]

When it comes to describing God in On Christian Doctrine, Milton finds it impossible to detach himself from this monistic viewpoint and he struggles to accept the orthodox Christian doctrine of the Trinity, with its vision of three Divine persons in perfect and eternal communion.[12] Yet the influence of this narrowly monistic vision of God in Paradise Lost is not as uncontested as Fish suggests. The problems surrounding God's inflexibility and need for control, real as they are at several points in the poem, are offset by Milton's doctrine of creation and his commitment to the idea that God makes a world with room for others. The range of theological ideas at work in Paradise Lost may explain why the poem encourages the plurality of critical readings that it does. Geoffrey Hartman, to take one example, reads 'God's omnipotent knowledge that the creation will outlive death and sin' as a 'counterplot' rather than the totalizing and overt theological vision described by Fish, while Harold Fisch, another influential critic, views the hermeneutic governing Paradise Lost as one that actively encourages a covenant or dialogue between author and reader.[13]

The readings offered by Hartman and Fisch share the sense that a religious account of Paradise Lost might find space for other perspectives. To appreciate the implications of this within the framework of Christian theology, it is useful to draw a parallel with the thought that Oliver Davies offers in The Creativity of God: World, Eucharist, Reason (2004): 'The creation of the world has something about it which is like the generation of a text. The scriptural record presupposes the priority of the voice, and of divine speaking, which calls all things into existence. It is the voice of God, or the triadic speaking of the divine Trinity . . . Moreover, the scriptural text itself, of both Old and

New Testaments, exhibits signs of the human voice answering to the divine voice.' Davies goes on to describe some of the forms that this human answering takes: 'hymnic, celebratory and testamentary passages'.[14] Given the presence of such forms in the Bible, it is unsurprising that *Paradise Lost* should adopt them in the way that it does. Reading the hymns in Milton's poem as a response to the voice of God rather than a direct continuation of that voice is central to the argument that Regina Schwartz proposes in *Remembering and Repeating: Biblical Creation in Paradise Lost* (1988). Starting with the notion that *Paradise Lost* does not 'depict the cosmic creation as a privileged beginning, a single event that occurred once-upon-a-time and for all time', Schwartz considers how the text continually seeks ways of reiterating its origins in new ways.[15] To illustrate the point, she argues that 'in this poem of many choices' we find 'two narratives of loss. Satan's fall is a myth of loss leading only to continual renunciation and relapse; Adam's fall is a myth of loss leading to repentance and recovery'.[16] According to Schwartz, the second of these two narratives can be seen through the poem's affinity with hymns – Adam and Eve punctuate their existence with songs of praise and these rituals serve to remind them of their contingency on God, the Creator and Sustainer of all things.

In contrast, Fish thinks that the hymns in *Paradise Lost* are just like the other songs that issue forth from the heavenly choir: mere echoes of an unalterable and totalizing Divine presence. Explaining that 'in a celestial song, no one can be said to be doing the singing; rather, everyone is sung by an informing presence whose precedence is endlessly and involuntarily declared', Fish believes that nothing can get beyond the 'omnific word' of God: the 'moment the omnific word emerges in the text, it renders beside the point the verbal manoeuvrings of the poem's other agents'.[17] Despite its rhetorical force, Fish's argument fails to acknowledge that the word 'omnific', like every other word used in *Paradise Lost*, is shaped by the vocabulary with which it co-exists. There are musical allusions throughout the poem which support the reading developed by Schwartz and indicate how God's creation makes more room for others than Fish is prepared to admit. The grammar of music offers significant theological resources for our view of creation, as Jeremy Begbie explains: 'Music offers a particular form of participation in the world's temporality and in so doing . . . it has a distinctive capacity to elicit something of the nature of this temporality and our involvement with it . . .'[18] Musical temporality signals, among other things, the inevitability of change and the mutual relationship of contingency and constraint that structures both music and human freedom.[19]

Taking a lead from Begbie's argument, we can see how the songs of praise that sound in *Paradise Lost* reveal the space opened up by creation for a multiplicity of voices to express their song together. Initially, space for different perspectives seems to be a characteristic of Pandemonium rather than Paradise. Describing the former, the first two books of *Paradise Lost* conjure up the image of a democratic gathering where a range of voices can be heard. In hindsight, however, Satan's verbal manipulation of Eve – 'in her ears the sound / Yet rung of his persuasive words' – mirrors his earlier use of rhetoric to get his own way in Pandemonium: although it is Beelzebub who pleads 'his devilish counsel' so persuasively, his counsel is said to have been 'first devised / By Satan, and in part proposed'.[20] Pandemonium may appear to construct a space for different voices but its democratic appearance dissipates by the end of the poem and is shown for what it really is, a 'dismal *universal* hiss' [italics mine].[21] In contrast, the voices that combine to express God's praise are said to be a 'charming symphony'; '[m]elodious' in their harmony.[22] The musical terms employed here register the presence of more than one voice. While Fish is unable to hear more than 'one note' in the celestial song of praise described in book IV of *Paradise Lost*, the language I have just drawn attention to suggests a plurality of notes and points to an underlying multivocality in Milton's account of creation.[23] A symphony may follow a prescribed score and be conducted by one person but it requires a variety of musicians to play their parts for the music to come to life. As *Paradise Lost* frequently reminds its readers, freedom is given to beings so that they may choose to involve themselves in the harmonious song intended for creation. It is this freedom that enables the musical diversity of the hymns sung by Adam and Eve:

> In various style, for neither various style
> Nor holy rapture wanted they to praise
> Their Maker, in fit strains pronounced or sung
> Unmeditated, such prompt eloquence
> Flowed from their lips, in prose or numerous verse,[24]

Mediated creation and the dark materials of language[25]

Although the creation imagined in *Paradise Lost* makes space for a harmonious multivocality, the harmony is not enforced and the narrative of the poem acknowledges the real difficulties of holding together the interests of the one and the many. Voices are free to say what they want and the sound they bring forth can vary from the 'odious din of war' to hymns of praise.[26] Disharmony is an ever-present possibility in a world that grants agents the freedom to choose for themselves, and the challenge of accommodating multivocality is considerable. Recognizing this, Gunton emphasizes the way in which God's activity is mediated through the world that he brings into existence and sustains by his Spirit: 'Against both ancient interpretation and modern distortion, an adequate notion of the mediation of creation enables us to hold together without strain the sheer multiplicity and variety of creation within the generous embrace of creation's God.'[27] Talk of the mediated quality of creation recognizes a distance between God and the world that he makes. Christian theologians do not think that creation gives us immediate access to the divine because, unlike pantheism, Christian theism insists that the creation is distinct from its Creator. The concept of mediation helps us appreciate how God finds room for and stays in relation with that which is foreign to His infinite and transcendent Being: 'The world is not simply a function of God's action, though that remains in the centre, but that action creates something that has its own unique and particular freedom to be.'[28] Significantly, Gunton does not think that the notion of a mediated creation is at odds with *creatio ex nihilo*, the traditional Christian idea that God creates the world out of nothing; rather, he believes that having brought the world into existence, God's involvement with it is pervasive. The idea that God can be present fully in something other than himself is developed further through the doctrine of the Incarnation: Christ, the one who is said to bring the world into existence, is also said to join the world to God through his ontological status as fully human, fully God and fully both.

Given that the divinity of Jesus was something Milton struggled to accept, it is hardly surprising that the body of thought permeating his understanding of creation is less coherent than the systematic account of Christian theology presented by Gunton. In Milton's theology, the emphasis on a God who creates the world out of pre-existing 'dark materials' sits uneasily alongside the belief that God is the starting point of everything.[29] Addressing this awkwardness, C. A. Patrides tell us that while Milton denied the doctrine of *creatio ex nihilo*, 'in his theological treatise explicitly, and in *Paradise Lost* implicitly, since chaos is nowhere said to have created of "nothyng"', he rejected the 'external-co-existence of God and the rude pristine matter, for he had no wish to become the prey of dualism. He claimed instead that chaos "originated from God at some particular time", so that ultimately all things derive their existence from God (*omnia ex Deo*).'[30] Milton's reluctance to accept *creatio ex nihilo* seems to be motivated less by a rejection of the doctrine per se and more by a desire to focus attention on the role of mediation in creation. What is important for Milton is the continuity between new life and pre-existing matter. Whether or not there is a hint of theological confusion here, the position Milton ends up with is not so different from the emphasis of Genesis 1. Acknowledging God as the Creator of all matter, Genesis 1 focuses on how God forms this world out of pre-existing materials, thereby opening up space for human beings to continue to participate in its development.

Much of the human activity described in *Paradise Lost* is destructive rather than developmental. Michael epitomizes this when tells Adam of the future descendents who will live with the consequences of Adam and Eve's disobedience: 'Doubt not but that sin / Will reign among them . . .'[31] A similarly bleak assessment of human participation in creation dominates the narrative of *Frankenstein*. One of the contributing factors to the destructive events that ensue in Shelley's novel is Victor Frankenstein's mistaken belief that he has unmediated access to and full control over all other elements in the world. Despite his scientific training and the fact that he is piecing together 'dark materials' rather than creating something from nothing, Frankenstein is remarkably reticent to admit the mediatory nature of that which he shapes. When he does refer to it, he seems perturbed, as though it interrupts his dream of authoring a new, unmediated reality that is under his complete control. His account of visiting 'charnel-houses' to gather materials is punctuated by negative descriptions of disturbing the 'secrets of the human frame' with 'profane' fingers and assembling the monster in a 'workshop of filthy creation'.[32] Elsewhere in the novel, he refuses to explain to Robert Walton the scientific basis on which he will finally animate the assembled creation. When the monster does eventually come to life, Frankenstein deflects his duty of care by finding only bad things to say about the creature he has brought into the world. This cumulative failure to accept the mediatory is interpreted by Alan Rauch in terms of the novel's concern with the social context of knowledge and Frankenstein's failure to grasp this sociality: 'The solitude and seclusion that Frankenstein seems to require for his work can result only in knowledge that can have neither context nor value. For Mary Shelley, this is . . . the most frightening aspect of her novel.'[33] As Rauch goes on to detail, Frankenstein's seclusion leads to one catastrophe after another, from his inability to see why 'he owes the creature companionship' to his failure to consider whether his scientific innovations might be used in other ways, to re-animate those who die in the novel, for example.[34]

A refusal of the mediatory is also evident in Frankenstein's disingenuous and evasive confessional narrative. He warns Walton that the monster 'is eloquent and persuasive; and once his words had even power over my heart; but trust him not', yet takes full advantage of Walton's fascination with his own 'unparalleled eloquence' to construct a narrative in which it is the monster, rather than his creator, who is seen to be at fault.[35] In an effort to offset the evasions of Frankenstein's account, Shelley employs a complex structure that draws attention to the way in which the truth of what has occurred is subject to the mediation of different narrators and forms. For Maureen McLane, this mediatory quality is especially apparent in the textual fabric of the novel:

> The letter proliferates in *Frankenstein*. Through this technology of the letter Shelley inscribes a network connecting literacy, literature . . . and epistolary form . . . Written marks propel the hauntings and recognitions of the novel: the monster constellates his identity crisis after he reads Victor's old labnotes, marks made by the hands that made him. The monster leads Victor on a global chase, perpetually taunting his maker with the bitterly eloquent sentences he leaves on the trees . . . These lettered practices – taking labnotes, reading Milton, learning Greek (Victor) or French (monster) – all point to a condition of made mediation. The intervention of the letter confounds any dream of *im-mediacy*.[36]

One of the aspects of *Frankenstein* where the intervention of the letter is most apparent is the range of texts that shape the monster's development. In *Reading Genesis in the Long Eighteenth Century: From Milton to Mary Shelley* (2006), Ana Acosta pays careful attention to the different books the monster reads – the texts he names explicitly (Volney's *Ruins of Empire*, Goethe's *Sorrows of Werter*, a volume of Plutarch's *Lives*, and *Paradise Lost*), the text he mentions without fully disclosing (Frankenstein's laboratory notes), and the texts he refers to implicitly (such as Genesis).[37] Acosta concludes that Milton's religious epic is given priority in this chain of textual inheritance: 'The creature thus receives his second version of origin after the "Old Testament" history of Volney, a new version that he chooses over the latter for its sublimity. Moreover, he will choose Milton's origin over that of his creator, the true Enlightenment utopia of the conquest of death recorded in Victor Frankenstein's notes.'[38] Accounting for this preference for a religious myth of origins, Acosta tells us that 'Shelley's reinsertion of opaqueness into Enlightenment clarity constitutes the ideological core of the novel'.[39] While Acosta's reading is persuasive and more nuanced than my brief summary can hope to show here, it is not certain that the hierarchy of sources in *Frankenstein* can be resolved so easily. If a critique of Enlightenment values is seen as constituting the core of the novel, then we must remember that this critique emerges, at least in part, from Frankenstein's Enlightenment perspective and it should therefore be treated with a degree of suspicion. Furthermore, on looking closely at what Frankenstein has to say, it is impossible to sustain a firm division between transparent Enlightenment values and Milton's opaque religious account of mythic origins. In the same way that the monster's vocabulary internalizes the language of *Paradise Lost*, so too does Frankenstein's. Towards the end of his narrative Frankenstein refers to the monster in a manner strongly echoing Milton's description of Satan whispering into the ear of Eve: 'I was answered through the stillness of night by a loud and fiendish laugh. It rung on my ears long and heavily; the mountains re-echoed it, and I felt as if all hell surrounded me with mockery and laughter . . . The laughter died away; when a well-known and abhorred voice, apparently close to my ear, addressed me in an audible whisper . . .'[40] Such textual echoes make it impossible to determine definitively whether Frankenstein's narrative is in opposition to religious myth or a continuation of it.

The difficulty for the reader of delineating the mediatory influences at work in Shelley's novel urges some level of sympathy with Frankenstein's failure to acknowledge the myriad of ways in which he manipulates language. At the root of this sympathy is the larger interpretive dilemma faced by all readers, of never being able to stand wholly outside the worlds they judge. Reflecting on the fear in *Frankenstein* that 'to tell a story eloquently is to exercise a power never securely distinct from violence, that persuasion is just a disguised form of domination', Peter Garrett warns that '[t]he same logic holds for our own response: if we question and try to replace the demonic version of the creature that Frankenstein constructs, we inevitably enter into a comparable struggle for control'.[41] Frankenstein's inadequate narrative forces the reader to take on responsibility for recovering and interpreting the dialogic traces of language that connect together the events of the novel and give meaning to the monster's existence, yet there is no uncontaminated position from which we might judge the characters in the novel. In a world that is far from harmonious, the forces that shape Frankenstein shape us, at least to some extent, and our reading risks perpetuating the same violent misreading imposed by Frankenstein.[42] While the same thing might be said of our reading of any literary text, *Frankenstein's* reworking of Milton's version of the Genesis story intensifies our awareness of being compromised readers in a world that is fallen. The account of Eden provided by Genesis is written in hindsight, and the problem of trying to describe perfection from the perspective of imperfection is one that Milton was all too familiar with. This is the basis for Stanley Fish's famous argument in *Surprised by Sin* (1967) that the primary intent of Milton's epic tale was to concentrate attention on our fallen reading of Paradise and the creatures that inhabit it. *Frankenstein* may not have the same homiletic focus as *Paradise Lost* but it does inculcate the reader in the same fallen world. Neither Frankenstein nor those who read his narrative are blameless – '[w]e are individually responsible for what we do, unless so constrained physically or by sickness that our actions are no longer our own' – but, as Gunton goes on to make clear in his subsequent comments on the fallen state we find ourselves in: 'The plight of the individual is that he or she . . . adopt, inevitably but voluntarily, the inheritance that we have received. Sin is a social reality because that inheritance is mediated to us by our history and by the social setting in which our lives take shape.'[43]

The only sensible response to the interpretive dilemma that confronts us in *Frankenstein*, Garrett tells us, is to acknowledge that all stories and utterances 'are never wholly our own; they can exist only in and through their dialogical relations with their surroundings, with the discourses that precede, follow, and penetrate them'.[44] It is a response that avoids the mistake made by Frankenstein, of thinking that a new chapter might be written without reference to anything or anyone else, and a response that points to the creative potential of the mediatory. If a Christian understanding of the Fall reminds us that nothing stands outside the sinful social settings we participate in, then a Christian doctrine of creation insists that is only through some level of mediation between God and those he has made that the world can be all that it was intended to be. The mediation that is required can be thought about in terms of reading, and it is this metaphor that Davies turns to in offering the following observation:

> Human beings are created as interpreters of the creation, in the fullest sense possible. Structured by and within language . . . [w]e constantly re-engage with the world by multiple acts of 'reading' the world and our place in the world, in a changing flux of localities, temporalities, languages, memories and relations. What these processes of 'reading' lead us to understand, therefore, is that the world is the domain of a continuing divine creativity which finds expression also within ourselves, in our understandings of and interactions with the world.[45]

Breathing new life into myth

Our re-engagement with the world through reading is shaped and enabled by the forms in which the story of the world is told. Form does not precede reading as such but exists in a mutually dependent relationship with it, so that our assessment of the literary forms that are passed down to us is inseparable from an active consideration of the human interpretation that shapes all textual inheritance. This understanding of a dynamic relationship between form and interpretation is evident in the hermeneutical framework we find in the work of Ricoeur. Reflecting on the forms that mediate our interpretation of the world, Ricoeur draws on Aristotle's work in the *Poetics* and considers the Greek root '*muthos* . . . which signifies both fable (in the sense of an imaginary story) and plot (in the sense of a well constructed story).'[46] To understand how myths structure and narrate our experiences, Ricoeur uses the concept of 'emplotment . . . the common work of the text and the reader . . . [I]t is the *act of reading* which completes the work, transforming it into a *guide* for reading, with its zones of indeterminacy, its latent wealth of interpretation, its power of being reinterpreted in new ways in new historical contexts.'[47] The new interpretations that myth begets are apparent when we turn to the reception of the highly condensed forms of narrative found in the Bible. While biblical forms vary, from legal discourse to lamentation, they share a mythic quality that tells the story of the world in a way that precipitates and requires new interpretations. This quality explains the midrashic reading that is so important for the Jewish interpretive tradition, as well as the willingness of Jesus and Paul to create new stories from the Hebrew Scriptures.[48] The fertility of the mythic also helps explain the use of biblical tropes and references in works across the English literary tradition, from *Paradise Lost* to Julian Barnes's *A History of the World in 10 ½ Chapters* (1989) and Jim Crace's *Quarantine* (1997). Like the account of creation described in Genesis, the literary creativity of the Bible brings with it an afterlife that exceeds every effort to contain its form and meaning. As Harold Fisch tells us in *New Stories for Old: Biblical Patterns and the Novel* (1998), 'what is valued is not only the story, but the ongoing life of the story, including the potentiality for change inherent in the process of recapitulation.'[49]

Declaring herself to be in the 'demythologising business', Carter is suspicious about the capacity of religious myths to encourage new readings.[50] Commenting in *The Sadeian Woman* (1979) on the function of myth and its consequences for feminism, Carter details her concerns about the form's imaginative fallout and lack of creativity:

> If women allow themselves to be consoled for their culturally determined lack of access to the modes of intellectual debate by the invocation of hypothetical great goddesses, they are simply flattering themselves into submission (a technique

> often used on them by men). All the mythic versions of women, from the myth of the redeeming purity of the virgin to that of the healing, reconciling mother, are consolatory nonsenses; and consolatory nonsense seems to me a fair definition of myth, anyway. Mother goddesses are just as silly a notion as father gods.[51]

It is easy to understand the reasons for this critique. Making a comparison between Carter's understanding of myth and the idea of performativity outlined by Judith Butler, Sarah Henstra notes the problem of 'a discourse so culturally invested with performative power that it overtakes and stands in for other renderings'.[52] Where myths organize our perception of the world in a way that prevents closer investigation and critique, the consequences can be disturbing. This is the reason, explains Carter, for the 'anti-mythic novel' she wrote 'in 1977, *The Passion of New Eve* – I conceived it as a feminist tract about the social creation of femininity'.[53] In the first part of the novel, the myth of Tristessa is used by Evelyn to justify his abusive behaviour. Later on, having perpetuated similar abuses under the guise of myth, the great goddess, Mother, is said to have 'voluntarily resigned from the god-head, for the time being. When she found she could not make time stand still, she suffered a kind of . . . nervous breakdown.'[54] Developing Roland Barthes's famous declaration that 'the very principle of myth' is its transformation of 'history into nature', Carter's narrative continually alerts us to the temporality and construction that myth can sometimes suspend and ignore.[55] In the case of the violent figure of Zero, the narrator reminds us, with more than a hint of irony, that 'his myth depended on their conviction; a god-head, however shabby, needs believers to maintain his credibility'.[56]

The possibilities that myth can be perverted means, as Ricoeur observes, that 'we can no longer approach myth at the level of *naiveté* . . . This is so not only because it expresses itself primarily through a particular apportioning of power functions . . . but also because several of its recurrent forms have become deviant and dangerous, for example, the myth of absolute power (fascism) and the myth of the sacrificial scapegoat (anti-Semitism and racism).'[57] Although the sort of critique that Carter offers in *The Passion of New Eve* is both necessary and astute, there is more to myth than a hermeneutic of suspicion might allow for: 'Myth is an ideological function. But it is also more than that. Once a hermeneutics of suspicion has unmasked the alienating role of myth as an agency of ideological conformism, there remains the task of a positive interpretation.'[58] For Ricoeur, a positive interpretation of myth involves recognizing the liberation that comes with the symbolic and expansive account of the world that myth narrates: 'Poetry and myth are not just nostalgia for some forgotten world. They constitute a disclosure of unprecedented worlds, an opening on to other *possible* worlds which transcend the established limits of our *actual* world.'[59]

The extent to which myth, properly critiqued, can yield, new supplementary readings is evident throughout *The Passion of New Eve*, despite its author's demythologizing intent. Myths are destructive in the novel when they are hermetically sealed: physically and spatially, in the case of Beulah, where the manufactured world involves a series of oppressive labyrinths and surgical procedures; linguistically, in the case of Zero, who does not permit his harem to speak human words and who perverts the idea of 'mediation' by subjecting the women to his phallic 'instrument'; and culturally, in the case of the so(u)ldier boys of the religious militia, whose fundamentalist beliefs prevent any response to cultural difference other than violence.[60] Yet many of the myths that feature in the novel are not sealed off and do not result in destruction. A case in point is the recurring reference to the desert, a symbol that evokes contemporary myths of America and older myths from the Bible. Commenting on Carter's use of the shifting expanse of the desert, Sarah Gamble notes that '[i]n *The Passion of New Eve*, the desert is the place of death, transformation and of simulation taken to the ultimate degree'.[61] Like the desert, other mythic references in the novel refuse to be contained. The fusing together of such references in playful and open-ended ways affirms the ability of the mythic to generate new readings without closing meaning down. Despite what one might think when looking at the limited number of themes dominating much of the criticism on the novel, Carter's book is extremely rich and indeterminate in the readings it produces. The title – with its allusion to, among other things, the final hours of Jesus's life, the character of Eve in Genesis, love and desire, and the dawn of a new epoch – offers one obvious example; another example might be found in the ambiguous ending, which is heavily reliant on the mythic. It is difficult to agree with Gamble's assessment that the ending of the novel purges myth through the discovery 'that Mother is no more than "a figure of speech"'.[62] Writers and readers of myth are usually profoundly aware of the figures of speech employed; the appeal of the form lies in its ability to use figurative language to narrate the world in expansive ways. It is far from clear that the ending to *The Passion of New Eve* exemplifies a transparent case of demythologizing. The novel ends with a multiplicity of mythic overtones, as Evelyn/Eve borrows a skittle to leave American by water, with the invocation: 'Ocean, ocean, mother of mysteries, bear me to the place of birth'.[63] Evelyn/Eve's previous experience as an academic literary critic makes it hard to accept that the proliferation of mythic references at the end of the novel is accidental or without significance, and his/her firm belief that he/she is pregnant as a result of all that has occurred means that the mythic becomes the bearer of new possible worlds.

A further example of the reproductive capacity of myth can be seen through the figure of Tristessa. While much of the novel is given over to critiquing the myth of Tristessa, the myth is transformed in the latter stages of the novel through one of the many biblical allusions that Carter includes. Having escaped Zero's violent attempt to erase a threat he perceives to be embodied in the Hollywood icon, the mythic figure of Tristessa is transfigured into 'a mad, old man with long, white hair like Ezekiel'.[64] The narrative continues: 'He ran a few places in the yielding sand, then flung back his head and raised his arms to heaven in the attitude of an Old Testament prophet interceding with his maker.'[65] Tristessa's prophetic intercession leads to a new period in her/his relationship with Evelyn/Eve, and the two begin a passionate if short-lived relationship in which genuine love seems to exist. The reference to Ezekiel is more than just a general reference to the prophetic, however. In addition to influencing our interpretation of Evelyn's/Eve's subsequent cry 'Eat me. Consume me' – the Eucharistic overtone of the cry builds on the image in chapter 3 of the book of Ezekiel, where God's servant is instructed to eat the word of God – the reference to this particular prophet from the Hebrew Bible calls to mind one of the most famous passages in the book of Ezekiel.[66] Chapter 37 finds the biblical prophet prophesying to a valley of dry bones and seeing them come to life.[67] Something similar takes place in *The Passion of New Eve*. Having previously overseen a waxwork collection described by Evelyn/Eve as an 'ingenious simulacra of corpses', without breath or bone structure, Tristessa/Ezekiel prompts a new physical awareness in Evelyn/Eve, who, after hearing the prophet speak, starts to appreciate the sexual possibilities of being a 'man-made masterpiece of skin and bone, the technological Eve in person'.[68]

The new life experienced by Evelyn/Eve illustrates Ricoeur's claim that '[i]t is by an understanding of the worlds, actual and possible, opened by language that we may arrive at a better understanding of ourselves'.[69] Evelyn/Eve's better understanding is not a final understanding though, hence his/her ongoing struggle to 'find words the equivalent of this mute speech of flesh as we folded ourselves within a single self in the desert'.[70] It is in full recognition of the limits of language that myth narrates events in the open-ended way that it does. Far from closing down the meaning of Carter's novel, the language of myth produces an overwhelming set of interpretive possibilities that transports the reader into new worlds. The infinite possibility of the mythic is one of the reasons why Frankenstein's monster describes the acquisition of language, rather than his creator's scientific knowledge, as a 'godlike science'.[71] What the monster realizes, like the myriad of writers who come before and after him, is that the ability of the story-teller to use language to plot new worlds echoes the creative work of God in speaking this world into being. The world narrated by the book of Genesis comes to us incomplete, waiting to be read, and pregnant with new possibilities – it provides writers such as Milton, Shelley and Carter with all the time and space they need to reanimate old myths and create new ways of seeing the universe.

Beings in Relation: Otherness, Personhood and the Language of the Trinity

Beginning with a concept of Creation that makes room for others to co-exist with God and participate in his creative activity, Chapter 1 emphasized the importance of the mediatory within the Christian understanding of Creation. As the chapter went on to observe, religious myth constitutes a rich form of literary mediation, with an inexhaustible capacity for begetting new narratives. Because of their involvement in God's creative activity, religious myths have an afterlife that brings with it space for other texts to continue the open-ended stories of their predecessors and narrate the story of the world in new ways. The relation between these narratives can sometimes be difficult, as Chapter 1 acknowledged, and much has been written by other scholars on the theological contribution to questions of intertextuality, canonicity and textual inheritance.[1] One of the issues at stake is how the relation between creator and creation is to be understood. The focus of this chapter – how beings (human and otherwise) relate to one another – follows on from matters raised in Chapter 1. A developed theology of creation may allow for ongoing creativity and a plurality of interpretive possibilities among those who inhabit the universe, but the question of how beings relate to God and to one another remains complex. Our history is punctuated with accounts of the violence that ensues when the purposes of individuals conflict, and the biblical narratives are full of instances where the efforts of an individual to assert his/her will over another erodes a proper recognition of Otherness, the quality that marks our difference from someone else. Establishing a framework in which individual desires might be accommodated and understood in a mutually constructive way is important for religion, as it is for any system of thought that seeks to say something about the relationship between beings.

There are considerable resources for understanding the relation between beings in the Christian doctrine of the Trinity, a doctrine articulated by the early Church in an attempt to formalize and make sense of the biblical accounts of the relation between Father, Son and Spirit. Over the course of this chapter, I will draw on the insights of several contemporary theologians who pay special attention to the Trinity in their work, and use them to reflect on some of the relational elements that we encounter in the poetry of John Donne, Emily Dickinson and Christina Rossetti. The religious interests of Donne and Rossetti are more closely tied to Christian theology than those of Dickinson but the poetry of all three writers lends itself to a trinitarian reading. After detailing the contribution that a trinitarian perspective can make to our view of the relation between beings, and following an exploration of the presence of associated ideas of personhood and language in the work of Donne and Dickinson, the chapter will conclude with a discussion of Rossetti's 'Goblin Market' (1862). The close attention Rossetti's poem pays to Communion, a Christian sacramental tradition that has also been described as a Love Feast, supplies a useful opportunity for bringing together some of the threads adumbrated in the chapter and reflecting further on the way in which Christian theology views the relation between beings. Communion's formal properties also provide a useful introduction to points developed in Chapter 3; however, rather than getting carried away with the structural relations that shape the rest of this book, I want to begin with two tropes that Dickinson and Donne employ to describe the relationship between God and those he has created: fumbling and ravishment. The sexual association of both words points to an embodied expression of personal desire, one that highlights the genuine attempt being made by both poets to engage with the challenges faced by different beings as they seek to relate to one another.

Dickinson's reference to fumbling can be found at the start of poem #315.[2] The poem is worth quoting in full, if only to acknowledge where the fumbling leads:

He fumbles at your Soul
As Players at the Keys

Before they drop full Music on –
He stuns you by degrees –
Prepares your brittle Nature
For the Ethereal Blow
By fainter Hammers – further heard –
Then nearer – Then so slow
Your Breath has time to straighten –
Your Brain – to bubble Cool –
Deals – One – imperial – Thunderbolt –
That scalps your naked soul –

When Winds take Forests in their Paws –
The Universe – is still –

There is more than enough religious vocabulary here to persuade readers that the unnamed figure at the start of the poem can be read as Divine; yet the refusal to name God directly also signals caution, both for those making claims about how the poem might be read and in the mind of the unnamed figure who begins by fumbling tentatively. Unlike the clumsier contact ('Paws') of an impersonal, omnipotent force ('Wind') that impresses itself on the universe and brings the alternate worlds of others to a premature end, the touch of the personal God referred to at the start proceeds hesitantly, at least at first, showing some recognition of the implications of extending influence to another. Ultimately, of course, the divine influence brings about a wounding effect on the person concerned, even if the violence of scalping is mitigated in part by the reference to the soul, traditionally seen as immortal, rather than a fragile, temporal body. The notion that one's influence might register some sort of lasting effect on another is not entirely alien to a constructive understanding of the relation between beings. Hélène Cixous insists that the ability of others to scalp or wound us through their words is a valuable quality; she quotes from a letter by Franz Kafka, written to his friend Pollak in 1904, to reinforce her point: 'I think we ought to only read the kind of books that wound and stab us. If the book we are reading doesn't wake us up with a blow on the head, what are we reading it for? . . . [W]e need the books that affect us like a disaster, that grieve us deeply, like the death of someone we loved more than ourselves . . .'[3]

In common with the rest of Dickinson's oeuvre, poem #315 invites readings that acknowledge minute details, not dogmatic readings that resort to reductive and clumsy interpretations. Responding to this invitation appropriately is easier said than done, but it is important to recognize that, like the music the poem opens with, the movements and allusions of this work are delicate and slight. Dickinson's poetry is full of suggestions that affect our thinking in subtle ways. It would be easy to miss the hint of a divine communion of persons signalled by Dickinson's choice of the word players, rather than player, as a simile for the divine author who fumbles at our soul. This is a pertinent example because the plural form that Dickinson uses directs our reading of the divine presence in the poem. When it comes to Donne's poem, 'Batter my heart, three-personed God', the reference to the Trinity is explicit from the start. The rest of Donne's poem continues in a similar vein:

> Batter my heart, three-personed God; for, you
> As yet but knock, breathe, shine, and seek to mend;
> That I may rise, and stand, o'erthrow me, and bend
> Your force, to break, blow, burn, and make me new.
> I, like a usurped town, to another due,
> Labour to admit you, but oh, to no end,
> Reason your viceroy in me, me should defend,
> But is captived, and proves weak or untrue,
> Yet dearly'I love you, and would be loved fain,
> But am betrothed unto your enemy,
> Divorce me, untie, or break that knot again
> Take me to you, imprison me, for I
> Except you enthral me, never shall be free,
> Nor ever chaste, except you ravish me.[4]

While Donne's holy sonnet is a rich and multidimensional piece of writing, the forcefulness of its imagery, with its references to assault and rape, has tended to dominate the attention of those who read it. Some critics have found it hard to rid themselves of the suspicion that the view espoused by the speaker of the poem ventriloquizes Donne's own attitude to women, while others have struggled to entertain the possibility that the triune God described in the poem might be opposed to the violent imagination of the speaker, not responsible for it.[5] It is easy to see why the violence of the poem can obscure literary and theological subtleties, and it is intriguing to see how this has led to recent interventions by two theologians, Gerald O'Collins and Sarah Coakley. In quite different ways, O'Collins and Coakley have sought to restore an appreciation of the poem's engagement with religious thought by highlighting the significance of the doctrine of the Trinity.[6]

Whereas O'Collins offers a straightforward and sometimes uncritical theological explication of the poem, Coakley's discussion begins by acknowledging the problems generated by the text: 'that Donne should have thematized his encounter with God as Trinity in terms of battery and seduction has not, of course, escaped feminist criticism.[7] For some of the feminist critics with whom Coakley engages, the presence of abusive sexual imagery in Donne's Divine Meditation is consistent with the patriarchal God of the Judaeo-Christian faith, a God who, as the Book of Hosea might be said to exemplify, seems all too willing to abuse women in the name of Divine Authority.[8] Sympathetic to the agenda of the feminist critics she cites, Coakley does not think that the development of the doctrine of the Trinity by the Church Fathers, or the use of the doctrine by Donne, should escape criticism, but she does insist that there is more to the Trinity than certain critics suggests. She complains: 'What none of these existing feminist critics examine, however, is the complex historic Western backcloth of Trinitarian theologies such as Donne's, with its roots in the Augustinian sense of tortured disjunction between human sexual love and love for God. Nor, indeed, do these critics face the primary and puzzling questions of why the doctrine of God as three, specifically, should find this erotic thematization in the Christian tradition in the first place.'[9] In her subsequent discussion of sexuality, desire and the Trinity, with particular reference to the writings of St Augustine and Gregory of Nyssa, Coakley makes it clear that the Christian doctrine of the Trinity offers the potential for framing a mutually constructive theory of the relation between different persons. Talk of this doctrine is not without its difficulties, but 'visions of God as Trinity see the inner trinitarian relationships (that is the relations between Father, Son, and Spirit) as a prototype or charter for right relationships' and are therefore worth pursuing.[10]

Coakley's interest in the Trinity as the starting point for theological enquiry and a prototype for right relationships between persons is part of a broader trinitarian turn among contemporary theologians: in the United Kingdom (see Sarah Coakley, Colin Gunton and Alan Torrance), mainland Europe (see Jürgen Moltmann, Christoph Schwöbel and John Zizioulas), and North America (see Miroslav Volf, Kathryn Tanner and Robert Jenson).[11] Reflecting on the renewal of interest in a doctrine that Immanuel Kant famously dismissed as having 'no practical relevance at all', Schwöbel explains:

> The reasons for the new trinitarian orientation are as diverse as the theological and ecclesial backgrounds of the theologians advocating it. Dissatisfaction with the theological possibilities non-personal, unitarian or unipersonalist conceptions of God leave open for a reasoned account of the central claims of Christian faith about the person of Christ and his saving work is among the reasons for the renewed interest in trinitarian theology, supported by disappointment with the

inability of many versions of Christian theism, conceived in terms of a metaphysics of substance or a philosophy of subjectivity, to do justice to the relational 'logic' of such central Christian statements such as 'God is Love'.[12]

The relational orientation of the Trinity not only helps Christian theologians make sense of statements about God that have long been central to the theological tradition; it also has something vital to contribute to both the recent critical emphasis on the importance of the Other and the way in which personhood is understood.[13]

Personhood

In orthodox theological accounts of the Trinity, the relation between divine persons is seen as completely harmonious, with each person oriented fully to the needs of the other; the three persons of the godhead are said to exist in perfect and eternal communion, possessing no existence or identity outside their mutual relations.[14] One of the consequences of this trinitarian reading of God is that the identity of Father, Son and Spirit can only be understood in terms of their relationship to one another. Another consequence, and one that we have already noted in Coakley's essay, is that Christian theologians insist on viewing human persons in the light of divine communion, a progression of thought that proves helpful for the discussion here. In part IV of Donne's 'Divine Litany', it is the 'entanglings' of the godhead, in which the relations and interdependence between Father, Son and Spirit penetrate their identity so deeply that it is impossible to distinguish between them clearly, that the speaker of the poem finds so attractive and seeks to partake of when he asks to be given 'a such self different instinct'.[15]

By locating communion at the core of God's being, rather than seeing the quality as an inconsequential addition to a prior divine substance, trinitarian theologians are able to see human beings, made in the image of God, as something other than an inadequate imitation of the divine being. John Zizioulas outlines the thinking that leads to this conclusion: 'If the ground of God's ontological freedom lies simply in His "nature", that is, in His being uncreated by nature, whereas we are by nature created, then there is no hope, no possibility, that man might become a person in the sense that God is one, that is, an authentic person.'[16] But, as Zizioulas goes on to claim, the Christian understanding that God exists as a relational being 'gives man, in spite of his different nature, his hope of becoming an authentic person'.[17]

Zizioulas is not alone in breaking with much of the Western philosophical tradition. In his essay 'What is a Person?', Alan Torrance traces a shift in the Western understanding of personhood, away from the individual substance of pure thought 'perpetuated in Descartes's famous definition of the self as a "thinking thing"' to currents of thought in the twentieth century that have sought to redefine the self in more 'relational terms'.[18] Drawing on the theological anthropology of Wolfhart Pannenberg, Torrance explains: 'No longer defined as thinking subjects whose primary relationship was to the world of ideas, or as mere agents defined by their relations to impersonal objects, human beings came to be defined as essentially *persons* constituted by their relations to other *persons*.'[19] Perhaps the most famous advocate of this move to a more relational understanding of personhood is the Jewish theologian, Martin Buber, whose influential work *I and Thou* was published in 1923. Buber distinguished 'I-It' from 'I-Thou' relations: the former involves treating others as a thing or object, to be mastered and then dispensed with; the latter involves treating the other as a person who, because they are not just an extension of oneself, requires a dialogic relation marked by respect and openness. While Buber's influence on twentieth-century Christian theology has been considerable, Christian theologians have thought about the relational dynamic of personhood in their own way and sought to interpret it with reference to the doctrine of the Trinity. In this respect, Torrance notes that 'it has been the theological anthropology of John Zizioulas that has done most to establish the significance for Christian thought of the concept of the person'.[20] Coming from an Orthodox Christian tradition in which, unlike its Western counterpart, the understanding of the triune life tends to begin with three persons who are one rather than one person who is three, Zizioulas orientates his theological understanding of human and ecclesial relations around the idea of a social Trinity. The consequences of this on the way in which Zizioulas views personhood is explained by Torrance as follows: 'By saying that the very essence of the person is such that rigid or static notions of capacity and incapacity do not apply, he [Zizioulas] defines a person . . . not in terms of internal features or qualities but in terms of relationships – where relating is not in any way conceived as a "constriction" or limitation of nature but precisely the opposite.'[21] Reflecting on how this view might shape our understanding of the relation between beings, Gunton writes: 'What flows from the conception of God as three persons in communion, related but distinct? First, there is something of the space we have been seeking. We have a conception of *personal space*:

the space in which three persons are for and from each other in their otherness.'[22]

The orientation to the other that is intrinsic to the person of God enables a generous relation between Father, Son and Spirit, and other, created beings, whose will does not fully accord with the divine life. In the opening to another of his Divine Meditations, Donne takes up the idea that humanity is invited to participate in divine communion:

> Father, part of his double interest
> Unto thy kingdom, thy Son gives to me,
> His jointure in the knotty Trinity
> He keeps, and gives me his death's conquest.

Part of the interest that accumulates in the opening to this poem is the description of divine movement and gift. The reference to the 'knotty Trinity' involves more than just the mysterious quality of the Godhead – it also speaks of entanglement, a word that connects Donne's attitude to metaphor and poetic language with recognition of the involved relations that mark the triune life of God.[23] While Donne's poem includes a contrast between the Son's jointure with the Trinity and the conquest of death that is presented to humanity, the giving of the Son to the world prevents the contrast from being absolute: at some level, the jointure extends an invitation to humanity to participate in the divine life. What Donne's poetry glimpses here, as it does on numerous other occasions, is the idea that there is no individuality outside our relationship with others. Instead of starting with individual identity and then trying to work outward to incorporate others, personal identity can only be understood with reference to our mutual relations.

It might reasonably be argued that the recent theological and philosophical emphasis on the relational fluidity of personhood reflects the late twentieth-century's preference for flux over fixity as the primary means of comprehending the nature of the world.[24] The critical privileging of flux manifests itself in a multitude of ways, and can be discerned in the tendency for recent Donne scholarship to reject some of the more rigid distinctions employed by earlier critics in their categorization of Donne's poetry. Although the literary forms used by Donne can be categorized with reference to the norms of the period – it is relatively simple, for instance, to distinguish between one of Donne's 'sacred' hymns and one of his 'secular' love poems – critics are increasingly alert to the crossover in subject matter and style between Donne's religious and non-religious work. Acknowledgement of the permeability and artificiality of the boundaries that separate the sacred from the secular in Donne is a starting point for a great deal of contemporary scholarship. Ben Saunders reminds us that Donne 'was not above addressing God Himself in tones of "immoderate desire," variously adopting the postures of demand, seduction, desperation, fidelity, and abjection in his poetic prayers', and Theresa DiPasquale finds little difficulty in tracing the sacramental in Donne's love poetry and exploring the way he 'plays upon the connections between the function of poetry and the function of sacraments'.[25] The brief reference made by Andrew Mousley to Donne's 'The Sun Rising' at the end of an engaging essay on 'Transubstantiating Love: John Donne and Cultural Criticism' provides further evidence of the current state of thinking in Donne criticism, as well as offering a more specific contribution to the present discussion: 'even in this poem, Donne writes arresting moments of epiphany which not only save love from being hollowed out by its cultural and ideological predators, but exist, in and for themselves, as testimony to love's transubstantiation of "you" and "I" into "us"'.[26]

Trinitarian perspectives on personhood offer readers of Donne an especially useful means of establishing connections between the themes developed in his poetry; they also open up the dramatic metaphors that Donne is famous for employing. Writing on Donne's 'The Triple Foole', Saunders tells us that 'The familiar Christian notion of the Holy Fool, and the concept of Trinitarianism, may also lend a positive spin to the ostensibly negative charge of multiplied foolishness; the connection is surely not too far-fetched, given the association between three-selves-in-one and the doctrine of the Trinity that Donne directly employs in sexual contexts elsewhere in his work (most famously in the seduction scene of "The Flea").'[27] Saunder's identification of three-selves-in-one as a recurring trinitarian motif in Donne's poetry encourages us to look beyond the more overt references to the Trinity in the 'religious' poetry, and consider other material in the Donne canon, such as the description of love in 'A Valediction: forbidding mourning'. While it seems reasonable to presume that Donne's familiarity with the Christian doctrine of the Trinity permeated his work in a variety of ways, a trinitarian reading of 'A Valediction: forbidding mourning' does not require a detailed case to be made for theological intent on the part of Donne; what matters is the extent to which the doctrine of the Trinity explains and is further elucidated by the treatment of love and the relations between persons in this poem.[28]

There are, however, certain difficulties with a trinitarian reading of 'A Vale-diction: forbidding mourning', the most significant of which is the way in which the poem's theological insights are compromised by a more selfish conception of love. The competing views become most apparent in the second half of the poem when the speaker sets out his response to the absence he has just been describing:

> But we by a love, so much refined,
>   That our selves know not what it is,
> Inter-assured of the mind,
>   Care less, eyes, lips, and hands to miss.
>
> Our two souls therefore, which are one,
>   Though I must go, endure not yet
> A breach, but an expansion,
>   Like gold to aery thinness beat.
>
> If they be two, they are two so
>   As stiff twin compasses are two,
> Thy soul, the fixed foot, makes no show
>   To move, but doth, if th'other do.
>
> And though it in the centre sit,
>   Yet when the other far doth roam,
> It leans, and hearkens after it,
>   And grows erect, as that comes home.
>
> Such wilt thou be to me, who must
>   Like th' other foot, obliquely run;
> Thy firmness makes my circle just,
>   And makes me end, where I begun.

Some indication of the speaker's confusion is evident when he claims to 'know not' love, only to give an extended account of what that love is like. The confusion stems from his desire to hold onto the idea of a love 'so much refined' that others are incapable of grasping it. In making this claim, the speaker is guilty of the sort of closed system of relations that Emmanuel Levinas observed and criticized in Buber's work.[29] Levinas complained that the 'I-Thou' relations proposed by Buber was likely to result in an exclusive relationship between 'I' and 'Thou', without room for others, and a similar tendency towards exclusivity pervades the thinking of the speaker in Donne's poem. The mysterious and unknowable love that the speaker admires undermines the contribution of the social and physical body ('Care less, eyes, lips, and hands to miss'), and threatens to transcend the receptive capacities of the less-enlightened common reader, who is condemned to observe the mystery of love from the outside.

Yet the exclusive view of love admired by the speaker of Donne's poem is undone by the poem's other, trinitarian insights. To appreciate this, we need to turn to an idea that Robert Jenson develops in volume 2 of his *Systematic Theology* (1999). Jenson argues that the room for others imagined by the Christian doctrine of Creation is made possible by a divine conversation between the persons of the Godhead. It is a conversation that avoids both the soliloquy of a selfish, monolithic God, and the closed communication that would result from a Godhead consisting only of Father and Son. Jenson explains: 'the only fully reliable otherness is that of persons, engaged in a discourse that is not merely between "Thou" and "I", that is not merely in the first and second persons. The word, "Let there *be . . .*" can truly be spoken only in *dramatic* discourse. The Trinity is such a conversation, the only one that can never collapse into dialogue or monologue, because the three who make its poles *are* the conversation.'[30] Jenson's account draws attention to the role of the Spirit – the breath of life – in animating this triune conversation. The Spirit is not easily located but his role in articulating a conversation between Father and Son helps constitute the divine life and make room for the participation of others in that conversation. By thinking about the Spirit as the enabler of divine conversation rather than as a fixed and discrete entity, Jenson supplies a new way of comprehending the love described in Donne's poem. 'A Valediction: forbidding mourning' recognizes a dramatic conversation from the start through the present tense of the subtitle but it develops the idea of dramatic space further through the extended metaphor used at the end. 'I' and 'Thou' are linked in a changing spatial relation that transforms the static description of a 'stiff' 'soul' with 'fixed foot' that 'makes no show / [t]o move'. By speaking about the distance between lovers in terms of their movement on a map, Donne's poem extends love beyond exclusive boundaries to cover a vast expanse of space. The talk of a hinged compass offers an analogy of the Spirit enabling relations between Father and Son, creating not a 'breach, but an expansion'. Donne's poem imagines a communion of persons in which the two arms of the compass are prevented from becoming locked into a fixed, immovable relationship by the movement of the thing that enables their relation; hence the description in the penultimate stanza of one who 'doth roam' and another who 'leans, and hearkens'.

Unlike the sort of monolithic deity that we saw Stanley Fish complaining about in the previous chapter, a trinitarian God offers a means of thinking about human relations in a way that accommodates the Other.[31] The space for the Other that Jenson roots in the triune conversation of the Godhead can also be seen in the violent chaos of Donne's holy sonnet 'Batter my heart', despite the speaker's impetuous demand to be transformed into the passive recipient of divine ravishment. Before the violence of the speaker's demand is allowed to solidify and become uncontested, the poem acknowledges that the work of God 'seek[s] to mend' the human, not 'o'erthrow' him. Instead of initiating the poem's violence, the triune life dramatically stands in its way, refusing to override the will of the human, despite his sinful ties, and inviting him into a divine conversation that allows the expression of desires that are not entirely harmonious with the will of God. In the sort of theological schema imagined by Fish, the demands that the speaker makes of God might be considered blasphemous; here, in the context of a triune God who seeks to restore the human and enable his/her agency, the demands are hallowed into a holy sonnet, a poem that is also a prayer. Donne's poem foregrounds the possibility of conversing with God, encompassing other readers and other perspectives as it does so.

Language relations

Donne's use of unexpected tropes to link together diverse persons and ideas is a trait shared by Dickinson. While the latter employs a more introvert and implicit style than Donne, she shares his willingness to use language in daring and expansive ways. Like Donne, Dickinson is aware of the relational dynamic at work in the world, and, like Donne, she explores this in her poetry, exploiting the capacity of words to connect unlikely ideas together. In one of the few pieces of scholarship to consider the relation between these writers, Judith Banzer writes about their mutual participation in what Louis L. Martz defines as the 'meditative tradition': 'Donne, practicing its three-fold mode of divine communion and Emily [Dickinson], moved by her theocratic environment to the constant contemplation of Essence, shared a conviction of the oneness of being. This produced in their poetry the continual creation of an explorative and unifying self.'[32] Banzer's decision to distinguish Dickinson's poetry from the trinitarian work of Donne is understandable given the limited number of references to the Trinity that we find in Dickinson's work but the distinction should not prevent us from thinking about Dickinson's poetry through the conceptual lens offered by the Trinity. The framework that the Trinity provides for thinking about what it means to talk of beings in relation is, as Janet Martin Soskice has remarked in another setting, the '*grammar* of Christian faith', and it is particularly well suited to appreciating the structural relations of language.[33] Jacques Derrida's famous insistence that there is nothing outside the text reminds us that all talk of persons and things is, in the first instance, talk, or text, and Dickinson is alert to the need for retaining a linguistic awareness as we apprehend and interpret the world.[34]

The profound link in Dickinson's work between words and worlds, and her insistence that one thing has to be understood in terms of another, asks questions of the description of solitude that has traditionally been given to her poetry. In recent years a plethora of critics have sought to qualify our understandings of Dickinson's solitude by emphasizing the importance of audience and social context in her writing: what I wish to suggest here is that this emphasis on a relational dynamic can be extended to a theological reading of the language in Dickinson's poetry.[35] Discussing the sacramental references in Dickinson's poetry, Margot K. Louis tell us that: 'In nearly all of the poems that I have been considering, the communion involves one recipient and her food; "two or three" are not gathered together; no-one administers the sacrament; no Redeemer has invited us to the feast, or is typified by his emblems of bread and wine. A solitary speaker looks at a rather blank table.'[36] The reading Louis develops in her essay is nuanced and thoughtful; yet the sacramental metaphor she explores (i.e. Communion) inadvertently hints at another, more relational reading of Dickinson's poetry.

Rejecting the idea that 'A word is dead / When it is said', Dickinson insists that a word spoken 'Begins to live'.[37] In making this claim, Dickinson pursues a similar line of thought to the Gospel of John, which equates the logos to a living person, Christ, who is said to enter the material world and become flesh.[38] At a more mundane level, Dickinson's insistence on the vitality of words reminds us that they take on a life that exceeds the limited comprehension of the author who articulates them. The entrance of words into the world resurrects a long history of negotiated meaning. Because words exist in an open-ended set of structural relations to other words, there is a sense in which all language exists on a metaphorical plane. Soskice tells us in *Metaphor and Religious Language* (1985) that 'metaphor is a speaking of one thing in terms which are seen as suggestive of another'. She continues: 'metaphor is a form of language use with a unity of subject-matter and which yet draws upon two (or more) sets of associations, and does so, characteristically, by involving the consideration of a model or models.'[39] The definition of metaphor that Soskice employs in her book is more specific than the use to which I am putting it here. She recognizes, quite rightly, the value of distinguishing explicitly metaphoric language from more technical vocabulary. But the relational dynamic that Soskice identifies as being at the core of metaphor can be extended to all language, nonetheless. All words acquire meaning through their association with other words; in doing so, they participate in a complex and indefinite set of relations, one that insists we think about the meaning of a word in relation to other words, and one that recognizes the futility of trying to impose a determinate structure on the equivocal relations between words.

Establishing a theological parallel between the relations that connect and define persons and the relations that connect and define words is an obvious response to the Christian belief in a trinitarian God who, having spoken the world into being, repeatedly uses the metaphor of the Word as a means of disclosing his personal identity. To talk of God as the source of human language does not have to lead us back to another version of the logocentrism criticized by Derrida in *Of Grammatology* (1967); for a start, as Gerard Loughlin has noted: 'One can tell the stories of Father, Son and Spirit in different directions, and thus speak of their radical dependence upon one another, of their coinhering and internarrativity, their mutual entailment and telling. There is a dynamic to trinitarian story-telling, an omni-directionality of narrative movement.'[40] Trinitarian theology starts with a notion of God in relation and finds itself in sympathy with many of the insights concerning the dynamic nature of language identified by post-structuralism. This is not to suggest that trinitarian theology renders the insights of post-structuralism redundant; nor is it to imply that trinitarian theology offers a simple solution to the problems of religious language. Trinitarian thought possesses considerable resources for conversing with the recent insights of post-structuralism but all doctrinal formulations are, themselves, forms of discourse, and theological attempts to speak of God as the Creator and Sustainer of the world push language to its limits. It is by no means certain that references to our experience in the world offer meaningful descriptions of the Divine, and there is no way of testing our analogies against a non-linguistic theology that reveals God as he truly is.[41]

Without wishing to name Dickinson as an early post-structuralist, her poetry does recognize the precarious state of language's referential capacity and the instability that marks the relations between words. Poem #568 explores the frailty of language against a recognizably theological background:

> We learned the Whole of Love –
> The Alphabet – the Words –
> A Chapter – then the mighty Book –
> Then – Revelation closed –

But in Each Other's eyes
An Ignorance beheld –
Divine than the Childhood's –
And each to each, a Child –

Attempted to expound
What Neither – understood –
Alas, that Wisdom is so large –
And Truth – so manifold![42]

Having begun with an admission of the link between personal relations ('love') and a variety of semantic units through which those relations are revealed, the poem moves on to confront the difficulties of communication. Words may connect us but they do not overcome 'Ignorance': partly because of the difficulty of translating our thoughts into words that others might understand and partly because our words are not even capable of translating our own thoughts clearly. Yet such limitations do not mean that language is to be despised; on the contrary, Dickinson's poem celebrates the indeterminacy of language and revels in the open-ended linguistic relations that take us beyond our immediate sphere of reference. The speaker of the poem sees the eyes of another and is linked to that person through a language that cannot be mastered or fully understood. Language, then, joins us to others, as words are joined to one another. Rather than giving up on language, the poet celebrates the mysteries of its relations. It is a moment of insight that indicates how Dickinson reconciles her awareness of linguistic limits with her willingness to write a vast number of poems.

One of the distinguishing marks of Dickinson's poetry is her use of gaps and silences. Things are frequently left unsaid and the number of words used is kept to a minimum. To understand why this is so, it is helpful to consider the argument that Regina Schwartz develops in an essay entitled 'Communion and Conversation'. Schwartz argues against instrumental views of language, which seek to 'inscribe, describe, explain, or capture'.[43] She continues: 'As such an instrument, language is destined to miss its mark, to misfire (the violence of these metaphors, not mine, is apt) . . . Misfires multiply: using language as a tool to convey meaning is one idolatry, but added to the misunderstanding are intentional misuses of language. Using language as a tool can look more like using language as a weapon.'[44] Against a view of language as something that describes – threatening to dominate its subject in the process – Schwartz entertains a view of language as something that 'praises or laments, rather than describes. To hear such language we would not attend to referential or predicational functions, but to rhythm, to the alternation of silence and utterance.'[45] While the distinction that Schwartz explores is not as rigid as she sometimes suggests, and while description is not always as violent as she sometimes fears, her account of silence as a sign that remembers the relational dynamic of language is astute. The argument that 'silence is where the conversation really takes place . . . for this is the silence of responsiveness, responsibility, and response' sheds light on some of the techniques used by Dickinson.[46] Seemingly aware of the limitations of words and the difficulties of genuine communication, Dickinson turns to silence, not because she gives up on communication but because she thinks that silence helps us to appreciate the relational ambition of language.

Words are joined in an infinite web of relations and they are the means by which persons relate to one another in personal communion. Yet the communicative value of words is easily lost. Language reveals the relatedness of the universe but our efforts to communicate often terminate those relations by subordinating words to our own, violent ends. Our tendency to miss or violate the relational dynamic of language in every area of life, including religious rituals, is a recurring theme in Dickinson's poetry. Poem #437 considers the danger to human communion with God posed by an instrumental view of prayer, which reduces this religious practice to a 'little implement'.[47] When the relational element of prayer is lost, humans simply 'fling their speech' in 'God's ear'.[48] Words are still in evidence but the connection that they are meant to enable is severed, and the communal aim of prayer is lost. In the light of this idea, we might see the careful and deliberate way Dickinson uses words elsewhere in her work not so much as an attempt to fix the meaning of the poems she writes but as evidence of a desire to respect the relational dynamic of language by providing space for words to be suggestive of something else. By not crowding her poems with too many words, Dickinson allows space for her readers to explore the infinite relations embodied through language. Dickinson creates room for her readers to see how words link the universe together, in one form or another, and to celebrate their joining of the universe to a God whose very being consists of persons in eternal communion.

On one of the rare occasions in which Dickinson makes direct reference to the Christian godhead, she tells us that 'The Jehovahs – are no Babblers'.[49] Again, the line does not suggest a reluctance to speak so much as a desire to avoid speaking incessantly. If language is to find space for speaker and listener to relate to one another and respond to each act of communication, silence has a role to play. The relational dimension of language, rooted in a perfect communion between Father, Son and Spirit, encourages Dickinson to choose her language carefully, so that the resonance of words is allowed to sound fully and invite a response. Writing in a different context – summarizing Derrida on the relation between language and silence – Graham Ward elaborates on the idea that silence creates space for words to be heard and responded to:

> Silence becomes analogous to the blank margins of a page, the space beneath the vaulting of a Cathedral, or a musical interval. The margin frames and focuses the text. The empty spaces here establish a certain tension between the arrangement of the letters, the words and the syntax into a communication and the empty margins which create a space for the cessation of intellection. It is a space for/of breathing. The margins, therefore, articulate, possibly at a somatic level, a certain rest, a certain Sabbath, a space for the activities of prayer and meditation. In silence a rest is written into the fabric of creation. There is articulation through this rhythm and in this rhythm. And every poet knows how to take advantage of the rhythm of the margins and make it part of the poem through enjambment, line length, and the spatial dynamics of the typesetting.[50]

The Love Feast

Like their theological counterparts, who seek to ground a Christian theology of personhood and the relation between beings in historic expressions of faith concerning the Trinity, poets turn to established forms to help realize the relational dynamic of the words they use. Poetic form varies considerably, as the choice of texts in this chapter illustrates, and poets are not bound by the forms they inherit. Although Dickinson writes in a distinctive style, her poems do not eschew formal considerations; even when she acknowledges the corruption of prayer as a religious form, for example, she re-imagines it, offering prayers of her own in the process. In this respect she is similar to a large number of poets in the Western literary tradition who borrow heavily from religious traditions and rituals. Such borrowing can be rooted in the creativity of the Christian faith: 'In its liturgical practices and reading of scripture, the Christian community creatively remembers and celebrates the incarnation of the Word of God ... The Christian who lives in a world of God's creation, and who sacramentally recalls God's own entry into the condition of createdness, speaks in a way that recalls Bakhtin's concept of "addressivity", whereby language itself ... is governed by a foundational relationality ...'[51]

The final section of this chapter will focus on 'Goblin Market' and its engagement with the Eucharist.[52] Communion has an important place within

Christian theology, and its intersection with ritual (enabling personal relations) and form (enabling the relational dynamic of language) is especially
helpful for understanding the relation between beings. In the Eucharist, words
and signs are repeated by the community of the Church in remembrance of
Christ, the Word made Flesh, who is believed to have given his life for
the world and made it possible for others to participate in the divine life of the
Trinity. Acknowledging the central place of this act of remembrance within
the communal story of the Church, Gerard Loughlin finishes his book on narrative theology with a discussion of the Eucharist. Drawing on the thinking
of Herbert McCabe, Loughlin writes: 'When people gather for the Eucharist,
they gather for a meal that is at the same time the language of their bodily
communication; and this language-meal is not their own, but comes to them
from beyond the site of their gathering, from beyond and after the revolution.
It is a language they can barely speak; but it is the language in which they can
most truly communicate; be most bodily, most alive.'[53] Loughlin's illuminating
connection of word and person, language and body, gets to the centre of this
important Christian sacrament, recognizing, as Jenson insists elsewhere, that
'sacraments *mean* something'.[54] Before going on to consider how sacraments
also '*do* something' Jenson takes a moment to explain the meaning of sacraments: 'In the terminology Augustine made standard, they belong to the
class of *signa*, "signs", things that point to something other than themselves;
what they point to is then the *res*, the "something" in question, the "matter"
of the occasion. "Sacraments" are those signs whose *res* is the grace of
Christ. Thus sacraments belong to the *discourse*, the "word", that is Christ's
self-interpretation to and in his church.'[55]

The allusion to the Eucharist in 'Goblin Market' is part of an extensive
world of symbolism inhabited by the poem. Resisting a straightforward alle-
gorical reading in which everything in the poem corresponds to one other thing
in a tight and linear schema, the poem's symbolism generates a variety of readings that confirms the literary fertility of Rossetti's immersion in Tractarian
theology. Readers are encouraged to bring other discourses into play as they
interpret the poem, and are not expected to uncover the religious lesson behind
the events of the text. At the centre of these overlapping discourses is the language of the Eucharist: having being rescued from her broken state through
Lizzie's sacrificial act, and having being invited by her sister to eat and drink
of the new life that is offered, Laura finishes the poem by urging her children
to join hands and remember her sister's love. The eucharistic reading of this

final act of remembrance is prompted by the language used earlier in the poem, most notably when Lizzie returns from her sacrificial encounter with the goblin men. Speaking to her sister, Lizzie cries:

> Did you miss me?
> Come and kiss me.
> Never mind my bruises,
> Hug me, kiss me, suck my juices
> Squeezed from goblin fruits for you,
> Goblin pulp and goblin dew.
> Eat me, drink me, love me;
> Laura, make much of me:
> For your sake I have braved the glen
> And had to do with goblin merchant men.[56]

Rossetti's use of erotic language here is reminiscent of the conjunction of sacrament and sex that we have already noted in the poetry of Donne. The theological idea that the bread and wine mediate Christ's presence in some form explains the attraction of the Eucharist for both poets as a site for thinking about the sacred in physical terms. Although the corporeal aspect of the Eucharist is a traditional point of divergence between Catholicism and Protestantism, recent theologians such as Marilyn McCord Adams and Robert Jenson have followed Martin Luther in combining their Protestant beliefs with a proper recognition of the role that the corporeal plays within the Eucharist.[57] Among other things, considering the corporeal dimension of the symbolism involved in the bread and the wine helps us to understand why Rossetti is so willing to speak of the Eucharist as an erotic and physically significant act of love.

Appropriately for a ritual so rich in meaning and capable of being understood in so many different ways, the Eucharist goes by other names, many of which confirm that the sacrament has something substantial to say about the relation between beings. Most obviously, the term Communion speaks of a union between different persons. Other terms for the Eucharist, such as 'The Lord's Supper' and 'The Love Feast', describe the Eucharist as a shared and life-giving act of physical intimacy. In 'Goblin Market' Lizzie's generous and costly provision of her own body proves sufficient for Laura's insatiable appetite, and enables a restoration of the relationship between the sisters. Adams explores a similar line of thought when she considers how those present at the Love Feast share with one another: 'The Lord's table is a groaning board . . . where adoptive sons and daughters gather to eat, drink, and be satisfied, to commune with one another and with God. But the carnal knowledge to which Christ invites us is more radically intimate: instead of eating the food He could have eaten or sharing a portion of the food He is eating, Christ sets the table with His flesh and blood, with the food that *is* Himself.'[58] Elsewhere in her account of the Eucharist, Adams becomes more explicit about the violent dimension of the feast that is shared; she explores how pain and celebration mingle together as those participating in the meal admit the pain suffered by all who sit at the table. For Adams, part of the sufficiency of the Lord's Supper is to be found in its provision of a meal at which beings can sit down together and share fellowship, despite their differences and previous, traumatic experiences. Reading 'Goblin Market' from this perspective reveals a Eucharistic celebration that is willing to acknowledge the harsh reality of physical abuse that Lizzie undergoes at the hands of the goblin men. In different ways, Adams and Rossetti imagine the Eucharist as a meal at which genuine horrors can be expressed, without fatally undermining the hope of a celebratory union that the event remembers and anticipates. Seeking to capture the nature of this hope, Adams writes: 'This family will not break. This quarrel is between lovers. Love bade us welcome . . . Love has held on to us, all the while comforting us with its touch. From time to time, eventually, the storm may break, the air clear, the bread and wine bear the passion of lovers' kiss, of pleasurable embrace, of taking in one another's life.'[59]

The Eucharist is not the only feast on offer in 'Goblin Market'. Lizzie receives an invitation to another type of meal when she goes to meet the goblin men and buy back her sister. The narrative warns us that their invitation is to be viewed with suspicion: 'They answered grinning: / "Our feast is but beginning"'.[60] Although the goblin men are keen to describe their feast in positive terms, the awkward syntax of their invitation 'Be welcome guest with us' offers a clear warning that something is wrong. The hidden cost of the feast that the goblin men offer makes it clear that the economy of this meal is different to the one involved in the Christian Love Feast. Thinking about the meals available in 'Goblin Market' in terms of their respective economies is something that readers are encouraged to do from the start of the poem. The goblin cry to 'Come buy our orchard fruits' reverberates throughout, '[w]ith its iterated jingle / Of sugar-baited words'.[61] Behind the superficial attraction of the goods that the goblins hawk lies a hidden system of exchange – 'Leering at each other, / Brother and queer brother; / Signalling each other' – that alienates Laura and subjects her to costs of which she has little or no appreciation.[62] As a number of critics have pointed out, the treatment of the sisters by the goblin men highlights the faults of an emerging Capitalist economy, in which consumers who participate in the economic system from a position of weakness are abused, and through which individuals (in this case, Laura) are prevented from ever being satisfied by the purchases they make.[63]

Some scholars have thought about the poem's engagement with Capitalism in more figurative terms. Alison Chapman, for instance, argues in her study of the afterlife of Rossetti that the coins in the poem 'are part of a semiotic circulation of things within a familiar economy that collapses production and consumption'. The 'economy of exchange' in the poem, she continues, involves a 'metaphorical process of substitution which further distances the text from the source and origin of its production and places it irretrievably within a rhetoric of reproduction'.[64] Chapman's reading of the economic language that circulates in the poem is productive, encouraging readers to think more extensively about the extent of the economic influence in 'Goblin Market'. While one meaning of the word 'economy' encourages us to define the word within narrow limits, the word can also be used more broadly to think about the general parameters that govern a system of relations. This broader use of the word 'economy' stops us from having to choose between a religious reading of the poem and a financial one, and allows us to appreciate the contrasting economies that emerge through the different feasts on offer in the marketplace of the poem.

In contrast to the meal economy urged on the sisters by the goblin men, the Love Feast that Rossetti refers to involves a radically different economic vision. The economic vision of Christian theology is something that Kathryn Tanner explores in *The Economy of Grace* (2005). Building on the idea that 'theological ideas are always internally constituted by a contestatory relationship with the beliefs and practices of the world in which Christians live', Tanner considers how trinitarian theology critiques key aspects of Capitalism and points to a different economic order.[65] Her reflection on the social and political consequences of the beings-in-relation envisaged by Christian accounts of the Trinity leads her to argue for three principles that might be used to shape our approach to a host of economic matters: unconditional giving, mutual benefit, and non-competitiveness.[66] While Tanner's discussion does not make reference to Rossetti's poem, the 'trinitarian' economy of grace she describes, in which goods are made widely available to all, without hidden cost, is evident in the eucharistic economy that we find in 'Goblin Market'. Rooted in the biblical texts available to both writers, this economy of grace offers a clear contrast to the system of exchange that lies behind the refrain of

'Come buy' repeated by the goblin men. The theological economy of the New Jerusalem that the writer of the book of Revelation imagines speaks of God's promise to 'give unto him that is athirst of the fountain of the water of life freely'.[67] It is a promise that echoes the words of Isaiah: 'Ho, every one that thirsteth, come ye to the waters, and he that hath no money; come ye, buy, and eat; yea, come, buy wine and milk without money and without price.'[68] Isaiah's prophetic call for people to 'buy' wine and milk 'without price' envisages an economy of love that is diametrically opposed to the economy operated by Rossetti's goblin men. The economy run by the goblin men ensnares unsuspecting victims and renders them incapable of continuing in a system of exchange that will allow them to give and receive. Recognizing the faults of such a system, Lizzie looks to the economic alternative offered by the Eucharist, in which the exchange of life-giving bodily fluids continues long after the immediate ecstasy of their initial consumption:

> That night long Lizzie watched by her,
> Counted her pulse's flagging stir,
> Felt for her breath,
> Held water to her lips, and cooled her face
> With tears . . . [69]

It is through the Eucharist that 'Goblin Market' imagines a reconciliation between two sisters who, post Laura's fall, have suffered a break in their relations. The poem's allusion to the Love Feast is not intended as a magical charm that can make all things right; instead, it offers some recognition of the way in which Christian theology understands the relational dynamic of the universe and it points to the means by which that relational dynamic is restored through the work of Christ. For Christian theologians, the possibility of understanding how beings relate to one another begins and ends in a vision of the communal life of the Trinity. Using this trinitarian language of love, we can attend to the events of a text such as 'Goblin Market' and try to make sense of the Christian imagery that is used. To understand the feast of love that Laura and Lizzie participate in, it is instructive to follow the links that Douglas Meeks traces when, in a non-literary context, he differentiates a trinitarian economy of grace from the obligation of debt that accompanies many commodity exchanges. Meeks considers the extent to which human giving might be said to reflect trinitarian giving: 'This giving is best seen in the life-serving shape of human life in the eucharistic existence gifted at the spreading of the Lord's table . . . Whereas commodity exchanges are anonymous, the emphasis in giving as God gives is on the persons brought into relationship, not on the objects that are exchanged. Gift giving creates communal relationships of interdependence.'[70] Communal relationships of interdependence are at the heart of Lizzie and Laura's identity in Rossetti's poem, and, as this chapter has argued, they are central to any understanding of personhood. In practice, such relationships are difficult to secure and respect, as both Dickinson's fumbling and Donne's ravishment acknowledge, but this merely confirms the importance of trying to find a means of enabling a loving relation between beings.

Mediating the Divine: Law, Gift and Justice

3

The previous chapter examined the contribution of Christian theology to our understanding of others and to the mutual relations that define our existence as human beings. Focusing on the poetry of John Donne, Emily Dickinson and Christina Rossetti, the chapter considered how personhood might be rooted in the relational economy of the Trinity. The chapter also explored the ways in which formal expressions of language can articulate an economy of love between persons. One of the most important forms in the Christian tradition is the Eucharistic, a ritual that looks back to the work of Christ on the Cross and looks forward to how that work might inaugurate a world other than the broken one we currently inhabit. As the last chapter discussed, the Eucharist, or Love Feast as it is also known, is central to the economy of love that Rossetti imagines in 'Goblin Market', standing in contradistinction to the crippling debt economy proffered by the goblin men. Reading the Eucharist in terms of its internal economy is a way of paying attention to the structural mechanisms through which we relate to one another, and it is with this in mind that the present chapter turns to the matter of the Law. In the Judaeo-Christian tradition, the Law casts it light or shadow over everything else. To speak of the Law is to evoke both the legal framework by which relations between beings are sustained, and the revelatory framework through which Jewish and Christian understandings of God are mediated. The intimate connection between these two elements is evident in the Book of Exodus, with the giving of the Ten Commandments following immediately after Moses has met with Yahweh on Mount Sinai and tried to communicate his experience of God to the people.[1]

By turning its attention to the Law, this chapter shifts the focus of discussion away from the individual expressions of love addressed in the previous chapter to something more universal and, in certain respects, more complex. The Law remains committed to understanding the Other but it does so using a more systemic language than the personal expressions of relationality considered in Chapter 2. Paul Ricoeur provides a helpful way of thinking about the distinction:

> Friendship, opposed in this context to justice, is the emblematic virtue of this immediate relationship that accomplishes the miracle of an exchange of roles between beings that cannot be substituted for each other. You are the you that says 'you' to me and to whom I respond, as Emmanuel Levinas loved to repeat, 'here I am' – me, in the accusative case. But however wonderful the virtue of friendship may be, it is not capable of fulfilling the task of justice, nor even of engendering it as a distinct virtue. The virtue of justice is based on a relation of distance from the other, just as originary as the relation of proximity to the other person offered through his face and voice. This relation to the other is, if I may so put it, immediately mediated by the *institution*.[2]

One of the consequences of approaching Otherness by way of the institution of the Law is a return to the mediatory element of the created world discussed in Chapter 1. Distance and complexity force us to re-examine our views of individual agency and autonomy, locating them in a more structured frame of reference that draws attention to the systems of truth and justice that mediate our actions. Thinking about Otherness in terms of the Law shifts our emphasis away from the individual agency of a will that expresses interest in another, towards the social framework in which the effects of the will are worked out. The hermeneutical implication of understanding the individual's will within its social framework is especially apparent in the case of legal wills: a legal will inscribes an individual's will and lawyers are then required to interpret this written testament to the way that a person wishes their material belongings to be distributed after death. Those seeking to interpret legal wills do not ignore the individual agency that shaped the will in the first place but their interpretation proceeds with a strong awareness of other social factors.

Despite seeking to codify an individual's desires clearly, legal wills are contested documents, subject to varied and disputed interpretations. There are few more pronounced examples of the legal problems that accompany conflicting readings of wills than Charles Dickens's *Bleak House* (1852–3), a novel in which difficulties are evident at every turn. The influence of the Jarndyce suit on every area of life highlights both the reach and the limitations of the Law. John Jarndyce rues the day when '[a] certain Jarndyce, in an evil hour, made a great fortune, and made a great Will', and the title of the chapter in which his comments are located – 'Covering a Multitude of Sins' – calls attention to the failure of the Law to do justice to the Will it interprets.[3] For Jarndyce, the Law has become 'such an infernal country-dance of costs and fees and nonsense and corruption, as was never dreamed of in the wildest visions of a Witch's Sabbath'.[4] By the time that a judgement on the Jarndyce case is finally reached, the damage caused by the suit is irreparable; there is no money left to pay out a financial settlement and no material resources by which the Law might atone for the injustices that have been perpetrated in its name.

Bleak House offers a disturbing account of how interpretive errors and economic complexities can undermine the divine vision of universal equity and order that the Law is meant to mediate. Commenting on the economy of failure in Dickens's novel, Gordon Bigelow tells us that:

> The danger posed by the systematized world of Chancery and the Bank can be described in [Roland] Barthes's terms as the 'metonymic confusion' of the bourgeois sign. 'Metonymic confusion' is Chancery's problem, in that the sideways-shifting network of writing threatens to bury the meaning of any of its documents. The detective, Mr Bucket, charged with solving all of the novel's 'connexions,' declares that he has so much knowledge about so many different people that 'a piece of information more or less, don't signify a straw'. That this might be true of all signs – that their true value might be rendered indistinguishable in their systematization – is the novel's central worry.[5]

A similar worry permeates the world of Franz Kafka's *The Trial* (1925), a novel that draws heavily on Dickens's text.[6] The multiple clues circulating in Kafka's narrative lead to a series of dead-ends, incapable of escaping the obfuscation of their origins; indeed, the more knowledge that Josef K acquires, the more he realizes the extent of his immersion in a system that he cannot hope to comprehend. Everyone that Josef K. comes into contact with following his arrest possesses some sort of ill-defined relationship to the Law, and the topography of *The Trial* continually leads the protagonist back to labyrinthine places under the jurisdiction of the court. At his first examination, Josef K. tries to convince those gathered around him that 'I can distance myself from the whole business, so I'm able to judge it calmly,' but the reality is the polar opposite: the one thing that Josef K. cannot do is stand outside the reach of the Law and enjoy an objective perspective on the 'agency' that mistreats him.[7] Jacques Derrida's playful essay on this novel explores the Law's inaccessibility and lack of agency, observing, among other things, that even the priest who seeks to explain the Law to Josef K. through the 'Before the Law' parable, is, himself, 'like the doorkeeper of the story . . . a representative of the law'.[8]

Given the accounts in *Bleak House* and *The Trial* of a Law that is unjust, inaccessible, and potentially meaningless, the focus of this chapter might seem ill-judged. Yet whether or not the novels of Dickens and Kafka do justice to the Law and identify its limitations correctly, one cannot ignore the challenge that the Law presents us with. There is no possibility of talking about the Jewish or Christian conception of God without heeding the central framework in which these conceptions are mediated, and Judaeo-Christian concerns with areas such as truth and justice insist that we think carefully about the workings of the Law. The Law raises other foundational questions about the way in which we relate to one another: for example, if a judicial system exists to govern our mutual relations with a sense of proportionality, then what does it mean to talk of loving someone and giving to them freely? Gifts pose a challenge for Judaism and Christianity because of the way in which the religions emphasize God's gifts to the world yet call for the people of God to respond with similar levels of generosity. Derrida explores the challenge in *Given Time: I. Counterfeit Money* (1991) when he shows how our gifts to one another always involve some expectation of a return. Placing Derrida's claim that a pure gift is impossible alongside the response of contemporary Christian theologians to this idea, the first section of the chapter will look at the exchange of gifts in *Bleak House* and *The Trial*. Using Kathryn Tanner's idea of an economy of grace, I will suggest that viewing gifts as an extension of benefits to others helps us sustain the coherence of the term gift and appreciate the purpose of the Law. Instead of presuming that the Law exists to circumscribe the Divine, we might think of the Law as a means by which God extends knowledge of himself to all people. The Law mediates God to the whole of society rather than to just a limited number of specially chosen individuals.

Of course, the purposes of the Law are not explained so easily. In the Christian tradition, the Law is said to find its fulfilment in the person of Jesus Christ; however, the obvious difficulty that the Apostle Paul has in explaining what this means results in multiple attempts on his part to try and reconcile the Law with the forgiveness and grace offered by Christ.[9] Paul employs several rhetorical devices to help him come to terms with the Law, including, in the second letter to the Corinthians, a distinction between letter and spirit. According to one reading of this dichotomy, a spiritual interpretation of the Law gives life whereas a rigid adherence to the letter of the Law brings death.[10] For all its interpretive power, there are major problems with this reading, not least of which is the negative view of Jewish interpretation that it promotes. The problems of seeking a solution to the Law via a spirit/letter dichotomy are detailed at length in *Bleak House*, and this is the focus of the second section of this chapter. Against the strict legalism associated with those linked to Chancery, Esther's narrative offers a spiritual interpretation that is no more satisfactory than the hermeneutic it seeks to replace. An alternative to separating literalistic interpretation from a spiritual counterpart is glimpsed during the death of Jo when the narrative makes use of the Lord's Prayer to inject an element of hope into an otherwise hopeless situation. This scene, in many ways the pivotal moment of the novel, affirms the life-giving words of Scripture and restores the possibility that the Law might offer something other than death. In the final section of this chapter I will explore the interpretive vitality of the Law further by turning to Midrash (a form of biblical exegesis that we find in *The Trial)* and relating it to the concept of justice.

Exchanging gifts

In the previous chapter I explored how the doctrine of the Trinity supports an inclusive view of human relations in which all are invited to share freely in the divine life of Father, Son and Spirit. The realities of Capitalism run counter to this vision, subjecting individuals to a series of debts that impoverish our ability to relate to one another. While it is tempting to see gifts as a simplistic answer to the problems of a debt economy, the behaviour of Harold Skimpole in *Bleak House* warns us that greater discernment is required. Skimpole's carefree attitude to money leads him to solicit gifts from everyone he comes into contact with. His attitude possesses a certain attraction for John Jarndyce – who sees in it a possible antidote to the system of financial relations that governs wider society and manifests itself most grotesquely in the figure of Grandfather Smallweed – but Skimpole's infinite capacity to take things from others, with no thought of return, makes him a social parasite. Throughout the novel characters are forced to impose limits on the charity they extend to

Skimpole and even Jarndyce ends up coming uncomfortably close to the 'spasmodic forms' of benevolence that he sees all around him and complains about bitterly.[11] Part of the problem with Skimpole is that his capacity to receive gifts is much greater than his ability to give things to others. The weakness of this selfish attitude of consumption manifests itself at one point in the form of an objectionable theodicy: considering the case of the Slaves in America, Skimpole argues that 'theirs is an unpleasant experience on the whole; but, they people the landscape for me, they give it a poetry for me, and perhaps that is one of the pleasanter objects of their existence'.[12]

The limits on generosity prompted by Skimpole's actions raise far-reaching questions about giving, casting suspicion on both the motivation behind charity and the extent to which gifts can be seen as genuinely disinterested acts. In *Given Time: I. Counterfeit Money* Derrida tells us that disinterested gifts are an impossibility: 'If there is gift, the *given* of the gift (*that which* one gives, *that which* is given, the gift as given thing or as act of donation) must not come back to the giving (let us not already say to the subject, to the donor). It must not circulate, it must not be exchanged, it must not in any case be exhausted, as a gift, by the process of exchange, by the movement of circulation of the circle in the form of return to the point of departure.'[13] The standard that Derrida sets for a gift to be considered completely free from the economy of exchange is demanding, perhaps too demanding; as Alan Schrift reminds us, it is not 'surprising' that 'the logic of the gift' is 'infused with assumptions of reciprocity . . . given that our fundamental notion of justice, embodied in the image of the balanced scales, is a notion of equitable exchange'.[14] Yet Derrida's critique of gift remains valuable, in part because it urges us to think more carefully about how the term 'gift' might retain meaning within the economic setting that we find ourselves in. The response of some of the theologians associated with the so-called Radical Orthodoxy school of Christian theology has been to turn to the idea of gift-exchange.[15] John Milbank insists that the Christian idea of God's love rests on the 'possibility or actuality' of 'purified gift-exchange . . . *not* "pure gift"'.[16] Claiming that an exchange of gifts involves delay and non-identical repetition (i.e. we do not get back precisely what we give), Milbank argues that Christianity imagines something other than contractual exchange. In the case of *Bleak House*, we might say that John Jarndyce *gives* Richard and Esther a home and a new future, for although he expects to benefit from his generosity, the benefit accrues over time and undergoes several unexpected changes. Similarly, the notion of gift-exchange helps us to make some sense of John Jarndyce's odd commentary on his gift to Allan Woodcourt at the end of the novel: '. . . take from me a willing gift, the best wife that ever man had . . . Take with her the little home she brings you. You know what she will make it, Allan; you know what she has made its namesake. Let me share its felicity sometimes, and what do I sacrifice? Nothing, nothing.'[17]

Tanner tells us that Milbank's attempt to contrast gift-exchange with the commodity-exchange of Capitalism is 'overblown'.[18] She explains: 'Exchange in both cases produces, moreover, a kind of increase or profit – that is the defining feature of capital, in the one case, and of giving across multiple recipients, in the other. Gifts in fact circulate similarly to the way money does when it becomes capital.'[19] According to Tanner, the more closely one looks at the sort of gift-exchanges promoted by Milbank, the more one finds evidence of the contractual language of commodity that Milbank wants to get away from. Tanner's critique finds support in the tangled world of exchange that Kafka imagines in *The Trial*. The novel thinks about systems of exchange on several levels, including, as Mark Anderson has observed, the use of repeated reference to the trafficking of clothes, but readers share many of the difficulties that Josef K. experiences as he tries to understand precisely what these systems of exchange signify and how one might distinguish between them.[20] Commodity-exchange looks remarkably similar to gift-exchange when, with Josef K., we enter the door to a concealed room at the bank to discover that Willem and Franz, the warders who arrested Josef K. at the start of the novel, are being flogged. Initially, the scene seems to underline the human cost of an economic system of commodity-exchange: the location of the punishment suggests we are accessing areas of Capitalism that normally lie hidden, and the theft that the warders are being punished for is one that Willem defends on the grounds that he has 'a family to support' and that such thefts are traditionally accepted.[21] Yet the system of exchange in the lumber room has as much in common with forms of gift-exchange as it does with forms of commodity-exchange: the language the novel uses in this scene alludes to both judicial punishment and the sado-masochism of a fetish club. Upon entering the room, Josef K. sees three men, dramatically lit by a single candle: 'The one who clearly dominated the others and first caught the eye was wearing a kind of leather outfit which left his neck down to the chest and both his arms bare.'[22] It is a scene that begins with 'sighs' rather than screams, and it is one that Josef K. observes with 'excitement', at least at first.[23] The theatricality of the episode leaves open the possibility that some level of sexual satisfaction is being experienced by the participants, although the subsequent cries of pain make it impossible to know whether the warders are enjoying gifts or enduring punishments.

Further problems with the idea of gift-exchange as a clear alternative to commodity-exchange emerge when one considers the bribe that Josef K. offers the whipper in an attempt to prevent the men from being punished. On the one hand, this is an act of generosity, a genuine attempt to help others (in spite of the knowledge that the 'gift' will be offset by some sort of return benefit); on the other hand, the exchange that the bribe signifies is so thoroughly corrupt that it contaminates all thought and closes down the possibility that an action can be directed towards the needs of another. The more that Josef K. reflects on his decision to flee the whipping room when Franz screams, the more he is consumed by the notion that the system of exchange makes all possible gifts too compromised to be worth risking:

> K. had noticed how his [the whipper's] eyes lit up when he saw the banknote. Obviously he had gone on with the whipping just to increase the bribe a bit. And K. would not have been stingy, he was really anxious to have the warders let off . . . But as soon as Franz began to scream, everything was of course at an end. K. could not allow the clerks and possibly all kinds of other people to come and surprise him in his dealings with the crew in the lumber-room. Nobody could expect K. to make this sacrifice. If he had thought of doing that, it would almost have been simpler to take his own clothes off and offer himself to the whipper as substitute for the warders. In any case, the whipper would certainly not have accepted this replacement, because by doing so he would be guilty of a severe violation of duty, without any advantage . . .[24]

Josef K. rejects a series of gifts – bribes, generous bribes, sacrifice, self-sacrifice – because they confer too many disadvantages and dangers. Unable to think outside a world of exchange, Josef K. can only think about weighing up the personal costs of giving to others.

Recognizing the limitations of an exchange system that encourages individuals to focus on the advantages that their gift might bring them, Tanner looks to an economy of grace that does not does not 'allow concerns over purity of motive to get in the way of the effort to benefit others . . . The priority is extending benefits. That is what unconditional giving is all about . . .'[25] Tanner is aware that the motivation behind a gift is of consequence, but she is also aware that such personal concerns threaten the primary purpose of a gift – the unconditional extension of benefits to others. She explains: 'Unconditional giving is not a matter of feeling or interior disposition but a social matter, an economic matter, a question of the way benefits are distributed to form social relations.' Tanner continues: 'And because it is not fundamentally an expression of emotion, the social relations it forms need not be restricted to those of close friends or kin, limited to exclusive tight-knit groups that approximate families ('brotherhoods'), or relegated to private worlds.'[26] One of the advantages of the model that Tanner develops is that it avoids the claustrophobic view of giving that suffocates Josef K. in *The Trial* and leads him, on discovering the whipping for a second day, to declare to his clerks: 'It's about time that lumber-room was cleared out! . . . We're being smothered in filth.'[27] Unconditional giving is focused outwards; it seeks to extend benefits, not reduce them in the interests of a solipsistic purification of one's motivation. The nature of the benefits might vary – as it does in the case of Skimpole, where those who extend charity to him most successfully realize that something more is needed than simply taking care of his latest bill – and the extension of benefits allows for some sort of personal return. Tanner argues that the latter can be reconciled with a view of gifts as the unconditional extension of benefits to others, by recognizing human contingency on God as the source of life: 'Finally, the unconditionality of God's giving is saved, despite all our failures of reception and response because anything that might look like a condition for the reception and good use of God's gifts is really itself the gift of God . . . this includes the acts by which we receive those gifts and put them to good use. The law and the real ability to act on it are made God's gifts . . .'[28]

The problem of the Law in *Bleak House*

Tanner's view of gift as the unconditional extension of benefits to others is rooted in the same Christian tradition that we find in the writings of the Apostle Paul. For both Tanner and Paul, the primary answer to sin is to be found in the gift of salvation offered through Jesus Christ. The gift of salvation is seen to liberate humanity from the predicament of sin; however, this perspective raises questions about the ongoing role of human systems and frameworks – if the world has been transformed by Christ's death on the cross, why do we need to think about the way society functions and what need do we have of the Law? Tanner's efforts to think about economics in the light of Christian revelation parallel Paul's attempts to make sense of the Law in the light of Christ. Commenting on the particular problem that Paul faces, the philosopher Alain Badiou explains: 'The polemic against the "what is due," against the logic of right and duty, lies at the heart of the Pauline refusal of works and law: "To one who works, his wages are not reckoned as a grace but as his due" (Rom. 4.4). But, for Paul, nothing is due. The salvation of the subject cannot take the form of a reward or wage. The subjectivity of faith is unwaged . . . It pertains to the granting of a gift . . .'[29] Christ's death and resurrection appear to make the Law redundant and it is this predicament that Paul wrestles with at length in his writing. If one argues, as Paul does, that the Christ event marks a radical turning point in human history, then one needs to explain why the Law was given in the first place. The problem is partly one of justifying God's past actions – if God is the same yesterday, today and forever, then the giving of the Law to Moses and the importance of the Torah within God's revelation has to be explained – and partly one of considering whether the salvation that the Son of God gives to the world removes any need for the legal and ritualistic apparatus that the Law provides.[30] Paul was more convinced than other members of the Early Church that the specific requirements of the Law had to be re-evaluated in the light of Christ; yet, for all his insistence on the liberation that Christ offers, his letters display an ongoing commitment to the Law and they devote considerable energy to articulating how individual and ecclesial behaviour might be regulated.

The letter in which Paul engages most extensively with the problem of the Law is the Epistle to the Romans. In the first few chapters of this letter, Paul's uses a variety of rhetorical manoeuvres to help him make sense of the Law. But it is in his second letter to the church at Corinth that we find Paul's most famous attempt to reconcile the Law with his revolutionary view of the Gospel. He writes: 'the letter killeth but the spirit giveth life.'[31] The distinction between a rigid attachment to the letter of the law and the new possibilities of a spiritual understanding is a crucial moment in Paul's theology. Geoffrey Hartman tells us that Paul's 'letter/spirit dichotomy' is part of a rhetorical strategy, one that in spite of its 'interpretive yield' and 'imaginative daring' has led to considerable 'ideological fallout'.[32] The fallout that Hartman complains of here is multifaceted: it includes the anti-Semitic belief that Judaism revolves around a hermeneutic approach committed to legalistic self-interest at the expense of others, as well as the tendency within certain Christian belief systems to seek false refuge in an unmediated and materially disengaged theology.

In the case of *Bleak House*, a novel with a legal system that involves striking parallels with the account of the Torah propagated by many Protestant churches in the nineteenth century, the use of the letter/spirit dichotomy to overcome the problems of the Law proves extremely problematic. At the most basic level, the division between letter and spirit does not work, and much of the novel's imaginative force comes from exploring the failures that a divided reading of the Law brings with it. The novel's acknowledgement that a rigid adherence to the letter of the Law can kill and destroy is matched by an acknowledgement that the spiritual alternative some commentators have identified in Paul is also a failure. Many of the central concerns of *Bleak House*, such as the interest in the modern economy of signs, and the anxiety whether words and actions can register a meaningful impact on the world, are also products of the misguided attempt to separate the letter of the Law from its spirit.

One of the critics that have been most alert to the religious influences in Dickens's novel is Janet Larson. At the start of her article on biblical books in *Bleak House* she notes that the *Book of Common Prayer* and the Bible are alluded to 'more often than . . . any other texts'.[33] The presence of religion in Dickens's text is most evident in the Law, a system that goes far beyond its immediate judicial remit and proves inseparable from the Law presented in the Pentateuch. It is significant that the presentation of the Law at the start of Dickens's novel echoes and perverts the account of Creation given in the Book of Genesis. In place of the Spirit who hovers over the waters and breathes life, the start of Dickens's novel presents us with a stifling fog. By the time the account of the fog reaches its epicentre in Chancery, the implication is not only that the breath of creation has been suffocated, but also that the work of Creation has been contaminated by the pollutants of civilization and human sin. The problem that this creates, of a Law that cannot extricate itself from the evil it seeks to judge and condemn, is a problem that Paul addresses at length. In his recent work *Reading Derrida/Thinking Paul: On Justice* (2006), Theodore Jennings tells us that 'Paul's argument about the law being taken possession of by "flesh" serves as a framework for understanding how it is that law always serves the self-interest of those who have the means to propose and enforce the law.'[34] It is a view shared by the anonymous narrator of *Bleak House*, who describes the High Court of Chancery as the 'most pestilent of hoary sinners'.[35]

Given the novel's strong link to the Torah, it is no coincidence that the route to the High Court of Chancery in the opening pages goes via *Temple* Bar, nor that the New Testament's complaint about religious leaders who are caught up in the letter of the law rather than its true spirit is echoed in the novel's depiction of lawyers who devote themselves to 'tripping one another up on slippery precedents, groping knee-deep in technicalities'.[36] Paul's warning that the 'letter killeth' is confirmed early on in *Bleak House* when the fog-bound Spirit finds itself constrained within 'walls of words', and Richard Carstone's soul-destroying hope of a positive legal judgement might be read in terms of the vain waiting for a certain eschatological vision of a new Messianic age that never arrives.[37] The Law in *Bleak House* offers nothing more than hollow judgements and it brings death to everything it touches. At one point we are told that 'the Will itself is made a dead letter' and the keepers of the Law are made to resemble the Jewish religious leaders maligned by Jesus and the early church.[38] Whether or not Jesus and Paul were more positive about their Jewish roots than the church has sometimes suggested, there can be little doubt that the majority of nineteenth-century Protestants, like many of their forebears, read the New Testament in terms of an unambiguous attack on a legalistic framework of belief allegedly blind to the real spiritual needs of the day. The keepers of the Law in Dickens's text have priestly overtones and are judged accordingly. Tulkinghorn is described as 'faithful, a zealous, a devoted adherent' of the Law, and descriptions of Vholes consistently point to a clerical figure of death.[39] When Esther first meets Vholes she describes him as '[d]ressed in black, black-gloved, and buttoned to the chin, there was nothing so remarkable in him as a lifeless manner'.[40] Her subsequent description of Vholes as a 'Vampire' is matched by the verdict of the anonymous narrator, who likens the lawyer to a 'cannibal'.[41] As a relatively low functionary of the law, Vholes's life-destroying qualities are easy to spot; more subtle, but equally chilling, are the qualities we find in Tulkinghorn. Whereas Vholes is shown actively draining the lifeblood from Richard, Tulkinghorn's wine collection, which he is often described as holding a key for, signifies a collection of lives already drained and stored for his enjoyment. Further evidence of the religious parallels offered by the text can be seen when Tulkinghorn is murdered – his judgement is witnessed by the Roman figure on the ceiling of his residence.

As the novel unfolds, Tulkinghorn's professionalism is recast as the conniving work of a remorseless villain. Lady Dedlock describes him as 'mechanically faithful without attachment, and very jealous of the profit, privilege and reputation of being master of the mysteries of great houses'.[42] Integral to Tulkinghorn's ruthlessness is his rigid insistence on the letter of the law. When he meets with Lady Dedlock to announce that he will no longer keep her history secret, Tulkinghorn insists that having 'put the case in a perfectly plain way, and according to the literal fact', she is 'not to be trusted', and accuses her of breaking both 'the letter and the spirit of our arrangement, [which] altogether precluded any action on your part'.[43] Despite introducing a linguistic distinction between the letter and spirit of their agreement, the legalistic Tulkinghorn proves incapable of recognizing any charity in Lady Dedlock's decision to send Rosa away. Elsewhere, his 'mechanical' and 'methodical' confidence in the letter of the law, which he approaches 'like a machine', renders him entirely incapable of comprehending the emotional figure of Hortense.[44] Just before his death, Tulkinghorn is unable to register the ambiguous meaning of Hortense's promise, 'I will prove you', given in response to his insistence that any return on her part to his chambers will result in being given 'over to the police'.[45]

In an influential essay on *Bleak House*, Hillis Miller lays great stress on the 'circle of signs' present in the novel.[46] Questioning the capacity of the text to offer an alternative that 'escapes from this situation' and 'step[s] outside the ring', Miller considers the role of 'Esther Summerson and John Jarndyce . . . the chief examples in *Bleak House* of Dickens's commitment to a Christian humanism compounded of belief "in the natural feelings of the heart"'.[47] Like the Evangelical religion against which he reacts so strongly, Dickens's Christian humanism involves a sharp division between the material and spiritual worlds. The preference of Esther and John Jarndyce for the spiritual comes close to Gnosticism, with its dualistic belief that salvation is revealed to the spiritual element of humanity and that the material world is fallen and incapable of redemption. One does not have to go along with those who suspect a sinister paedophilia behind the philanthropy of John Jarndyce to see that his actions in the novel are an inadequate response to the destructive activity of the Law. In particular, his frequent retreat to the Growlery and his preference for euphemistic references to the direction of the wind when faced with challenging life events constitute a fundamental attempt to evade the harsh reality of the material world. Through their evocation of one of the meanings of the Greek and Hebrew words for 'Spirit', John Jarndyce's references to the 'wind' pursue a spiritual alternative to the textual preoccupation of the figures associated with Chancery. Esther can be seen in a similar light to her guardian. At one point she explains that her appreciation of Allan Woodcourt has 'risen above all words . . . but I hoped he might not be without some understanding of what I felt so strongly'.[48] It is easy to sympathize with this desire to rise above the corrupt and failing language systems we encounter in the novel, but Esther's confidence in an unmediated spiritual feeling proves to be as misplaced as her guardian's.

Much has been written about the way in which Esther's narrative offers an alternative to the pessimistic writings of the anonymous narrator.[49] For Alexander Welsh, writing in *Dickens Redressed* (2000), the happy ending of her narrative 'stands over against the wrongs of the world' and is a 'triumph'.[50] Yet it is difficult to see how the happy ending can be taken too seriously, considering the 'all for the best' theodicy upon which it is predicated; and there are other factors that stop us from taking Esther's narrative at face value.[51] Part of the problem is Esther's slippery relation to the words that she uses. One of the earliest incidents she recalls is reading to her godmother a story from the Gospel of John, of a woman caught in the act of adultery. Understandably, most critics read this episode in *Bleak House* in terms of its reference to fallen women, but another dimension of the biblical story is the precarious status of words themselves. In the passage, as Esther notes, Jesus responds to the charge that the woman should be stoned according to the Law, by stooping down, 'writing with his finger in the dust'.[52] It is a response that highlights the temporal nature of the words that articulate and constitute the judgement of the Law. This is not the only time Esther's narrative reminds us how transient words are. For instance, when Esther first meets Krook she draws attention to his refusal to mark letters in any sort of permanent manner. Having observed how Krook writes and rubs out the letters 'J' and 'a', Esther continues: 'He went on quickly until he had formed, in the same curious manner, beginning at the ends and bottoms of the letters, the word JARNDYCE, without once leaving two letters on the wall together.'[53] Although Esther admits to finding Krook's actions strange, she is similarly quick to erase the trace of the words she interprets. Noting the 'biblical allusions associated with Esther's major crises in the second half of the novel', Janet Larson explains that they offer 'the emotional attractiveness of religious language to authorize her mechanisms of evasion. Her resolutions of major conflicts, often culminating in a biblical allusion or echo, are for most of the novel, unstable and temporary.'[54] Esther's 'happy ending' is built on a series of biblical stories that she does not fully believe, and this leads her to try and wipe out all trace of her textual inheritance. However, her attempts to erase the trace of the text are doomed to failure. The problem, to return to the words of Hartman, is that 'the letter as vehicle, or the prior, once-authoritative text, can never be erased: It is, by the sheer fact of alphabetic existence, as well as its inertial meanings, the ghostliest of creations, at once opaque and transparent, persistent and barely noticed.'[55]

In spite of Esther's attempt to conclude her narrative with a new 'spiritual' beginning, the elisions of her narrative and the material residue of what she does tell us remain apparent. When at the end of the novel Esther feigns surprise at the praise she enjoys from local people and her immediate family and friends, the narcissistic tendencies that mark much of her narrative are exposed, casting suspicion on her spiritual vision of an idealized future. Esther may present herself as a sympathetic individual but her benevolence is rooted in a selfish economy of words, despite her disclaimers: 'I don't know how it is, I seem to be always writing about myself. I mean all the time to write about other people, and I try to think about myself as little as possible, and I am sure, when I find myself coming into the story again, I am really vexed . . .'[56] At key moments the selfish orientation of Esther's narrative is made explicit, such as the occasion on which she turns on Skimpole, writing him out of an extremely long and detailed novel with a sudden, dramatic indictment of his behaviour. Esther recalls a sentence of his memoirs that she claims to have 'chanced' upon: 'It was this. "Jarndyce, in common with most other men I have known, is the Incarnation of Selfishness."'[57] The jarring nature of this description suggests that Esther is putting words into Skimpole's mouth, revealing, in the process, her own manipulation as a narrator. Esther's willingness to deploy the word Incarnation for the purpose of criticism is telling (the quotation may be Skimpole's but the narrative is clearly Esther's). Given that this is the one occasion in the novel when Esther makes any reference to the Incarnation, we are left to presume that she has little interest in a religious doctrine that affirms God's commitment to the material needs of the world. Esther's answer to the problem of the Law – laughter at its hollow judgements; a belief that the suffering of those around her has been necessary to Providential design; a 'new beginning' where several deaths are conveniently forgotten; and her relocation to a provincial setting where it becomes far easier to position herself at the centre of life – offers a spiritual vision that is doubly false, to the painful reality of Chancery for those who are forced to deal with it and to a Christian belief system that speaks of God's commitment to those who suffer.

Esther's narrative may have the last word in the novel but it is never allowed to remain entirely uncontested. Among the many images provided by the anonymous narrator that persist in our minds long after we have read them is the death of Jo. His death, at the hands of a system 'based on words', remains a profoundly tragic event, and the tragedy is intensified by the lack of help given by figures such as Tulkinghorn, Bucket and Rev. Chadband, who all claim to speak on behalf of the law in its different forms.[58] Yet the letter that killeth also brings with it new possibilities. When Allan Woodcourt, an idealized character committed to addressing the material needs around him, realizes that the dying Jo knows no prayers and is unable to articulate a call for the world to be transformed, he decides to lead him in the Lord's Prayer. It is significant that the repetition of the prayer, line by line, is not accompanied by a spiritualized gloss, despite the wealth of sentiment and interpretive comment elsewhere in this scene. Of course, the prayer is never finished, and Jo dies before he can hear and express the lines: 'Thy Kingdom come. Thy will be done on earth as it is in heaven.'[59] Beyond the obvious poignancy of a biblical text that is never fully realized, the fragment is an acknowledgement that the Law contains new possibilities within it. The words of the Lord's Prayer appear in the Sermon on the Mount, Jesus's reinterpretation of the Torah. Jo's death reminds us that however much the Law alienates and excludes those it is meant to help, it also contains the possibility of transformation and new life.

Reading *The Trial*: just interpretation

Jo's death in *Bleak House* not only exposes the failures of the Law; it insists that a more just and equitable interpretation of the Law is available to those willing to read the text differently. The scene highlights the dynamic nexus that the Law establishes between justice, judgement and reading: justice requires ongoing judgements, and those judgements are acts of interpretations that read the Law in different ways. In recent decades the emergence of law and literature as a burgeoning field of scholarship has led to a number of influential critics writing about the way in which *Bleak House*, along with other literary texts, opens up hermeneutical concerns that are crucial to our understanding of justice.[60] Whether we are thinking about playful readings or major judicial edicts, interpretation involves acts of judgement with consequences that extend beyond the immediate sphere of literature. Words impact the world, and although the significance of our reading may vary, acts of judgement confirm the strong link between hermeneutics and justice. Commenting on this, Paul Ricoeur writes:

> In the usual sense of the word, the verb *to judge* covers a range of major senses that I propose to arrange in what I shall call an order of increasing density. First, in a weak sense, to judge is to opine. However, an opinion is expressed about something. In a slightly stronger sense, to judge is to value, to assess. In this way, a hierarchical element is introduced, expressing a preference, an evaluation,

an approbation. A third degree of force expresses the encounter between the subjective and the objective sides of judgement. Objective side: someone takes a proposition as true, good, just, legal; subjective side: he subscribes to it. Finally, at a deeper level than the one assumed by Descartes in his Fourth Meditation, judgement proceeds from the conjunction between understanding and will. The understanding that considers the true and false – the will that decides. In this way we have reached the strong sense of the word 'judge': not just to opine, value, take as true, but in the final analysis, to take a stand.[61]

Regardless of the significance that one attaches to the interpretive stand that is taken in any given situation, no judgement is final. All judgements remain open to re-evaluation and while certain judgements can be wrong, even destructive, just judgements are not definitive so long as the Law remains available for new readings. The divine truth that the Law mediates is less static than the severity of judicial edicts might sometimes suggest. In contrast to the belief voiced by Sir Leicester Dedlock at the start of *Bleak House,* that the Court of Chancery has been devised 'for the eternal settlement (humanly speaking) of everything', readers of Dickens's novel are encouraged to recognize that the Law is in a continual state of flux and subject to differing interpretations.[62] The twin narration of Dickens's novel reminds us that there is always another way of judging what has taken place, and this may explain why the characters that seem to flourish, such as Skimpole and Chadband, are those who possess a propensity for interpretive acrobatics.[63] It is easy to see why Miller's argument that '*Bleak House* is a document about the interpretation of documents' has been so influential.[64] Sir Leicester Dedlock may begin the novel with a 'fixed opinion' of the Law but other judgements eventually combine to overwhelm his household and change his understanding of what justice might look like.[65]

Given the debt that *The Trial* owes to *Bleak House,* it is no surprise that Josef K. makes a similar mistake to Sir Leicester Dedlock in presuming that the Law is a fixed thing. When Josef K. seeks help from Titorelli, the painter, he finds himself disturbed by a picture of Justice and the goddess of Victory. Josef K. complains: 'That's hardly a good combination . . . Justice has to be motionless or the scales will waver and there's no possibility of a correct judgement.'[66] One of the reasons why Josef K. finds himself so confused by the judgements that the Law passes is that he remains wedded to a notion that the judgements of the Law are immutable. The desire for a Law that is fixed affects Josef K.'s reading of the events that occur and leads him to interpret stories in an erroneous and perverse manner. When, for example, he listens to the priest's account of the 'Before the Law' parable, Josef K. seizes on a narrow interpretation, only to be admonished for being too 'hasty' in his judgement.[67] The hastiness of Josef K.'s initial judgement is symptomatic of a wider failure of reading on his part in *The Trial*. Earlier in the novel, when Josef K. returns to the Examination Room, he complains about the inaccessibility of Law books, and insists on having an opportunity to read them for himself. Yet when he is allowed to look at 'old, well-worn books', with 'sections hung together by threads', he fails to register the history of reading that the wear and tear reveals, complaining instead that the books are 'dirty'.[68] On one level, Josef K.'s assessment is right – the first book turns out to contain an indecent picture of a man and woman sitting naked – but on another level, Josef K.'s reading is a failure: we are told that having finally been given an opportunity to open the books of the Law, Josef K. 'looked no further' than the picture of the first book and 'merely opened the second book at the title page'.[69] Later on in the novel, Josef K.'s superficial reading habits are explicitly challenged by the priest in the Cathedral, who invites Josef K. to go beyond his immediate judgement and reflect more carefully on what the text of the Law might mean.

Northrop Frye famously described *The Trial* as 'a kind of "midrash" on the Book of Job'.[70] The historic form of Jewish biblical exegesis that Frye finds in Kafka's novel is most evident in the extended interpretation that the priest and Josef K. engage in when discussing the parable, although it is the Law rather than the Book of Job that is the main biblical source behind this episode. As a Jewish writer with interests in a wide range of traditions and sources, Kafka was familiar with the playful and detailed attention to verses of the Bible that characterizes older collections of Midrash.[71] Following the publication of Geoffrey Hartman and Sanford Budick's influential work *Midrash and Literature* (1986), contemporary literary critics have been encouraged to join Kafka in exploring the interpretive richness of Midrash. Introducing 'the Hebrew word *midrash*', James Kugel, one of the contributors to *Midrash and Literature*, explains that it 'might best be translated as "research", a translation that incorporates the word's root meaning of "search out, inquire" and perhaps as well suggests that the results of that research are almost by definition recherché, that is, not obvious, out-of-the-way, sometimes far fetched'.[72] The characteristics that Kugel outlines are evident in the discussion that follows the parable in *The Trial*, but their importance goes further than the case that they make for Kafka's engagement with his Jewish heritage. Midrash acknowledges the preeminence of the Law by refusing to ignore or leave behind the words it pronounces. The importance of Midrash for our reading of *The Trial* lies in its affirmation of ongoing acts of interpretation, reminding us that the Law is a text to be interpreted rather than a judgement to be received.

The midrashic commitment to ongoing acts of close interpretation reads the letter of the Law as a source of life rather than death. Struggling to comprehend this, Josef K.'s immediate response to his midrashic discussion with the priest is dismissive:

> He was too tired to follow all the deductions that could be drawn from the story; they led him into unaccustomed trains of thought, removed from reality and more suitable for academic discussion among court officials. The simple story had become perplexing, he wanted to be rid of it; and the priest, showing great delicacy of feeling, let him do this, receiving K.'s remark without a word, although it certainly did not coincide with his own opinion.[73]

Josef K. wants the Law to be simplified but the story Josef K. looks back to, nostalgically, is neither simple nor straightforward. What Josef K. struggles to understand is that 'unaccustomed trains of thought' are intrinsic to the just interpretation of the Law he is seeking. If the Law is an ethical framework given by the infinite God who is the source of all truth – in other words, a genuine mediation of something or someone Other – then it cannot be internalized, mastered and dispensed with. The Law is not to be interpreted in a familiar way, for it requires new ways of reading. Recognizing this, Midrash extends our understanding of the Law, imaginatively, without losing sight of the words that constitute the Law and without succumbing to the temptation of thinking that what the text means can be definitively grasped in a single gloss. Midrash insists that readers of the Law engage in ongoing acts of judgement. Josef K.'s refusal to meet this demand during his experience in the Cathedral circumvents the possibility of justice. With no possibility of new words and sentences, the only sentence that the Law can pass is an ending, death; in this respect, Josef K. acquiesces in his own death during the chapter that follows the Cathedral scene and that concludes the novel.

Criticizing Josef K.'s reading of the Law risks an injustice of another sort. It is impossible to isolate his reading of the Law from the Law itself, and a wide range of environmental forces conspire to shape his interpretive practice throughout the novel. Other characters in the novel also appear to read the Law badly, without being punished, and readers of *The Trial* experience their own interpretive failures when they seek to explain precisely what the Law means. As Harold Fisch reminds us, there is a certain inevitability about the misreading that takes place: 'Joseph K. will never . . . understand the Law by which he is condemned, nor will the reader . . . We are moved to seek the meaning of these figures and institutions. But we shall find only an absence, a closed door which inhibits final interpretations.'[74] Nevertheless, the lack of access to an interpretive vantage point that is uncontaminated by the Law does not justify every instance of misreading. The characters in the novel all read the Law differently, as do readers of Kafka's novel, and the lack of uniformity suggests that different judgements are possible. As a result, Josef K. must accept some responsibility for his reading of the Law, despite the limits on his freedom and autonomy.

Although we are aware that the reading of the Law pursued by Josef K. and the other characters in *The Trial* is limited and skewed, the majority of the text offers little indication that a more just interpretation is close at hand. Aware of this, and in an effort to insist that another reading of the Law is possible, the description of Josef K.'s death in the final chapter of the novel deliberately evokes the Genesis story of God instructing Abraham to sacrifice his son Isaac. The Genesis story is a problematic one, for obvious reasons, but it treats Abraham's willingness to sacrifice his son as a positive thing and is part of the Pentateuch's vision of the Law as something that enables people to access Yahweh's justice. Beth Hawkins describes Kafka's interest in the story of Abraham as an 'obsession', surfacing in his parable 'Abraham' and also 'in his metaphorical reworkings of the story (the most graphic of which might be identified as Josef K.'s execution upon a makeshift sacrificial altar)'.[75] In *The Trial*, the 'obsession' with Abraham results in the remembrance of a Law quite unlike the one that dominates the preceding pages of the novel. Reflecting on the knife that is driven into the heart of Josef K., the narrative concludes: 'With his failing sight K. could still see the gentlemen right in front of his face, cheek pressed against cheek, as they observed the decisive moment. "Like a dog!" he said. It was as if the shame would outlive him.'[76] In place of the account of a Law that sees death as an inevitable end, the murder of Josef K. is refigured as a sacrifice. It encourages a new reading of the Law that recalls the way in which generations of Jews and Christian have found new life in the teachings of the Pentateuch.

Jill Robbins insists that 'all the writings by Kafka on Abraham that we possess are glosses on Kierkegaard's Abraham'.[77] If this is so, then the Law that the allusion to Abraham recalls at the end of *The Trial* is one shaped by Soren Kierkegaard's writing on Abraham in *Fear and Trembling* (1843). In this work Kierkegaard sees Abraham as an exemplar of the knight of faith, a figure that challenges the closed ethical systems which certain philosophical readings of religion associate with the Law. Refusing to close down the meaning of God's revelation, Kierkegaard starts his book with four fictional glosses on the story of Abraham and Isaac, a textual strategy that is, in its own way, a form of Midrash. Kierkegaard's suggestion that the story in Genesis can be read in different ways is part of a broader insistence that the knight of faith can always break with established readings of the Law. At the end of *The Trial* Kafka draws on this possibility to insist that, in spite of all we have read in the novel, the Law remains capable of being read *differently*.

Commenting on the open style of interpretation that Midrash encourages, Hartman writes: 'The accreted, promissory narrative we call Scripture is composed of tokens that demand the continuous and precarious intervention of successive generations of interpreters, who must keep the words as well as the faith.'[78] Midrash insists that to do justice to the Law and appreciate all that it offers requires close attention to the words themselves, rather than seeking to transcend them through a spiritual interpretation. Spiritual readings are suspect for a variety of reasons, not least of which is the separation they bring between the person pursuing them and the interpretive communities that have read the Law previously. By definition, the Law is given to a people rather than a person, and if the Law really mediates God's justice, then the letter of the Law is the source from which justice is to be found. While some literal readings of the Law can bring death, as both *Bleak House* and *The Trial* are acutely aware, the danger lies in interpretive closure rather than in a close attention to the text. To read the Law closely, to read it justly, is to heed its call for new readings that might extend justice to all.

4 Interpretive Communities: Scripture, Tolerance and the People of God

Chapter Outline

The focus of this chapter is the reading undertaken by religious interpretive communities: not the content of their reading so much as the way in which it is undertaken. Echoing the title of Gerard Loughlin's book on narrative theology, the chapter explores how those who call themselves the people of God *tell God's story*.[1] In pursuing this subject, the chapter acknowledges that interpretive communities read sacred texts in different ways. The interpretive possibilities that sacred texts open up can be seen in fictional reworking of biblical texts, as well as a tradition of religious reading that refuses to see the meaning of sacred texts as static or fixed. Scripture's afterlife is certainly in evidence throughout the multiple readings of the Law that occur in *The Trial* (1925) and *Bleak House* (1852–3) and it is especially evident in the way that Kafka's novel uses the midrashic tradition found in the Jewish faith. Kafka is not the only writer to see the potential of Midrash, as Terry R. Wright has shown in his recent study of the ways in which twentieth-century novelists have drawn on the midrashic tradition to rewrite stories from Genesis.[2] Other writers and theorists have also shown interest in the range of readings that Midrash encourages, including Emmanuel Levinas, who tells us that:

> The reading processes that we have just seen at work [within Midrash] suggest, first, that the statement commented upon exceeds what it originally wants to say;

that what it is capable of saying goes beyond what it wants to say; that it contains more than it contains; that perhaps an inexhaustible surplus of meaning remains locked in the syntactic structures of the sentence, in its word-groups, its actual words, phonemes and letters, in all this materiality of the saying which is potentially signifying all the time.[3]

Midrashic approaches to interpretation are not the only way of realizing the surplus of meaning in the biblical text. *Bleak House* utilizes other ways of reading, including, most notably, the reinterpretation of the Lord's Prayer at the moment of Jo's death. Jo's fragmentary prayer reminds us of the capacity of sacred words to contribute to a new vision of how the world might look. Something similar takes place in Margaret Atwood's dystopian novel, *The Handmaid's Tale* (1985), where the narrator juxtaposes the protagonist's broken reworking of the Lord's Prayer with the more rigid interpretive practice of the Republic of Gilead, and uses the former to expose the religious abuses of the latter. Faced with a world of patriarchal fundamentalism that not only circumvents a woman's ability to make decisions about her own body but erodes the words that form the building blocks for individual thought and decision-making, Offred turns to the words of the Lord's Prayer to articulate a prayer for justice and hope:

> My God. Who Art in the Kingdom of Heaven, which is within.
> I wish you would tell me Your Name, the real one I mean. But *You* will do as well as anything.
> I wish I knew what You were up to. But whatever it is, help me to get through it, please. Though maybe's it's not Your doing; I don't believe for an instant that what's going on out there is what You meant.
> I have enough daily bread, so I won't waste time on that. It isn't the main problem. The problem is getting it down without choking on it.
>
> . . .
>
> Deliver us from evil.
> Then there's Kingdom, power, and glory. It takes a lot to believe in those right now. But I'll try it anyway. *In Hope*, as they say on the gravestones.[4]

In many respects, Offred's reworking of the words of Jesus is more faithful to the sacred text than the religious pretensions of those who exercise control over her: whereas the Republic of Gilead dispenses with the dynamic vitality of prayer, replacing it with a series of soundbites – 'soul scrolls' – that seek to prescribe precisely what it is that one should be saying, Offred sees prayer as an opportunity for honest, meaningful expression.[5] Moreover, as the Lord's Prayer that the Gospels record is probably a summary of the main themes of Jesus' teaching on prayer, Offred's willingness to improvise on the biblical text can be seen as theologically preferable to the rigid interpretation practised by the novel's oppressive religious government.

The freedom with which Offred reinterprets the Lord's Prayer is consistent with comments made elsewhere in the novel about the Bible as a text waiting to be rescued from the Republic of Gilead. Describing the way in which individual households keep the Bible locked up and off-limits, Offred reflects: 'It is an incendiary device: who knows what we'd make of it, if we ever got our hands on it? We can be read to from it, by him [the Commander], but we cannot read.'[6] The etymology of the word 'incendiary' carries a plurality of meanings that point to the liberating potential of reading the biblical text.[7] In addition to Offred's sense of the Bible as an inflammatory set of teachings that might lead to social agitation, there are the ideas of the Bible kindling ('incend') passionate feeling or producing the odour of religious rituals (from the cognate word, 'incense') that testify to another way of living. A comparable sense of the Bible as a potentially liberating text, waiting to be read differently, pervades Jeanette Winterson's *Oranges Are Not the Only Fruit* (1985). Like Offred, the first-person narrator of Winterson's novel comes from a fundamentalist religious community that reads the Bible in a highly selective manner – in place of 'soul scrolls' we are told of 'an elephant's foot Promise Box; two layers of little scrolls, all rolled up, each with a promise from the Word. My mother had tears in her eyes, as she put it carefully on top of the sideboard' – and like Offred, Jeanette responds to her oppressive environment by thinking of the Bible as a text waiting to be rediscovered.[8] Describing her decision to leave her mother's house, Jeanette speaks of taking 'my books and my instruments in a tea chest, with my Bible on top'; her ongoing commitment to the sacred text is evident in the narrative structure of *Oranges Are Not the Only Fruit*, which follows the first eight books of the Bible.[9]

Although the fictional worlds imagined by Atwood and Winterson seek to rediscover Scripture's 'surplus of meaning', they do so through an emphasis on individual reading. In both cases, the view of the Bible as a liberating text requires the protagonists to read against the grain of the religious interpretive communities within which they find themselves. The emphasis of both novels is open to the criticism that Scripture's interpretive vitality has more to do with the creativity of the rebellious reader than the text's inherent qualities. Any attempt to address this criticism quickly propels us into larger hermeneutic issues, such as the validity of distinguishing between the meaning of a text and our reading of it. Hans-Georg Gadamer argues that distinguishing between the meaning of a text and our reading of it is a mistake: in *Truth and*

Method (1960), probably the most important twentieth-century work in the field of hermeneutics, he insists that reading is a dynamic activity, where meaning emerges from the interaction between reader and text rather than existing prior to that interaction. Gadamer's ideas are rightly seen as pivotal in the development of reader-response criticism later in the twentieth century, yet his commitment to the idea that reading communities participate in the construction of a text's meaning should not be understood as a belief that texts are a blank slate, waiting to be read in any way one chooses. The distinction becomes apparent in *Truth and Method* when Gadamer likens hermeneutics to a conversation between reader and text. He explains: 'We say that we "conduct" a conversation, but the more genuine a conversation is, the less its conduct lies within the will of either partner. Thus a genuine conversation is never the one that we wanted to conduct. Rather, it is generally more correct to say that we fall into conversation, or even that we become involved in it.'[10] Acknowledging that a text is not the same thing as a person with whom we might converse, Gadamer still insists that reading a text 'is like a real conversation in that the common subject matter is what binds the two partners'. He continues: 'But from this it follows that hermeneutical conversation, like real conversation, finds a common language, and that finding a common language is not, any more than in real conversation, preparing a tool for the purpose of reaching understanding but, rather, coincides with the very act of understanding and reaching agreement.'[11]

The implied dialogue of the prayer described in *The Handmaid's Tale* suggests that reading sacred texts involves engaging in a conversation. In the pages that follow, I will consider how these conversations are conducted and who is involved in them. The communal focus of the hermeneutics explored in this chapter acknowledges that reading should not be seen as an isolated activity; as Stanley Fish has argued, our reading of texts is shaped by the interpretive communities from which we emerge and in which we participate. Fish's work on interpretive communities is taken seriously by narrative theologians such as Loughlin and Stanley Hauerwas, who have written at length on the way in which religious communities read the Bible within their own interpretive tradition. The question of whether or not such reading is legitimate is addressed in the first section of this chapter, which considers the distinctions that are sometimes made between sacred and secular interpretation. While some literary critics have claimed that secular reading is free from the interpretive baggage associated with religion, their claim is hard to sustain: the history of literary theory in the second half of the twentieth century can be seen as a successful attempt to expose the assumptions and biases accompanying the supposedly value-free reading promoted by F. R. Leavis and some of the New Critics on the other side of the Atlantic. Something of the ideological blindness that besets all reading communities, religious or otherwise, is apparent when we turn to George Eliot's *Silas Marner* (1861). Eliot constructs a narrative trajectory that seeks to move from the simplicity of religious fundamentalism to the sophistication of a secularized religion of humanity, yet the trajectory proves problematic – like the fundamentalism it seeks to replace, Eliot's secular reading involves its own bias and compromise.

To insist on the ideological bias of all interpretive communities is not an attempt to exempt religious communities from critique. The need for critique is a major theme of the second section of this chapter, which examines Salman Rushdie's *The Satanic Verses* (1988) and the furore surrounding the novel's reception. Fundamentalism and the cultural clash between different faith positions offer a salutary reminder that reading sacred texts is never a purely 'academic' matter. The seriousness of the clash between opposing interpretive communities highlights the need for competing readings to co-exist and talk through their differences; however, enabling and sustaining genuine conversation is extremely difficult. Commenting on *The Satanic Verses* and the hostility that the novel attracted, Rushdie claims that the novel is a form of art that models the capacity of the secular state to tolerate competing interpretive communities.[12] But there are limits to the extent that secularism is willing to tolerate the claims made by certain religious communities, and fundamentalism's refusal to acknowledge tolerance as a substantive good creates a particular problem for secularism. The failure of tolerance to arbitrate between competing readings of the world requires alternate mechanisms that enable co-existence and conversation. One of the alternatives to emerge in *Oranges Are Not the Only Fruit* is a first-person narrative that combines critique with imaginative sympathy, and in the final section of the chapter I use this as a stepping stone for thinking about hospitality as a means of negotiating the clash between different interpretive communities. Drawing on the political theology of Luke Bretherton and the eucharistic theology of Loughlin, the chapter concludes by exploring the role of hospitality in *The Handmaid's Tale*, and *Oranges Are Not the Only Fruit*. Through the welcome that it extends to strangers, hospitality provides the people of God with a metaphor that indicates how they might host other perspectives as they read and tell God's story.

Interpretive communities, the secular and the sacred

Following the eclipse of earlier critical schools of thought that privileged the formal qualities of a text and urged individual readers to try and identify precisely what it was that a text was intending to say, new schools of literary theory in the second half of the twentieth century sought other ways of approaching the issue of textual meaning.[13] The critical move to broader hermeneutic issues was epitomized by Stanley Fish, who shifted his attention away from Milton's *Paradise Lost* (1667) to the role played by interpretive communities in the production of textual meaning. Fish's work in the 1970s on interpretive communities culminated in the publication of *Is There A Text in This Class?: The Authority of Interpretive Communities* (1980). In this book he argues that 'meanings are the property neither of fixed and stable texts nor of free and independent readers but of interpretive communities that are responsible both for the shape of a reader's activities and for the texts those activities produce'.[14] To support this claim Fish deploys a series of anecdotes, including the now legendary account of a seminar he gave to a group of students who were studying English religious poetry of the seventeenth century. The group 'had been learning how to identify Christian symbols and how to recognize typological patterns and how to move from the observation of these symbols and patterns to the specification of a poetic intention that was usually didactic or homiletic'.[15] Fish recalls the day on which the students entered his classroom and saw a group of words on the blackboard from a previous seminar on linguistics: the new group of students were told 'that what they saw on the blackboard was a religious poem of the kind they had been studying' and were asked to interpret it.[16] Describing the inventive religious readings that resulted, Fish concludes that it was the interpretive practice of the community that shaped the reading rather than the words themselves. Of particular interest here is the religious dimension of the anecdote: while there are other non-religious examples in Fish's book, and while he is careful to argue that it is the dynamics of interpretive communities rather than the qualities of religion per se that are responsible for the events he describes, an inevitable, if unintended, suggestion of the story is that interpretive communities for whom religion is a central thread are especially susceptible to bringing their own prejudices to the texts that they read.

The close association between religious reading practice and the role played by interpretive communities has been embraced by some theologians, who see nothing wrong in the claim that that there is something fish-y about the way in which the Church reads the biblical text. Looking back at the development of Hans Frei's narrative theology in the second half of the twentieth century, and aware of its parallels with developments in literary theory, Loughlin observes a shift away from Frei's early sympathy with Anglo-American New Criticism, with its claim that texts possess a 'self-evident intelligibility' that can be accessed through 'formal analysis of its stylistic devices', to a later position, influenced by the ecclesial emphasis of George Lindbeck's theology.[17] Loughlin explains that Frei came to emphasize 'a communal reading of the scriptural text', recognizing 'that it is possible to discern a unified story in the biblical narratives and other writings only by dint of a community that so reads them'.[18] By the early 1990s other theologians were encouraging a wider Protestant audience to think about the importance of interpretive communities. In *Unleashing the Scripture: Freeing the Bible from Captivity to America* (1993) Stanley Hauerwas exposes the negative side-effects of a North American tendency to make the Bible 'the possession not of the Church but . . . of the citizen, who has every right to determine its meaning', and insists that 'the debate between fundamentalists and biblical critics is really more a debate between friends who share many of the assumptions'.[19] The critique of biblical criticism here needs further explanation. Hauerwas is reacting against an individualistic tradition in biblical studies that privileges neutral exegesis and plays down the politics of interpretation. It is a tradition that also has the effect of making the 'Church incidental' to theology.[20] Reflecting on the alternatives to fundamentalism and 'biblical criticism', Hauerwas casts an approving eye in the direction of two thinkers who are an unlikely source of instruction for the Protestant audience that Hauerwas is addressing. Naming the two thinkers in a chapter entitled 'Stanley Fish, the Pope, and the Bible', Hauerwas goes on to observe that the two 'are on the same side when it comes to the politics of interpretation. Both men assume that the text, and in this case the text of Scripture, can be interpreted only in the context of an "interpretive community".'[21]

While theologians such as Loughlin and Hauerwas have welcomed the links between interpretive communities and religious readings of sacred texts, a number of novelists have been more sceptical about the benefits of allowing the people of God to be the main custodians of the way in which Scripture is read. The reservations of Winterson and Atwood over the interpretive competence of those who claim to be the people of God are not new. Long before contemporary novelists registered their concerns over fundamentalism, writers such as George Eliot were asking searching questions about the direction religious hermeneutics should take. Although the narrator of *Silas Marner* should not be seen as providing unfiltered access to Eliot's own beliefs, it is commonly acknowledged that Eliot's personal scepticism regarding faith, which includes a rejection of the Evangelical beliefs of her youth, affects the narratives she constructs.[22] *Silas Marner* opens with an extremely negative account of what happens when religious sects are left to undertake the work of interpretation. When the main protagonist is falsely accused of a crime, his religious community follows an interpretive practice recorded in the Acts of the Apostles and draws lots to confirm his guilt. Commenting on the inadequacy of the hermeneutic employed by the religious community at Lantern Yard, the narrator observes: 'This resolution can be a ground of surprise only to those who are unacquainted with that obscure religious life which has gone on in the alleys of our towns.'[23] A few lines later, the condemnation of the interpretive community in which Silas finds himself at the start of the novel continues: 'We are apt to think it inevitable that a man in Marner's position should have begun to question the validity of an appeal to the divine judgement by drawing lots; but to him this would have been an effort of independent thought such as he had never known; and he must have made the effort at a moment when all his energies were turned into the anguish of disappointed faith.'[24]

The narrator's disparaging attitude to the folk beliefs of religious communities reflects some of Eliot's reading in nineteenth-century philosophy and biblical criticism.[25] Although thinkers such as August Comte, Charles Darwin, David Strauss and Ludwig Feuerbach do not reject religion altogether, they do locate belief within a naturalistic and humanistic framework that has little interest in maintaining the content of the theological vocabulary used by the Church. The interjections of the narrator in *Silas Marner* provide some indication of Eliot's preference for a more secular approach to interpretation but the preference is clearer when we consider the novel's narrative trajectory. Having found himself estranged from the community of Lantern Yard, Silas goes through a period in which his obsession with material goods cuts him off from meaningful human interaction and he eventually finds happiness through participation in the community at Raveloe. Silas's experiences at Raveloe lead him to re-interpret his Job-like ordeals in a more secular fashion, and the wisdom of the novel favours a love for one's fellow humanity over theological beliefs or the pursuit of material wealth.

Although the language used by the community at Raveloe maintains the semblance of religion, it contains remarkably few references to God and virtually no recognizable theological content. When Dolly makes a cake for Silas, engraved with the letters I. H. S. (the first letters of the name of Jesus in Greek), she explains: 'I can't read 'em myself, and there's nobody, not Mr Macey himself, rightly knows what they mean; but they've a good meaning, for they're the same as is on the pulpit-cloth at church.'[26] A similar commitment to words that are good for no discernable theological reason is apparent later in the novel, when Dolly seeks to comfort Silas by speaking of her own inability to understand what's going on: 'I can never rightly know the meaning o' what I hear at church, only a bit here and there, but I know it's good words – I do.'[27] The theological vacuity of the religious language that Dolly seeks to impress upon Silas is consistent with Feuerbach's religion of humanity, an interpretive framework favoured by Eliot that values religious beliefs for their insight into human aspirations rather than their claim to reveal something about the Divine. Rejecting the specific claims of the Christian faith (or any other distinct religious belief system) in favour of a secular and universal human alternative, the narrator offers the following comment on Nancy's hermeneutic endeavours:

> It might seem singular that Nancy – with her religious theory pieced together out of narrow social traditions, fragments of church doctrine imperfectly understood, and girlish reasonings on her small experience – should have arrived by herself at a way of thinking so nearly akin to that of many devout people whose beliefs are held in the shape of a system quite remote from her knowledge: singular, if we did not know that human beliefs, like all other natural growths, elude the barriers of a system.[28]

By treating the interpretive work of a particular religious community as being of little or no consequence, the narrator suggests that such work does not need to be considered in detail; readers are encouraged to explain away the theological vocabulary that primitive groups of people allegedly use when they interpret the world. While the narrative continues to speak of religion, the novel shows virtually no interest in the specificities of religious interpretive communities, and it is difficult to avoid the conclusion that Dolly, Nancy and the other inhabitants of Raveloe are vehicles for Eliot's own secular approach to hermeneutics.

My criticism of Eliot's treatment of religious interpretive communities in *Silas Marner* is not meant to suggest that there has to be a radical divide between the people of God and those outside the Church when it comes to interpreting sacred texts. Hauerwas and Loughlin are right, I think, to argue that because the people of God are those whose story is narrated in Scripture, they are in a good position to continue interpreting that story, but not every instance of sacred interpretation is preferable to its secular counterpart and it is not always possible to make a clear distinction between sacred and secular interpretive communities in the first place. The proliferation of reading communities that attend to the reading of Scripture and the crossover between these communities mean that interpretive options extend well beyond the stark choices offered by the Lantern Yard community and Eliot's religion of humanity. One of the consequences of the co-existence of different interpretive communities, religious and otherwise, is the possibility of critique. Loughlin is right to observe that the 'Church reads its Scripture according to certain rules or doctrines'.[29] But he is also right to point out that these 'imperfect rules, attempts after the event to model in a formal system the vagaries of the Church's language', are continually subject to critique by virtue of the fact that they 'jostle with the other language-games we play . . . there must be credible relations between what we say in religious discourse and what we say elsewhere'.[30]

Satanic verses: fundamentalism and the limits of tolerance

Loughlin argues persuasively that the refusal to subordinate theological hermeneutics to other modes of reading does not have to be seen as irrational; he also makes a convincing case for the ability of religious interpretive communities to prioritize theological assumptions while remaining open to external critique. Yet not every religious hermeneutic is as theologically astute as the one promoted by Loughlin. Fundamentalists may constitute a small subset of a much larger religious interpretive community but their forceful presence in the modern world and their violent antipathy to the work of the imagination explain why a number of commentators with an interest in literature have expressed concern about the potential danger of religious interpretive communities. The danger was underlined in 1989 when the Ayatollah Khomeini sought to capitalize on the protests among sections of the worldwide Muslim community at the publication of Rushdie's *The Satanic Verses* by issuing a fatwa against the author of this 'blasphemous' novel. The fatwa strengthened the image of the Ayatollah as the world's leading defender of Islam and Rushdie was sent into hiding for much of the following decade, prompting a variety of literary and cultural commentators to question the place of religion in a world made up of multiple interpretive communities.[31]

Specific objections to *The Satanic Verses* ranged from the way Rushdie 'retells an old legend that some of the Qu'ran's original verses originated with Satan and were later deleted by Mohammed' to anger at the novel's suggestion of sexual impropriety among the wives of the Prophet and the 'choice of the name "Mahound" (a medieval demonisation of Mohammed)'.[32] In many respects, the specificities of Rushdie's text were incidental to the protests that followed the novel's publication: a vociferous section of the Islamic community who charged Rushdie with blasphemy did not accept that their objections required a close personal engagement with the text. Understandably, Rushdie was frustrated and bewildered at learning that 'people, millions upon millions of people, have been willing to judge *The Satanic Verses* and its author, without reading it'; yet his complaint does not fully take into account the dynamics of different interpretive communities.[33] A tradition that privileges personal autonomy and insists on the need for every individual to make their own interpretation about what a text is saying expects those criticizing a piece of writing to read it first; other interpretive communities, however, operate with different assumptions, including the willingness to hold a belief on the basis of a judgement made by a more senior member of the community.

In an astute essay on the aftermath of the fatwa against Rushdie, Ruvani Ranasinha complains about 'literary and sociological discussions of the Rushdie Affair' that 'routinely' sideline 'the vocal "non-readers" who constitute a significant interpretive community'.[34] Ranasinha's use of quotations marks when referring to the 'non-readers' who played such an influential role in the Rushdie Affair provides a useful insight into the great paradox of fundamentalist reading. On the one hand, fundamentalism's use of an inconsistent and narrow hermeneutic that makes more sense to those within the community than those outside it can be seen as a failure of reading; on the other hand, this 'non-reading' community continually interpret the texts they come into contact with. To dismiss fundamentalists as non-readers is to make the mistake of conceding one of the central premises of fundamentalism: that interpretation can be avoided, that it is an unnecessary addition of the modern world, a desire on the part of unbelievers to explain away the sacred text and ignore its plain message. Following the publication of a series of pamphlets

(*The Fundamentals: A Testimony*) in the United States between 1910 and 1915, the term fundamentalism was coined to describe people from different religious traditions who display an unwavering commitment to a truth they believe to be at risk from the sophistication and complexity of modern life. Like the writers of *The Fundamentals*, who wrote their pamphlets in response to great cultural change and a pressing call to read the world differently, fundamentalists cling aggressively to beliefs that they hold to be timeless.

The belief that every aspect of modernity threatens the integrity of the Christian faith may be questionable on a philosophical level but it is not surprising as a human response to change. A fear of cultural change lurks behind the emergence of fundamentalism across the major world religions. One does not have to share Steve Bruce's commitment to secularization as the inevitable trajectory of the modern world to acknowledge the truth of his observation that fundamentalism 'is a rational response of traditionally religious people to social, political and economic changes that downgrade and constrain the role of religion in the public world'.[35] Fundamentalism is far from being the only response that religious communities make to modernity but the violence of the retreat into fixed and inviolable modes of interpretation marks it out for special attention and encourages us to pay close attention to the cultural factors at work. Among these factors, the link to modernity is especially crucial: 'although reformist tendencies can be found at any period in history, fundamentalism's quarrel with secularization and the specific and unique of concepts of society and culture produced by Western modernity place its beginnings firmly in the twentieth century. It is a reaction against modernism . . .'[36]

Ironically, the lack of a nuanced hermeneutic in fundamentalism's response to the questions posed by modernity is mirrored by the interpretive generalizations and unsympathetic language shown by some 'secular' commentators as they seek to articulate their own worries about fundamentalism. Steve Bruce's sociological study of fundamentalism may contain plenty of helpful material but the abrupt and aggressive opening – 'This book is about the modern zealots. One of their signs is intolerance.' – betrays the author's hostility to any and every expression of religious enthusiasm.[37] Bruce's use of the Rushdie Affair as both an exemplar of fundamentalist intolerance and an indication of the dangers to which religion is prone echoes the response of many liberal commentators at the time of the Rushdie Affair. While these responses often articulate legitimate complaints about the violence of the fundamentalist reaction to *The Satanic Verses* and the clumsiness of 'blasphemy' as an analytical term, they also communicate an ideological position that is more questionable.[38] Ranasinha draws our attention to this when she quotes from Homi K. Bhabha, who highlights 'the limits of liberalism as evidenced in some liberal responses to fundamentalism that emerged in the wake of the Rushdie Affair'. Ranasinha continues: 'Signalling the dangers implicit in the opposition between fundamentalism and traditional notions of secularism, Bhabha unpacks such constructions of secularism and suggests they can be imperialistic.'[39] But the critique that Bhabha offers in 'Unpacking My Library . . . Again' has limits of its own. Objecting to views of secularism that are grounded in 'an unreconstructed liberalism . . . devoid of the *crucial interpolation* of its colonial history', Bhabha advocates a more self-reflexive secularizing of the public sphere, enabling a 'social space which has to be communally shared with "others," and from which solidarity is not simply based on similarity but on the recognition of difference'.[40] It is a conclusion that perpetuates the idea of the secular as a neutral alternative to religious intolerance.

Despite the linguistic violence of the exchanges between fundamentalism and modern liberal thought, the two camps share more in common than either side cares to admit. Fundamentalists who try desperately to purge their beliefs of all traces of modern thought are as blinkered as the liberal critics who seize on the worst excesses of fundamentalism and use them to argue for the total removal of religion from the public sphere. Those within the fundamentalist community who see themselves as a bastion of uncontaminated religious belief are misguided about the purity of their position. Fundamentalism makes considerable use of the resources of modernity and Klaus Stierstorfer is not alone in describing fundamentalism as 'parasitic'.[41] Likewise, some advocates of modern liberalism, including Rushdie, fail to acknowledge the 'religious' shibboleths of their secularism. Rushdie is a sophisticated thinker who is certainly not guilty of the widespread hostility to religion that some religious commentators have accused him of, but he does have a tendency to position his own narrative as a neutral alternative to the closed systems of thought that he associates with religion. Thus Joel Kuortti is right to describe *The Satanic Verses* as a text that sets 'secular words against the absolute words of revelation. The narrative is to a great extent a wrestling match between different verses, satanic and otherwise. It contrasts various types of fundamentalism – Sikh terrorism, Christian Creationist fundamentalism, Hindu communalism, Muslim chauvinism – with a liberal humanist worldview. The Islamic history is used as one of the settings in which these fundamentalisms are criticised.'[42]

The reading of *The Satanic Versus* that Rushdie provides in his essay 'In Good Faith' differs from the reading provided by Kuortti. Rushdie insists that: '*The Satanic Verses* celebrates hybridity, impurity, intermingling, the transformation that comes of new and unexpected combinations of human beings, cultures, ideas, politics, movies, songs. It rejoices in mongrelisation and fears the absolutism of the Pure.'[43] John Maslama's description of Gibreel Farishta as 'a rainbow coalition of the celestial; a walking United Nations of gods . . . in short, the future' is indicative of the generous intermingling of ideas that Rushdie highlights in his gloss on the novel. *The Satanic Verses* is full of instances of hybridity, from characters that cross different cultures and physically mutate, to the inventive juxtaposition of ancient myths and contemporary magic realism.[44] Yet the distinction Rushdie makes between the religious 'absolutism of the Pure' and his own celebration of impurity and hybridity is questionable. In an attempt to show that the impure belongs purely to the secular literary imagination, the novel slips continually between references to religious ideology and references to fundamentalism, as though the two things were the same. It is easy to sympathize with the political reasons for this commitment to the secular as the place where different ideas can co-exist and be explored – Rushdie explains: 'To be an Indian of my generation was also to be convinced of the vital importance of Jawaharlal Nehru's vision of a secular India. Secularism, for India, is not simply a point of view; it is a question of survival.'[45] At the same time, Rushdie's commitment to the necessity of the secular ignores the affirmations of the profane and impure that feature in a number of theological belief systems. When Salman the Persian (very obviously an allusion to the author) talks of 'polluting the word of God with my own profane language', he implies, wrongly, that religion is always on the side of the pure.[46] Bhabha sides with Salman the Persian when he tells us that 'Rushdie's sin [in the eyes of those who attacked the novel] lies in opening up a space of discursive contestation that places the Koran within a perspective of historical and cultural relativism', yet the reality is that Islam, along with other belief systems, has a long history of opening its sacred text to different readings.[47]

A further problem with Rushdie's description of his novel as a site where difference can be celebrated is that *The Satanic Verses* only tolerates certain voices. Those who refuse to acknowledge difference and impurity as substantive goods are silenced, most notably in the case of Eugene Dumsday, the creationist scientist who sits next to Saladin Chamcha on the hijacked plane.

When Dumsday accidentally bites off his tongue during a struggle with the terrorists, he is literally deprived of a voice. But the silencing of Dumsday begins before the accident occurs. Openly sceptical of what Dumsday has to say, the narrator refuses to give the creationist a proper hearing, and the narrative trails off before all the details of Dumsday's position can be heard: 'He . . . began shouting hysterical incoherences. A stream of dribble ran out of the corner of his mouth; he licked at it feverishly with his tongue. *Now just hold hard here, busters, now goddamn it enough is ENOUGH, whaddya wheredya get the idea you can* and so forth . . .'[48] In a novel the length of *The Satanic Verses*, the 'so forth' of this quotation is particularly dismissive: it reveals the bias of a narrative that has no real interest in what fundamentalists have to say and no intention of giving them a proper hearing.

The difficulty surrounding the voices that are allowed to speak in *The Satanic Verses* parallels the difficulty that the novel chooses to raise when it incorporates a legend that some of the verses in the Qu'ran originated with Satan and had to be deleted. When the Prophet Mahound realizes that the words of revelation he has listened to are from the Devil rather than Allah, 'not godly, but satanic. He returns to the city as quickly as he can, to expunge the foul verses that reek of brimstone and sulphur, to strike them from the record for ever and ever . . .'[49] As Rushdie's narrative quickly reminds us, the Prophet's desire to purify his message proves difficult, partly because the revelation comes via the ambiguous figure of Gibreel – '*it was me both times, baba, me first and second also me*' – and partly because Mahound's efforts to strike the verses from the record make noises that are outside the Prophet's control.[50] Mahound's attempts to modify the text mirror the interventions of the narrator in *The Satanic Verses*; for, whereas Mahound wants to purify the record, the narrator wants to contaminate the story using a series of post-modern narrative techniques. Like Mahound, the voice of Rushdie's narrator makes itself heard and a dismissive attitude to fundamentalism echoes throughout the novel. Describing the city of Jahilia in one of Gibreel's dreams, the narrator observes: 'This is the world into which Mahound has brought his message: one one one. Amid much multiplicity, it sounds like a dangerous word.'[51] Rushdie's distrust of religious absolutism resounds in his novel, albeit in more complex ways than some of the novel's opponents have appreciated. Critics who seized on the novel's title as proof of Rushdie's satanic orientation misunderstood what *The Satanic Verses* was about and missed the novel's debt to William Blake; at the same time, the narrator does align himself with some level of diabolic intent when he identifies himself as the one with 'the best tunes'.[52] The verses that follow in the novel may not be devilish in the sense of pursuing evil, ungodly aims, but their silencing of certain religious voices and their re-arrangement into a secular song are unmistakeable.

Rushdie's secular reading of religion in *The Satanic Verses* goes some way to satisfying the criteria of writing laid down by the satirist Baal: 'To name the unnameable, to point at frauds, to take sides, start arguments, shape the world and stop it from going to sleep.'[53] If there is a complaint to be made against Rushdie's secularity, it lies in the failure to register its bias against religion rather than the bias itself. The limits of secularism as a guarantor of freedom and diversity need to be acknowledged. Rushdie comes close to acknowledging these limits in his essay 'Is Nothing Sacred?' when he poses the question: 'Do I, perhaps, find something sacred after all? Am I prepared to set aside as holy the idea of the absolute freedom of the imagination and alongside it my own notion of the World, the Text and the Good?'[54] But before the question can be considered adequately, Rushdie allows himself a convenient distraction from the challenge of confronting his own shibboleths, asking: 'Does this add up to what the apologists of religion have started calling "secular fundamentalism"?'[55] By reframing the limits of secularism in extreme terms that can then be dismissed as the conspiratorial counter-accusation of religious fundamentalists, Rushdie allows the assumptions of his own thinking to remain hidden. The result is a theory of the novel that falls short of his aspiration that literature should be 'the arena of discourse, the place where the struggle of languages can be acted out'.[56]

Hospitable stories

Securing such an arena of discourse is notoriously difficult, and both *The Satanic Verses* and its detractors show a lack of tolerance towards one another. The limits of tolerance might be seen as an inevitable consequence of democracy's underlying fragility but they might also be seen as a sign that toleration is an inadequate mechanism for sustaining a heterogeneous society. Much of the problem concerns the inability of tolerance to provide a framework for negotiating difference and determining truth. While it is easy to decry truth as an outdated transcendental, easily dispensed with in a modern culture that believes all ideas to possess equal validity, this perspective ignores the ongoing need for some level of common agreement in the face of competing perspectives. Finding common agreement is hard: the severity of the conflicts that occur in the modern world places considerable demands on the idea of a universal truth and urges caution upon those who wish to declare that their story of the world is a true one. Yet truth claims are an unavoidable part of tolerating something or someone, as Luke Bretherton explains when he outlines the conditions that tolerance needs to meet:

> First, there must be some conduct about which one disapproves, even if only minimally or potentially. Second, although such a person or group has power to act coercively against, or interfere to prevent, that of which they disapprove, they do not. Third, not interfering coercively must result from more than acquiescence, resignation, indifference or a balance of power. One does not tolerate that which one is not concerned about; nor is it tolerance simply to accept what one cannot, or is not willing to, change . . .[57]

Because many of the calls for tolerance concentrate on passively allowing other perspectives to co-exist rather than developing active steps to enable that co-existence, the framework that tolerance offers can struggle with the questions that arise in a multicultural society – for example, should we tolerate teachers on the far right of the political spectrum who incite religious hatred among the children in their care, or should we tolerate the efforts of a particular religious community to put to death an individual who has offended them? For all its idealism, tolerance is difficult to sustain in practice. All too often it finds itself exposed as an empty concept, a synonym for our relative disinterest in the activities of others so long as we are not personally affected.

Conflict resolution is a central concern of the semi-autobiographical *Oranges Are Not the Only Fruit*, a novel in which Winterson searches for some level of reconciliation with the fundamentalist community that has been so damaging to her during childhood. Recognizing the incoherence of a philosophical outlook that refuses to tolerate fundamentalist intolerance, Winterson searches for a more robust framework to hold together different interpretations of the world. Her novel combines an extensive critique of fundamentalism with an imaginative sympathy for it that never stops trying to understand the community that shaped her upbringing. Much of the book's imaginative sympathy is sustained by a humour that stops the narrative from becoming too vitriolic or vengeful; towards the end of the novel, the humour is joined by moments of reflection in which the narrator explains how she is able to combine critique with sympathy: 'I miss the company of someone utterly loyal. I still don't think of God as my betrayer. The servants of God, yes, but servants by their very nature betray . . . I don't even know if God exists, but I do know that if God is your emotional role model, very few relationships will match up to it.'[58] An awareness of human fallibility is important to the sympathetic perspective that Winterson adopts; equally important is her belief in the power of the imagination. She writes: 'I have a theory that every time you make an important choice, the part of you left behind continues the other life you could have had . . . There's a chance that I'm not here at all, that all the parts of me . . . for a moment brush against each other. That I am still an evangelist in the North, as well as the person who ran away.'[59]

It is significant that Winterson's most explicit comments on the need for imaginative sympathy occur in the section of the novel named after the Book of Ruth, a biblical text focusing on the experience of being an alien in a foreign land and the choices required of those who profess loyalty and love. While the religious community that Winterson leaves behind is neither tolerant nor sympathetic to others, the people of God have not always been so hostile to their neighbours. The many expressions of love for one's neighbour in religious history are as conspicuous as the failure to show such love has been on other occasions. Bretherton points out that 'the emphasis on the relative newness [post-Enlightenment] of tolerance as a concept can be overstated . . . tolerance and freedom of conscience have been a constant theme in the Christian tradition'.[60] However, for Bretherton, 'hospitality constitutes a better way of framing relations with strangers than tolerance'.[61] Arguing that the 'motif of hospitality is a root metaphor and practice embedded in the Christian tradition that encapsulates its crucial elements with regard to how the church relates to it neighbours', Bretherton argues that 'it allows for Christians to retain their specific criteria for evaluating the veracity of moral claims, while at the level of moral practice experiencing both continuity and discontinuity with their neighbours'.[62]

Bretherton's focus on hospitality offers a useful way of approaching the subject matter of this chapter – hospitality invites us to consider how religious communities interpret the story of God and how they relate to those who tell a different story of the universe. Rooting hospitality in the work of Christ, and focusing on the parables in the Gospels that invite outsiders to a shared meal with the heavenly host, Bretherton argues that those who identify themselves as followers of Christ should extend hospitality to those with whom they disagree. In spite of the obvious differences between the hospitality advocated by Bretherton and the hospitality shown by literary writers who find a place for dissenting and objectionable characters in their fiction, the act of welcoming a stranger is common to religion and literature.[63] If Mikhail Bakhtin is right to insist on the dialogic quality of the novel, then it is a short step to think of the novel as a hospitable form of writing.[64] For the four authors under discussion in this chapter, stories are open forums with an ability to host something or someone outside our common experience. In the case of Eliot, the mythic element that haunts her tale is derived from an intertextual reference to the Book of Job; in the case of Atwood, the story moves between past and present, constantly reminding us that what we read is a reconstruction that could have been written differently; in the case of Rushdie, fantastic dream sequences are used to challenge the complacency that creeps into our notions of reality; and in the case of Winterson, the juxtaposition of a fairytale within a semi-autobiographical narrative reminds us that deeply held beliefs can always be interpreted differently All four writers see stories as an opportunity for accommodating other perspectives, with the narrator of *Oranges Are Not the Only Fruit* explaining: 'that is the way with stories; we make them what we will. It's a way of explaining the universe while leaving the universe unexplained, it's a way of keeping it all alive, not boxing it into time.'[65]

The commitment to hospitality that we see in stories is also a fundamental aspect of language. This is one of the many ideas to emerge from 'The Critic as Host', the essay that J. Hillis Miller wrote in response to the attack by conservative literary critics on deconstruction during the theory wars of the 1970s. Challenging the claim that deconstruction "'is plainly and simply parasitical" on "the obvious or univocal reading"', Miller explores the capacity of a few simple words to host a multiplicity of different readings.[66] He reflects:

> To get so far or so much out of a little piece of language, context after context widening out from these few phrases to include as their necessary milieux all the family of Indo-European languages, all the literature and conceptual thought within these languages, and all the permutations of our social structures of household economy, gift-giving and gift-receiving – this is an argument for the value of recognizing the equivocal richness of apparently obvious or univocal language, even of the language of criticism. Criticism is in this respect, if in no other, continuous with the language of literature. This equivocal richness, my discussion of 'parasite' implies, resides in part in the fact that there is no conceptual expression without figure, and no intertwining of concept and figure without an implied narrative, in this case the story of the alien guest in the home.[67]

Equivocation ensures that language continually hosts alien ideas, even if, as Miller is aware, authors do not always embrace the strangers that turn up in their work. Authors may not always welcome strangers but the immersion of the writer in a world of words ensures that showing hospitality to others is an ever-present possibility.[68]

The authors of the totalitarian government in *The Handmaid's Tale* are not very hospitable people, and Offred is justifiably suspicious when the Commander she is attached to invites her to his study. Once there, she is asked to play Scrabble with him, a request that challenges the unequivocal instruction she has received from Aunt Lydia previously, that men 'only want one thing'.[69] The word-games that Offred participates in with the Commander form part of the novel's interest in language as a means of resistance to tyrannical modes of thought.[70] Playing Scrabble helps Offred recover her earlier familiarity with language – she used to work in a library – and eventually leads to an instance of literary equivocation that allows her to see the world in new, unregulated ways: 'It's strange, now, to think about having a job. *Job.* It's a funny word. It's a job for a man. Do a jobbie, they'd say to children, when they were being toilet trained. Or of dogs: he did a job on the carpet.'[71] Offred's exploration of the word 'job' also leads her to think of the Book of Job. Although the mention of the biblical text is not followed by any sort of explicit commentary, the allusion is enough to encourage her to ask the same defiant and open-ended questions of her predicament that Job asks of his.

Literary equivocation is never far removed from the concerns of theological narratives, as Miller shows us when he finds unexpected links between equivocation and the Eucharist in the course of an etymological exploration of the words 'parasite' and 'host':

> A curious system of thought, or of language, or of social organization (in fact all three at once) is implicit in the word parasite. There is no parasite without a host. The host and the somewhat sinister or subversive parasite are fellow guests beside the food, sharing it. On the other hand, the host is himself the food, his substance consumed without recompense, as when one says, 'He is eating me out of house and home.' The host may then become host in another sense, not etymologically connected. The word 'host' is of course the name for the consecrated bread or wafer of the Eucharist, from Middle English *oste*, from Latin *hostia*, sacrifice, victim.[72]

A similar proximity between wordplay and the Eucharist can be found in *The Handmaid's Tale* when Offred starts to play word-games with the Commander. Describing her handling of the 'plasticized wooden counters' that are used to play Scrabble, Offred tells us: 'I hold the glossy counters with their smooth edges, finger the letters. The feeling is voluptuous. This is freedom, an eyeblink of it. *Limp*, I spell. *Gorge.* What a luxury. The counters are like candies, made of peppermint, cool like that. Humbugs, those were called. I would like to put them into my mouth. They would taste also of lime. The letter C. Crisp, slightly acid on the tongue, delicious.'[73] The vocabulary used here entertains freedom in different ways – new words, implements that can be put to unexpected uses, erotic feeling and food as a source of sensual delight – but the allusion to the host eaten during the Eucharist is the richest part of this linguistic alternative to the Republic of Gilead.[74] The allusion *counters* the strict order of Gilead by welcoming us into a new realm of words, a Republic of Letters. As well as narrating a story of liberation, the Eucharist invites Offred's active participation in that story rather than treating her as a nameless and subordinate element within a tightly controlled account.

It is quite possible that a theological reading of the Scrabble episode in *The Handmaid's Tale* is not what the teller of Atwood's story has in mind, yet stories play host to a multiplicity of religious ideas and perspectives as they are interpreted by readers. This is also true of the stories recorded in Scripture. Arguing that the story found in the Christian Bible is meant to remain open to new readings *and* outline a specific narrative, Loughlin turns to the Eucharist to end his book about the telling of God's story. As well as recalling a particular event, the Eucharist invites those who participate in this act of remembrance to find a place within a much larger story. In contrast to the lack of hospitality displayed by fundamentalist accounts of the story of God, the grand narrative to which the Eucharist points is altogether more inclusive, open and communal: 'The Eucharist is story and meal, narrative and food. When the meal is over, the one who has gathered his friends together shows the depth of his love for them by taking bread, breaking it and giving it to them . . . He gives the story that the Eucharist first and quite simply now gives. It is given by him for all.'[75]

The Stain of Sin: Tales of Transgression in the Modern World

5

In the context of a discussion about interpretive communities and the way in which the people of God read different narratives, the previous chapter interrogated Salman Rushdie's interest in impurity. Although Rushdie is right to insist that the stories we tell are impure, his implicit assumption that impurity can only be accommodated in secular narratives is unsatisfactory. Secular readings of the world are more compromised than Rushdie is willing to admit, and, conversely, religious stories of the world are more attuned to contamination than the subtext of *The Satanic Verses* (1988) suggests. Theology is a discourse that foregrounds contamination: theologians employ an extensive vocabulary to name imperfection and, historically, they have had a great deal to say about what is wrong with the world. Moreover, theological narratives embody contamination, in their mingling with other stories that describe and construct our view of the world. The extent of the mingling is such that it is often unclear what distinguishes a theological narrative from a non-theological narrative, as Samuel Taylor Coleridge's 'The Rime of the Ancient Mariner' (1798) makes apparent. The strange quality of Coleridge's poem explains why the wedding guest is not the only one 'stunned' by the tale that he hears. Interpreters have been unable to agree whether the poem's movement between pagan and Christian allusions allows for a theological reading.[1] The poem contains undeniable allusions to Christian ideas of Original Sin but these are contaminated, perhaps overwhelmed, by other ideas, and the Mariner's final state seems quite different from the one imagined by traditional Christian teaching on the Atonement and Redemption. Recognizing that '[t]heological attempts at reading *The Ancient Mariner* have a chequered history, though in some ways they remain the poem's contested paradigm', Peter Larkin suggests that '[i]t is not the business of Coleridge's poem to exemplify any theological motif, but in its very un-innocence before experience and disorder it presents the existential material out of which its own marginalised and tentative theological self-reading can begin'.[2] Larkin's thoughtful and nuanced theological reading of the poem makes it clear that Rushdie's secularism is not the only means of taking contamination seriously.

While the Christian tradition has sometimes emphasized sin at the expense of other theological ideas, wrongly implying, like the less successful readings of Coleridge's poem, that this is the main point of the tale, the majority of theologians locate sin within a broader theological reading of the world. Gerard Loughlin writes: 'One of the most important lessons in learning the scriptural story of Christ is learning its story of the world; learning to see the world as it is envisioned in Scripture: as the gift of God. This first requires that we learn our sinfulness . . . we learn it in the same story in which we learn that the world is God's gift and that we are convicted and forgiven sinners.'[3] Given the influence that the Christian story of the world has exerted on the history of Western literature, there is little surprise in finding that sin is a recurring theme in literature, a perpetual stain on the tales of transgression that writers tell. This chapter looks closely at works by Coleridge, William Shakespeare, Nathaniel Hawthorne, Philip Roth and Ian McEwan, but these authors are far from being the only ones to have something to say about sin. Ronald Paulson surveys a wider array of writers in *Sin and Evil: Moral Values in Literature* (2007), exploring the multiplicity of ways in which their works register notions of transgression and wrong-doing. Paulson concludes his book with some final reflections on the two main words of his title. Although he acknowledges that all words are human constructs, subject to competing ideological positions, he points out there is little disagreement regarding the 'evil' quality of some events, such as the Holocaust. Paulson is more suspicious, however, about the word sin, which he describes as 'one fictive lens through which ideologues saw the actions of their opponents'. He continues:

Alongside the monstrous evil/evils of the twentieth century, sin appeared trivial – a diversion from harsh realities of enormous death and suffering; but it has, unfortunately, been slipped back into discourse under the guise of evil. Much of what is *called* evil is only sin. Sin is the term for the large gray area covered by custom and ideology: whether a woman's head should be covered, or her breast; whether members of the same sex should marry. We must conclude that evil as an act has remained a constant, sin a variable.[4]

It is easy to sympathize with Paulson's critique of the prejudice that sometimes masquerades as sin, and it is difficult to deny his claim that individualistic notions of sin have little to say to the structural complexity of all that is wrong with the world. Yet the critique of sin that Paulson offers does not do sufficient justice to the theological tradition. His constriction of the Christian theological tradition appears to be influenced by the re-emergence of fundamentalism as a force in contemporary American life, and his aversion to the grammar of sin can be traced to the way in which that grammar is deployed by Christian fundamentalists. Paulson is right to locate fundamentalist rhetoric within an older trajectory of American Protestant theology. But one should not forget that the history of American Christianity can be told in other ways, and that the history of Christian theology offers a broader perspective on the world, one that affirms the value of sin as a means of naming the predicament in which we find ourselves. When Paulson notes the way in which twentieth-century 'mainstream theology' has shifted its emphasis 'from personal salvation to acts of charity and love, from religion as soteriology to a concern with living in this world', he attaches the label 'Christian Humanism', implying that a theological account of the world that moves beyond the personal and individualistic requires the addition of a non-theological term, 'Humanism', to a narrower theological referent.[5] On my reading, however, the Christian understanding of sin is more flexible and resourceful than the pronouncements of fundamentalists might lead us to think.

Aware of the intellectual resources of the Christian tradition, one recent theologian, Charles Mathewes, explores the contribution that St Augustine offers to our modern context, observing, as he does so, that 'our culture seems to lack the ability, and more particularly the moral imagination, to respond usefully to evil, suffering and tragic conflict'. Mathewes continues: 'Indeed the whole intellectual history of modernity can be written as the story of our growing *in*comprehension of evil, of our inability adequately to understand both the evils we mean to oppose, and those in which we find ourselves implicated.'[6]

Whether or not one agrees with this assessment of modern thinking about evil, Mathewes' appeal to the intellectual vitality of theological reflection on sin and evil is worth heeding. One of the claims of this chapter is that the Christian language of sin does not have to remain a parochial preserve, because it offers a sharp and honest assessment of the state of the world. Many Christian theologians are aware of the need to address the structural failure of the modern world and their references to sin are alert to complex manifestations of suffering and evil. Mathewes is not the only theologian to recognize that evil 'challenges our *moral anthropology*, because it reveals that human agency – and in particular human autonomy – is a much more problematic concept than many believe, and more dubiously attributed to people than we usually assume'.[7]

The detailed reflections on the problems of agency that we find among Christian theologians who explore the language of sin are paralleled by the work of Jewish philosophers and theologians, who have re-examined perspectives on guilt and wrong-doing in the wake of the Holocaust. Perhaps most famously, Hannah Arendt's reflections on the trial of Adolf Eichmann led her to conclude that evil was not the result of dramatic acts by monstrous individuals so much as the culmination of countless 'bureaucratic' decisions.[8] Commenting on the 'grotesque silliness' of Adolf Eichmann's clichés as he went to the gallows after his trial in 1961, Arendt wrote: 'It was as though in those last minutes he was summing up the lesson that this long course in human wickedness had taught us – the lesson of the fearsome, word-and-thought defying *banality of evil*.'[9] It is significant that Arendt's persuasive assessment of the banality of evil does not do away with the idea of individual wrong-doing and personal responsibility. She is adamant that Eichmann is guilty and she is convinced that he should be sentenced to death. By retaining a clear belief in the responsibility that one has for the things that they do, Arendt's talk of banality complicates rather than severs the link between human agency and evils of unimaginable magnitude.

Another Jewish writer who addresses the stain of sin is Philip Roth. In *The Human Stain* (2000) Roth's fictional narrator, Nathan Zuckerman, tells the life story of Coleman Silk, an academic whose successful career starts to unravel when a reference in class to two missing students as 'spooks' leads to an allegation of racism. The irony of the incident is that Silk has been passing himself of as Jewish for many years and hiding his true ethnicity. This is not the only secret to come out in the novel, and Zuckerman explores the complex web of interconnections that link individual actions to the stains that make their presence felt in society. Having opened the novel with an arresting juxta-position of the local reception of Silk's impropriety (in having a relationship with someone half his age) and the national reaction to President Clinton's marital infidelity at the turn of the millennium, Zuckerman later returns to muse on the underlying forces at work in American society:

> The *tyranny* of propriety. It was hard, halfway through 1998, for even him to believe in American propriety's enduring power, and he was the one who considered himself tyrannized: the bridle it still is on public rhetoric . . . As a force, propriety is protean, a dominatrix in a thousand disguises, infiltrating, if need be, as civic responsibility, WASP dignity, women's rights, black pride, ethnic allegiance, or emotion-laden Jewish ethical sensitivity . . . A century of destruction unlike any other in its extremity befalls and blights the human race – scores of millions of ordinary people condemned to suffer deprivation upon deprivation, atrocity upon atrocity, evil upon evil, half the world or more subjected to patho-logical sadism as social policy, whole societies organized and fettered by the fear of violent persecution, the degradation of individual life engineered on a scale unknown throughout history . . . all the terrible touchstones presented by this century, and here they are up in arms about Faunia Farley. Here in America either it's Faunia Farley or it's Monica Lewinsky! The luxury of these lives disqui-eted so by the inappropriate comportment of Clinton and Silk! *This*, in 1998, is the wickedness they have to put up with. *This*, in 1998, is their torture, their torment, and their spiritual death.[10]

Influenced by the tales told by Silk, an evasive, smooth-tongued wordsmith, Zuckerman seeks to attenuate the gap between individual impropriety and collective suffering. And yet, like Silk, Zuckerman's language betrays him, pointing to a more intimate relation between our words and actions, and the lives of others. The reference to 'pathological sadism' roots collective social policy in human agency; the comparison with President Clinton reminds us that however much an individual views their behaviour as private and inconsequential, some level of social scrutiny is inevitable. Though the charges levelled against Clinton and Silk register a distorted and sometimes perverse political agenda on the part of those who articulate them, they also affirm the presence of some sort of relation between individual action and social conse-quence. The term 'wickedness' may be a disproportionate description but Silk's life, like that of his colleagues, is not without its faults, even if they are not always what his opponents think they are. The 'terrible touchstones [or tombstones] presented by this century' may render an affair with someone con-siderably younger and from a different cultural background inconsequential, yet Silk's participation in a personal history of social estrangement, prejudice and bitterness is continuous with those forces that lie behind the historic touchstones.

Much of the power of Roth's novel is rooted in the way it talks about the human stain, an idea that the Church has traditionally named sin. Aware of the sort of dangers that Paulson identifies in the discourse of sin, and suspicious of the labels that we sometimes attach to the failures of others – 'No motive for the perpetrator is necessary, no logic or rationale is required. Only a label is required' – Zuckerman reflects at length on what the human stain entails.[11] He locates it within a multifaceted narrative and offers the possibility that something of that which blights our lives is intrinsic to our humanity. While not all of Zuckerman's insights are ones shared by Christian theologians, he does pursue several ideas that converge with Christian theology. In the remainder of this chapter, *The Human Stain* will be read alongside other literary texts with something important to say about the stain of sin. I will begin by examining the ways in which Roth's novel and Shakespeare's *Macbeth* (1606) use the language of sin to try and overcome the difficulty of talking about evil. Sin offers a grammatical framework that helps substantiate evil. Through its vocabulary of contingent terms such as depravity, falleness and corruption, sin operates within the parameters of Monotheism and avoids a dualism that grants evil its own ontology. As well as naming evil in a way that respects the needs of a particular theological tradition, sin draws attention to evil's material and worldly trace. The second section of the chapter explores this further by turning to the indelible stains that feature in *The Human Stain* and Hawthorne's *The Scarlet Letter* (1850). Because of their mutual preoccupation with the physicality of evil, both novels locate their tales of transgression in this world rather than the ethereal realm sometimes favoured by American Protestant theology. The focus on this world does not stop Roth and Hawthorne from thinking about the wide reach of evil, and both novels implicate their narrators in the web of sin that they describe. Roth's novel refuses to see this contamination entirely negatively, suggesting instead that the stain of sin might constitute our humanity rather than simply detracting from it.

Having explored the theological consequences of sin's indelible stain, the final section of the chapter considers the response of Roth and McEwan to a world contaminated by sin. Like so many of the other writers who make reference to transgression in the stories they tell, Roth and McEwan are aware that transgression can be transformed. Not all stories end happily but the aesthetic treatment of sin and suffering cannot avoid the suggestion that destructive moments can be thought and read differently. The transformation of sin through writing is not peculiar to contemporary writers. In Coleridge's 'The Rime of the Ancient Mariner', for instance, the Mariner's guilt is not erased but it is given an afterlife through the telling of the tale. While the events of the twentieth century have combined with a postmodern suspicion of grand narratives to leave contemporary writers cautious of happy endings and narratives that claim to redeem sin, these writers are still faced with the age-old challenge of doing something with the tales of transgression they describe. The concluding section of this chapter rethinks Roth's vision of a stain that humanizes Silk in light of the evocative account articulated by the narrator of McEwan's *Atonement* (2001). Even writers who reject the Christian narrative of sin and its resolution, or at least remain ambivalent towards it, continue to draw on theological resources as they tell tales of transgression in the modern world.

Dirty talk: the grammar of sin

Describing evil and conveying human suffering create genuine difficulties for writers and theologians. No one wants to reduce the depth of human suffering to a few trite phrases, and no-one wants to misrepresent the more catastrophic aspects of human experience. Part of the difficulty arises from the way in which suffering cuts across an array of human experience. Unable to isolate precisely where it begins and ends, writers and theologians have to concede that suffering, like human experience per se, is a mystery. Reflecting on the deaths of Silk and Farley in *The Human Stain*, Zuckerman admits how little he knows about them and their awareness of one another's secrets, insisting: 'Now that they're dead, nobody can know. For better or worse, I can only do what everyone does who thinks that they know. I imagine. I am forced to imagine. It happens to be what I do for a living.'[12] The imagination of writers extends readers' understanding of the world, as Zuckerman reminds us, yet the severity and extent of human suffering asks a great deal of the imagination and pushes language to its limit. It is no surprise that Lester Farley, the Vietnam veteran who wreaks havoc in *The Human Stain*, is often seen as the least successful of Roth's characters in the novel.[13] Representing another person's suffering is difficult, and the concern that all of us experience at some level, that the lot of human suffering might be made worse through inappropriate language, is especially acute for authors who write about suffering at length. Inappropriate language is central to the 'spooks' episode that plays such a major role in *The Human Stain*, as well as surfacing in Zuckerman's description of Delphine Roux. Zuckerman's conservative prejudices paint a particular picture of the young, female Head of Department, reminding us that the narrator's tale is part of the world that Roux finds so oppressive.

Suffering and evil are difficult to talk about constructively; indeed, they are difficult to talk about at all. While the problem of evil presents more disturbing dilemmas than finding the right words to describe what is taking place, the problem of evil remains closely entangled with the problem of language. Our talk about evil adds additional layers to an already complex situation, ensuring, perversely, that we never find our way to the root of the problem. Rejecting religious discourse as a means of describing reality does not remove this dilemma; it merely causes us to substitute another set of assumptions as we seek to make sense of the world. Language is unavoidably contaminated. Our reading, says Hartman, discloses 'a structure of *words within words*, a structure so deeply mediated, ghostly, and echoic that we find it hard to locate the *res* in the *verba*'.[14] Like our actions, our language is tainted by participation in the world and the things that we learn from others. Our collusion with the very problem of evil that we identify makes it difficult for us to bring any clarity to our talk about evil. Though evil sometimes manifests itself in extreme forms that capture our attention and appear qualitatively different from the normal course of affairs, catastrophies such as genocide and global poverty are inseparable from the activities and linguistic currency that make up daily life. The participation in the world that so often seems inconsequential or innocuous accumulates, over time, a destructive capacity that we struggle to free ourselves from. This is one of the central insights of *The Human Stain*: the novel refuses to locate the source of evil discretely or explain precisely why things are the way they are. A refusal to hold anyone or anything solely responsible for the state of the world is apparent in the fate of Coleman and Faunia. Their deaths follow from Lester's intervention but the chain of causation is indirect – he runs them off the road rather than colliding with them – and the surrounding narrative identifies plenty of other contributing factors to the tragic events that transpire.

Recognizing something of the involvedness and intricacy of evil in the world, Christian theologians turn to Original Sin, a doctrine that has been conceived in several ways and does not have to dwell on pre-modern ideas of physical inheritance. Rejecting the idea of a deprived and infected human nature that is passed down biologically, Robert Jenson continues to adhere to the doctrine of Original Sin, insisting that 'there is no difficulty in seeing how idolatry, lust, injustice, and despair are both my acts and acts of all of us historically together'.[15] Original Sin allows theologians to acknowledge that evil is endemic to human activity and indissolubly associated with the most basic aspects of our experience. It is a doctrine that links evil to human activity without making the crass and simplistic suggestion that the world's faults are directly attributable to the sins of a particular person.

Discussing the fate of Coleman and Faunia after the funeral, first with Faunia's father, Harry, and his partner, Sylvia, and then with Coleman's sister, Ernestine, Zuckerman reflects on the inherited dimension of evil and the social aspects of suffering. Despite being estranged from their families, Coleman and Faunia are still affected by the trials and tribulations of previous generations. Lester's victims are part of a long history of suffering and hardship, and it this that Zuckerman draws our attention to in the aftermath of his aborted conversation with Harry and Sylvia: 'If suffering was passed around in that family like a disease, there was nothing to do but post a sign of the kind they used to hang in the doorways of the contagiously ill when I was a kid . . .'[16] Characters such as Faunia and Coleman are victims of generational suffering, but they are also perpetrators. Reflecting on the potential consequences of Coleman's decision to feign Jewish ethnicity, Zuckerman worries about the biological impact on Coleman's future descendents who, ignorant of his true ethnicity, might one day give birth to a black child and fail to understand why this has happened.

By viewing the human stain in generational terms, as something inherited and passed on, Zukerman adopts language commonly associated with Original Sin. The idea that sin is somehow inherited is developed further by the way that *The Human Stain* draws on other writing about sin from the Western literary tradition. In keeping with Original Sin's account of the ghostly and interconnected human relations that mark our actions, the literary sources of the stains described by Roth cannot be delineated definitively. Yet the novel's link with Shakespearean tragedy is difficult to ignore. Inheritance, language and betrayal conspire to devastating effect in *Macbeth*, a play by one of the writers admired by Silk's father: 'The father who had another way of beating you down. With words. With speech. With what he called "the language of Chaucer, Shakespeare, and Dickens".'[17] Like *The Human Stain*, *Macbeth* employs symbols that locate evil in a theological context – Shakespeare's original audience would have seen Lady Macbeth's attempt to wash the blood off her hands as a clear sign of Original Sin – and, like Roth's novel, Shakespeare's play situates personal wrongdoing within a broader political framework.

Reading the play against the backdrop of the 1605 Gunpowder plot and its aftermath, Rebecca Lemon claims that *Macbeth* 'imagines treason beyond ideologically confining polemical discourses that proliferated at the time of its production'. She argues that the treatment of treason in the play rejects triumphalist accounts from the period in favour of an exploration of 'the charismatic power of treason: staging the crime charms audiences on and off stage with apparent truths or sheer imagination, infecting the ways in which we perceive the social and political world'.[18] Lemon's reading is concerned with political and legal history rather than religion; however, the language she uses and her attentiveness to the treasonous capacity of words are confluent with a more theological discussion. Those who insist on the presence of Original Sin in the world recognize that all our talk about the state of the world is permeated by human sinfulness and self-interest.

The treasonous core of language and human endeavour is central to *Macbeth*'s tragic narrative, hence the play's refusal to treat any individual as wholly innocent. Although some of the characters (e.g. Duncan, Malcolm and Macduff) are often described as virtuous or unwitting victims, their innocence is moot, and not just because some of the most saintly descriptions of them emanate from the corrupt mouth of Macbeth.[19] Our first sight of Duncan occurs amid a war and political struggle for power, reminding us that Macbeth's subsequent actions are far from unique, and the discovery that Duncan and Macbeth are 'cousins' stops us from presuming that the King of Scotland is completely removed from the machinations of his treasonous general. When Malcolm speaks to Macduff later on in the play, describing Macbeth as a 'tyrant, whose sole names blisters our tongues', the description registers the way in which we become contaminated by the sinful activities of others.[20] If treason permeates the words and actions of every agent who acts in the world, then the idea of individual 'demonic violence' offers little by way of additional explanation or clarification.[21] This is apparent from the very start of *Macbeth*, with the unholy trinity of witches providing one of the play's most arresting and philosophically ambiguous images. The extent of the witches' power is never resolved, and Macbeth's subsequent reliance on what they say about his future becomes something of a self-fulfilling prophecy. At the same time, as Janette Dillon observes, the placement of the witches at the start of the play and the decision by Shakespeare to echo their vocabulary in the first words that Macbeth utters raise the 'question of what kind of world Macbeth occupies and what kind of agency he has within it'.[22] Although the world of *Macbeth* is one in which the supernatural forces of darkness may exert some level of influence, the witches point to evil rather than constituting evil. Recognizing that the presence of the supernatural serves to complicate our understanding of evil, Shakespeare refuses to treat the demonic as the causal loci of evil. All agents, human and otherwise, are caught up in a world where evil pervades everything and cannot be localized.

In one of the play's most memorable quotations, Macbeth asks the witches what they are doing and is given the reply, 'A deed without a name'.[23] The intriguing quotation provides a subtitle for the chapter on *Macbeth* in Alexander Leggatt's *Shakespeare's Tragedies: Violation and Identity* (2005). Leggatt writes: 'Throughout *Macbeth*, the language dwells obsessively on unnameable deeds; and these deeds are done by unnameable agents. The question of identity shifts into the question of agency. "Who's there?" becomes "who did this?"'[24] In its response to the question of agency, *Macbeth* carefully avoids dualism, the belief that forces of good and evil exist in tandem and compete with one another to influence the world. While this may tell us little about Shakespeare's own beliefs, it does, as John D. Cox argues, say something about the 'beliefs of the community in which he [Shakespeare] found himself'.[25] These beliefs include the monotheism of the Christian faith. Believing there to be one God who is responsible for everything that exists, monotheism resists the temptation of holding the Devil responsible for all the evil that occurs in the world. This is why there is such an emphasis on the contingency of evil in the Christian tradition. Two of the most influential theologians in the tradition, Augustine and Aquinas, define evil as a privation: the absence of a good that is due.[26] Within the context of the Christian doctrine of creation, the idea of privation equates sin with any activity that contributes to the corruption or distortion of an existence that is understood to be good. This understanding of evil as loss emerges from the conclusion to Leggatt's reading of a deed without a name:

> In Macbeth and Lady Macbeth we are taken, with terrible authority and conviction, into the minds of two people who have centered their life together on doing a deed of violation, we watch those minds infecting each other and the world, and in their destruction, greeted by other characters with easy satisfaction, something of us is destroyed – because they themselves have exemplified so powerfully the very human bond they have violated.[27]

The concept of privation makes it hard for us to imagine what evil is like.[28] Loss, violation, corruption and tragedy may provide figures of speech that link evil to something real and substantive, yet evil itself lacks solidity. This is a recurring theme in *Macbeth*. The second half of the witches' famous incantation at the start of the play – 'Fair is foul, and foul is fair: / Hover through the fog and filthy air' – describes evil using language that conveys a lack of substance, and the rest of the play makes extensive use of ghostly images to conjure up appearances without a clear name or substance.[29] The dagger that haunts Macbeth just before the murder is both real and imagined, bloody and ethereal; the entrance of Banquo's ghost precipitates a scene of intense physical drama, even though the other characters cannot see what Macbeth and the audience see; and, having previously chided Macbeth for seeing things – 'This is the very painting of your fear' – Lady Macbeth ends up washing her hands compulsively in a futile attempt to remove the stain of blood.[30] In each case, the borderline state of the ghostly, evoking that which is neither live or dead, neither real or imagined, is used to indicate the presence of evil without ascribing evil an independent metaphysical existence.

Roth approaches the insubstantial nature of evil from a related perspective. In place of ghostly manifestations, he makes uses of what Hartman refers to as 'the ghostly life of the letter'.[31] After a successful career, it is one treasonous word – 'spooks' – used by Coleman to describe two absent students, that brings about his downfall: 'I was using the word in its customary and primary meaning: "spook" as a spectre or a ghost. I had no idea what color these two students might be. I had known perhaps fifty years ago but had wholly forgotten that "spooks" is an invidious term sometimes applied to blacks.'[32] No amount of gloss from 'Mr Determined', the Professor of Classics who has controlled events at Athena College over the years and who prides himself on a mastery over words, can erase the charge of racism that the reference to 'spooks' conjures up.[33] Silk fails to comprehend that language is not under his full control; rather than containing meaning, words act as a vehicle through which other voices communicate and speak from the dead. Along with the past decisions that catch up with Silk over the course of his life, the haunting afterlife of words undermines Silk's confidence in himself as a man in control of his own destiny: 'First "spooks", now "lily-white" – who knows what repellent deficiency will be revealed with the next faintly antiquated locution, the next idiom almost charmingly out of time that comes flying from his mouth? How one is revealed or undone by the perfect word.'[34]

Indelible stains

The history, sociality and indeterminacy of language ensure that words have a material trace. Transcending our full comprehension, these traces are still present in the world, and, as a result, they are capable of being read. Language is not unlike evil in this respect: for all its ghostliness, insubstantiality and pervasiveness, evil leaves behind a stain that is all too apparent. The metaphysical convergence between language and evil is one of the reasons why *The Human Stain* is able to depict the problems of human experience in the way that it does. Roth's novel is not alone in registering the indelible stain of human existence. The recognition that words have the power to embody and pass on the reality of evil is indebted to an American literary tradition that has had a great deal to say about the human stain. Like many of his literary forebears – including Hawthorne, Herman Melville, Henry James, William Faulkner and Ralph Ellison – Roth is aware that talking about the human stain poses a predicament: texts that embody the human stain are liable to contribute to its spread.[35] To write fiction always involves some level of participation in the world and it always leaves behind a material trace.

The speech that Herb Keble delivers at Silk's funeral epitomizes the tendency for writers and speakers to propagate the very problem that their words are seeking to resolve. Herb's speech may attempt institutional and personal purification by acknowledging the 'blight on the integrity' of Athena College but it results in a further stain, as Zuckerman's accompanying narration is keen to point out. Zuckerman is not alone in recognizing the persistence of the human stain. Herb uses Coleman's funeral to locate events at Athena in a bigger and older narrative tradition that tells a similar story: 'Here, in the New England most identified, historically, with the American individualist's resistance to the coercions of a censorious community – Hawthorne, Melville, and Thoreau come to mind – an American individualist . . . was once again so savagely traduced by friends and neighbors that he lived estranged from them until his death . . .'[36] While Melville and Thoreau have a great deal to say about evil and suffering, it is Hawthorne's infamous account of sin in *The Scarlet Letter* that leaves the strongest mark upon Roth's novel. The ghostly trace of evil that Silk's reference to 'spooks' embodies and that Zuckerman finds so intriguing has an antecedent in the embroidered letter that the narrator of Hawthorne's tale discovers during his time at the Salem Custom House. Recounting the 'sensation not altogether physical, yet almost so, as of burning heat' that causes him to drop the fabric to the floor, the narrator goes on to contemplate the history behind his discovery. Like Zuckerman, he links material history to words, perceiving an onus on writers to tell tales of transgression: 'With his own ghostly hand, the obscurely seen, but majestic, figure had imparted to me the scarlet symbol, and the little roll of explanatory manuscript. With his own ghostly voice, he had exhorted me . . . to bring his mouldy and moth-eaten lucubrations before the public.'[37] Yet passing on the lucubrations has a cost, namely, contamination by the tale that is told.

One of the contaminants of *The Scarlet Letter* is the Puritan tradition at the centre of the tale. Traces of Puritanism, with its emphasis on personal morality and purity, remained influential in nineteenth-century American life. Noting the conservative social politics of the period, Erika M. Kreger tells us that 'Hawthorne had given reviewers what they wanted: a book that encouraged self-restraint and adherence to conventional community values and yet did not directly address readers with intrusive, didactic remarks.'[38] Although Kreger's reading recognizes Hawthorne's agency as a writer, it insists, quite *rightly*, on reading the narrative voice of *The Scarlet Letter* in conjunction with the predominant morality of the period: 'Hawthorne carefully guides his audience to the "right" ethical conclusion through his depiction – both physical and emotional – of his central characters. All of these characterizations underscore the narrative's conservative lesson about the need for self-denial and social responsibility ...'[39] *The Scarlet Letter* guides the interpretation of its readers through a series of embodied signs, from the Reverend Dimmersdale to the embroidered letter that Hester is made to wear as a 'living sermon against sin'.[40]

Like Hawthorne, Roth offers continual reminders that history and its telling leave an indelible material trace: 'we leave a stain, we leave a trail, we leave our imprint. Impurity, cruelty, abuse, error, excrement, semen – there's no other way to be here.'[41] Discussing this quotation and related passages from *The Human Stain*, David Brauner observes that: 'For Zuckerman (and Roth) to be alive, to be human, *is* to be stained, not simply in the Christian sense of the taint of original sin, but also in a more worldly sense: it is our bodily needs and functions – eating, pissing, shitting, ejaculating, crying, vomiting – that makes us human.'[42] Hawthorne's tale displays a similar preoccupation with material stains, hence the extensive account of the history of the Custom House in the introduction, and the association at the start of *The Scarlet Letter* between a moral crime and the 'rust on the ponderous iron-work' of the prison's 'oaken door'.[43] The interest that Roth and Hawthorne show in the physical stain of human activity parallels their interest in the material trace of language and testifies to an intimate relation between words and material history. Silk's reference to 'spooks' leaves an indelible stain on his career. In the case of Hester, the requirement that that she wear an embroidered letter testifying to her immorality is meant to ensure that lessons are learnt. Yet the strategy of guarding against future misdemeanours by recording transgressions is questionable. The stain of language is more pervasive and more penetrating than those who believe in the moral efficacy of story-telling realize. In Roth's novel the question that Coleman's daughter, Lisa, asks her father in a moment of despair – 'What do you do with the kid who can't read?' – is subsumed by another question: what do you with the person who can read?[44] The fact that Faunia is more literate than she lets on makes little difference to her moral agency, and, as the figure of Coleman reminds us so forcefully, the power to read does not protect one from transgression.

Like Coleman, Delphine's expertise as a reader does not stop her from making mistakes when it comes to communicating with others. For all her regret at sending an anonymous letter to her former Departmental Chair, she follows it with a more calamitous mistake when she inadvertently e-mails a personal ad to the staff in her department rather than the *New York Review of Books*. Delphine knows that words are capable of being manipulated and she acts accordingly; however, she fails to appreciate that the material trace of language renders all manipulation partial and incomplete, and she experiences limited success when trying to undo her acts of communication. The anonymous letter is easily identified by Coleman and the handwriting specialist he brings in, and her allegation that Coleman has broken into her office and sent the personal ad from her computer is eventually uncovered by Zuckerman.

Delphine's preference for e-mail is predicated on a misplaced confidence in the insubstantial and inconsequential nature of cyberspace. Oblivious to the material traces that e-mails leave behind, Delphine makes the mistake of thinking that the electronic age creates a safe distance between agents and their actions. The danger of thinking about technology in this way helps explain Zuckerman's disquiet at the anonymous online posting he is unable to source in the aftermath of the Coleman scandal. While it is easy to dismiss Zuckerman's disquiet as the reaction of a Luddite, he voices the same sort of concerns about modernity and human responsibility that Arendt and others articulated in the wake of the Holocaust. Zuckerman explains: 'I still had no way of knowing who at the college might have had the turn of mind to conjure up the clytemnestra posting – the most diabolical of art forms, the on-line art form, because of its anonymity – nor could I have any idea of what somebody, anybody, might next come up with to disseminate anonymously.'[45] His fear that anonymity might encourage humans to avoid taking responsibility for the state of the world finds support in the content of the message that is posted. Having accused Coleman of being to blame for a range of depravities, the unnamed author goes on to speak of an 'impenetrable darkness that those who are not violent by nature or vengeful by design . . . can never know'.[46] Fearing that this sort of language tries to detach the speaker from the stain that marks out humanity, Zuckerman turns to the language of Original Sin. With the aid of vocabulary such as 'germs of malice', 'epidemic' and 'pathogens', Zuckerman re-inscribes a pseudo-theological vision of the human stain that insists on some level of responsibility: 'The pathogens were out there. In the ether. In the universal hard drive, everlasting and undeletable, the sign of the viciousness of the human creature.'[47]

Although Zuckerman is prone to the deceptions practised by all writers as they narrate the story of the world, his insistence on the indelible stain of human sin and the attention he pays to the material trace of language stop him from thinking that he is entirely blameless.[48] Having uncovered the sins of Roux in a narrative that is frequently hostile to the female Academic, Zuckerman manages to muster a degree of sympathy for her. Introducing Roux's fabricated account of Silk breaking into her office, Zuckerman writes: 'All she had was the very human wish to be saved.'[49] This passing moment of sympathy discloses an acute awareness on the part of Zuckerman that writing rarely, if ever, satisfies an author's desire for absolution. A more pronounced example of this awareness can be found at the end of the novel when Zuckerman sees a truck he recognizes as Farley's and sets off along deserted fields to find the man he believes to have killed Silk. Discussing the significance of this scene, Brauner notes 'Zuckerman's sense of himself as an interloper, contaminating the prelapsarian environment with his very presence'.[50] Brauner goes on to explain, '[a]lthough at first sight Farley seems to achieve some sort of salvation in his pastoral idyll, it becomes clear in the final paragraph of the novel that his Utopian dream of inhabiting a pure realm can never be realised, since he himself is a symbolic human stain on the otherwise unblemished landscape'.[51] Zuckerman realizes that the idyllic landscape in which he stands is contaminated by 'a man, the only human marker in all of nature, like the X of an illiterate's signature on a sheet of paper'.[52] This is a revealing conclusion to the novel, for though 'the illiteracy of the human marker' is ostensibly concerned with Farley, it is also a reference to literate, well-educated members of the human race such as Zuckerman. The final paragraph asks questions of the narrative that has just been concluded and of Zuckerman's career as a writer. It reminds us that the stories writers tell about the human stain contribute to the history of transgression and reveal something of the teller's complicity in the state of the world. Tales of transgression testify, literally, to the indelible stain of sin.

Atonement in the modern world

Despite being indelibly present in all writing, the stain of sin is always waiting to be transformed. Hester's embroidered letter may be intended as a permanent sign of wrongdoing but, as chapter 13 of Hawthorne's tale reminds us, the equivocation of language ensures that there is always 'another view of Hester', another way of reading the stain that words record: 'The letter was the symbol of her calling. Such helpfulness was found in her, – so much power to do, and power to sympathize, – that many people refused to interpret the scarlet A by its original signification.'[53] Recognizing that the stain of sin can be read differently, writers share a common function with priests: offering others a mechanism by which sin can be transformed. The tendency of writing towards profligacy typically hides this link to priestly activity, yet what else are writers doing when they transform some of our darkest experiences into a narrative that other people might want to read? Writers are complicit in what Faunia Farley calls the 'appalling' 'fantasy of purity': 'What is the quest to purify, if not *more* impurity?'[54] Zuckerman may be sympathetic to Farley's dislike of purity and he may write a novel that embraces the human stain, but he recognizes that a writer's commitment to aesthetic creation leaves him or her with a case to answer. Although it is Silk who identifies correctly the writer's craft that Zuckerman practises during their conversations – 'Letting him listen. Sharpening the writer's sense of reality. Feeding that great opportunistic maw, a novelist's mind. Whatever catastrophe turns up, he transforms into writing' – the words of Silk come to us via the pen of Zuckerman.[55] For all his evasiveness, Zuckerman's writing can be surprisingly self-reflexive. It offers moments that confront the challenge of writing about the human stain, and the narrative techniques employed frequently register the seriousness of Farley's accusation that 'cleansing is a joke. A barbaric joke at that.'[56]

Like Zuckerman, Briony Tallis, the narrator of *Atonement*, links the problem of the human stain to the problem of writing. She uses important events and characters from her own history to construct a narrative that seeks atonement for the way that she has mistreated others. The link between writing and the human stain is not the only parallel between the two narrators: they share a pronounced awareness of their own mortality and the stories they disclose interweave stains and secrecy in a manner that is, to borrow a term from Zuckerman, 'counterconfessional', hiding the thoughts inside one's head rather than making them known.[57] Where *Atonement* differs, however, is in the explicitly self-conscious way it engages with the ethics of writing. In this respect, *Atonement* marks a shift from McEwan's earlier work. Brian Finney explains: 'McEwan has explained his fascination with evil or illicit behaviour by arguing that this "projected sense of evil in 'his' stories . . . is of the kind whereby one tries to imagine the worst thing possible in order to get hold of the good." *Atonement* still embodies this premise, but it employs a degree of self-consciousness which far exceeds that found in any of his previous novels.'[58] As Finney argues, the self-consciousness at the end of *Atonement* is continuous with the intertextual references that pervade and disrupt the semblance of realism earlier in the novel.

The coda to *Atonement* links purification and writing in a climactic moment of revelation. Having completed an evocative narrative of wrong doing, guilt and reconciliation, Briony admits that her account of Robbie and Celia during and after the war is fabricated. She confesses:

> The problem these fifty-nine years has been this: how can a novelist achieve atonement when, with her absolute power of deciding outcomes, she is also God? There is no one, no entity or higher form that she can appeal to, or be reconciled with, or that can forgive her. There is nothing outside her. In her imagination she has set the limits and the terms. No atonement for God, or novelists, even if they are atheists. It was always an impossible task, and that was precisely the point. The attempt was all.[59]

Despite appearing in an account that reminds us of the fictional nature of all fiction, this final note of confession is revealing, admitting, as it does, the limits faced by writers who seek to transform experiences into something else. Briony's commentary on the difficulty of making amends is not altogether convincing, partly because if '[t]he attempt was all', one wonders why she needs to pass comment and explain the point of writing her imaginary narrative, and partly because her use of the theological concept of atonement is not easily integrated into a narrative that shows little interest in stepping outside its implicit atheism. Without a God who is able to forgive sins and bring about reconciliation, atonement becomes a ritual emptied of its meaning. The reference to atonement makes for a moving finale but it is moving because of the glimpse that it offers into the futility of Briony's attempts to put things right.

Briony's inability to imagine how atonement might work leaves us with unanswered questions about the possibility of co-opting theological ideas in a modern world that no longer thinks of itself as religious. Atonement is particularly hard to deal with outside of an explicitly theological frame of reference. The Christian doctrine is closely related to theological claims about God's activity in creation, and it involves reading human history as a plot that finds its epicentre and culmination in the life, death and resurrection of Jesus Christ. These theological details make it difficult to translate atonement into nonreligious language. Colin Gunton confirms this when he describes Immanuel Kant's doctrine of Radical Evil as a 'philosophical translation of the traditional Western Christian doctrine of original sin'. Gunton goes on: 'Where Kant differs decisively from the tradition to which he is closely related is in his view of what that redemption is and how it takes place . . . he ascribes it not to God through faith in the justifying death of Christ but to God operating through human moral reason.'[60] The difficulty that Kant has in translating atonement adequately finds an analogue in *Atonement* and *The Human Stain*. In the former, Briony's inability to appeal to a higher power means that she has exhausted the narrative resources available to her; in the latter, Zuckerman's attempt to weave the human stain into a meaningful narrative ends up shifting the focus away from atonement towards demystification. Reflecting on the completion and consummation offered by Coleman's funeral, Zuckerman admits to 'obstinately thinking that this ending, even if it were construed as having permanently re-established Coleman's place as an admired figure in the college's history, would not suffice. Too much truth was still concealed.'[61]

Narrative revelations and reconciliation tell us something about 'at-one-ment' but the theological claims of the doctrine of atonement go further. They require reference to God, creating problems for atheistic novelists who want to incorporate theologically laden terms into their work without an accompanying religious narrative. Such problems, however, are not so different from those experienced by theologians who actively try and refer to God's atoning work. Gunton admits:

> Here we meet a problem which is complicated and philosophically controversial, but which must be faced in any discussion of theological language: the nature of reference. How, if at all, do we refer to God, and what is the status of such reference? We have reached here the crux of the matter of the realistic use of metaphor, because with the metaphors of atonement we propose to refer to the action of God by the use of words which are customarily used to refer to something else: *sacrifice* to the slaughter of an animal on an altar, *victory* to the outcome of a military engagement.[62]

No theologian speaks about the atonement directly, and no account, not even those recorded in Scripture, is pure. The language of theology is always a contaminated commentary on a story that itself borrows metaphors freely from different traditions. This does not prevent reference (to God or the world) but it does complicate that reference and render it incomplete. Paul Fiddes argues that complications of this sort are a good thing: 'But no theory of atonement was ever declared to be definitive by the church, so that hearers of the story were encouraged to find new meaning in their own responses.' He continues: 'The story of the cross could always acquire new meaning, and – when placed alongside stories of suffering elsewhere in human life – could enable meaning to be gained in new situations when it did not seem to be intrinsically present.'[63]

Although Briony's narrative fails to find the absolution it searches for, it does tell us something about the scope and nature of atonement. At the end of the main narrative, just before the revelation of the coda, Briony writes of her meeting with Celia and Robbie and her attempt to make amends: 'She was calm as she considered what she had to do. Together, the note to her parents and the formal statement would take no time at all. Then she would be free for the rest of the day. She knew what was required of her. Not simply a letter, but a new draft, an atonement, and she was ready to begin.'[64] Briony's use of the word 'draft' offers an instructive translation of 'atonement', one that thinks in terms of a series of iterations and suggests that existing material will eventually be turned into something better. The emphasis on transformation offers an important corrective to a tendency in church history for the problem of evil to be answered by arguing that the good things God provides for the world (e.g. human freedom) offset the suffering that results. Seeking to balance off evil in this way, or relying on the promise of a future, perfect life (i.e. heaven) to mitigate the suffering that we experience in the here and now, constitutes an impoverished conception of the atonement. Among those who have objected to such approaches is Marilyn McCord Adams. She argues that an adequate account of atonement has to go much further and envisage a way in which every experience of evil and suffering can be transformed: 'for God to be *good to* a created person, God must guarantee him/her a life that is a great good *to him/her* on the whole and one in which any participation in horrors is defeated within the context of his/her own life.'[65] Adams employs a range of theological resources (including the atonement, the incarnation and beatific visions) to try and find a way of explaining how the worst of our experiences might be transformed and made new.[66] By approaching the stain of sin in the way that she does, Adams seeks to meet the challenge posed by Briony, of seeing our failures, individual and collective, as a draft waiting to be written into a different and more meaningful story.

Novelists do not possess the divine omnipotence that Briony speaks about at the end of *Atonement*; they are not able to extricate themselves from the stain of sin that Zuckerman finds himself caught up in. Yet imaginative attempts to deal with sin and describe its transformation are meaningful. Like corresponding theological accounts, literature expresses something significant about the nature of the atonement, despite the 'draft' status of such expressions. The discovery of hope in the depths of human depravity plays an important role in 'The Rime of the Ancient Mariner', even though the Mariner struggles to find redemption through the re-telling of his 'ghastly tale'.[67] Larkin argues that the Mariner's compulsive and seemingly hopeless retelling of his story testifies to a liturgical hope that our tales of transgression can result in a new narrative. Focusing on the ecclesial allusion of the procession to the kirk at the end of the poem, Larkin argues for 'a more benign repetition with difference, a celebrative participation in time and community' while recognizing that this path 'eludes the main body of the tale and lingers at a margin'.[68] Larkin's location of theology at the margins of the poem offers a way of appreciating the incompleteness of language and humanity's fallen state: 'Only in aspiring towards the liturgical can the Mariner rediscover his own lostness, and from within a repetition echoing divine distinction and difference cease to centre that loss obsessively on his own self-narration.'[69] The lostness of which Larkin speaks manifests itself in several ways, including, I suggest, the weak interweaving in the poem of Christian ideas of original sin and redemption. Paulson tells us that the addition of a redemptive subtext in the poem involves 'conflating the Ancient Mariner's sin against nature (inhospitality, etc.) with fallen humankind's evil treatment of Christ'.[70] The conflation reminds us of the limits of reading the tale as an analogy of the Christian story of atonement, and it is understandable why so many critics have stressed the tenuous grounds on which the analogy rests. Nevertheless, the poem does speak theologically. Its language parallels the limited insights of theologians regarding how a world stained by sin might be made new, as well as the inadequate metaphors of atonement found in Scripture. As Gunton reminds us, these metaphors are 'finally unfathomable and present to the theologian ever new possibilities for insight and development. For the same reason, no final account can be given of what they mean, certainly not this side of eternity: they are eschatological concepts, giving up their secrets only by anticipation and through the gift of the Spirit.'[71]

A Hope and a Future: Suffering and Redemption in Eschatological Perspective

6

Having begun this book with *Paradise Lost* (1667) and the idea that creation makes time and space for others, and having concluded the previous chapter by exploring the use of repetition in Samuel Taylor Coleridge's 'The Rime of the Ancient Mariner' (1798), I want to start this final chapter with a play that resists any teleology and appears to go nowhere. Samuel Beckett's *Endgame* (1958) plays out the final stages of a game of chess: the two main characters, Hamm and Clov, jostle with one another as they move endlessly around the stage; two isolated figures in a game with no hope of resolution. *Endgame* is an evocative piece of drama with a different 'sense of an ending' than the dramatic vision at the heart of Christian eschatology.[1] The former revolves around an ahistorical setting; the latter involves what Ben Quash, following Hans Urs von Balthasar, has termed 'theodramatics', the orientation of the play of history around the person of Christ.[2] One play offers little hope of redemption; the other makes redemption the central act. The contrasts go on – many of them the result of Beckett's intertextual use of the Christian tradition. Whereas Beckett's drama mostly imprisons its central characters within the bare interior of one room with two small windows, the Christian drama, as Richard Bauckham and Trevor Hart describe it, 'is the biblical story of the world from creation to consummation'.[3] Bauckham and Hart continue: 'It is the story of the trinitarian God's relationship with his creation. It sees God as the beginning and end of all things, their source and their goal, Creator and Lord, Redeemer and Renewer, the one who was and who is and who is to come. It shares with the Jewish and Islamic metanarratives, but few others before modern times, the characteristic of a story which is not yet completed.'[4]

The narrative précised by Bauckham and Hart is significantly different to the one enacted in *Endgame* but the 'not-yet-complete' status of the Christian drama invites further comparison with Beckett's work and its preoccupation with time. Paul Fiddes insists that there are other ways of configuring the relationship between Beckett's plays and the Christian drama, telling us that the 'interest for the theologian in entering this [Beckett's] imaginative world is not simply that of finding a *contrast* with Christian eschatology . . .'[5] One of the reasons for being cautious about an oppositional reading of the eschatological perspectives in Beckett and the Bible is that *Endgame* is neither mimetic nor didactic, at least not in any straightforward sense. Like all plays, *Endgame* says something about the world; yet to interpret Beckett's work as anti-Christian or illustrative of a world bereft of God is to miss the multitude of ways in which Beckett plays with his readers.[6] Not only is the play a tragic-*comedy*, it is attentive to the fact that it is a *play*, with all the linguistic and referential complications that brings. This playfulness has prompted Theodor Adorno to criticize those who read Beckett's work as an exemplar of the Theatre of the Absurd. Questioning the view that the play makes a case for twentieth-century Existentialism, Adorno insists that 'Beckett shrugs his shoulders at the possibility of philosophy today, at the very possibility of theory'.[7] Taking his cues from the ashbins that house an older generation and from the play's numerous allusions to earlier works of literature and philosophy, Adorno argues that *Endgame* is best understood as a commentary on the poverty of Western thought, one which is acutely aware of its own contaminated status as commentary: 'In *Endgame*, a historical moment unfolds . . . After the Second World War, everything, including a resurrected culture, has been destroyed without realizing it; humankind continues to vegetate, creeping along after events that even the survivors cannot really survive, on a rubbish heap that has made even reflection on one's own damaged state useless.'[8]

Recognizing that critique is a crucial component of Beckett's work, Fiddes reads *Endgame* in conjunction with *Waiting for Godot* (1954) and tells us that the hopelessness of both plays serves as a reminder of 'a kind of waiting for the future which *is* futile from a theological perspective'.[9] The futility involves waiting for a deity that is man-made and shaped by human reason alone – whether that is *Waiting for God's* Pozzo, William Blake's figure of Nobodaddy, *The Passion of New Eve's* Zero, or countless other examples from Western literary history. Such deities are static and destructive, an extension of that which exists already, the actual; in contrast, says Fiddes, the God of the Bible is genuinely transcendent, a figure who breaks into this world and offers to transform it:

> What we expect from God is possibility, and God has revealed what is possible in the resurrection of Jesus from the dead. The possibilities for new creation in God challenge the actual tendencies of the present, or its potentials; they break in from the future. If we think possibility as mere *potential*, we are really simply subordinating it to actuality again, for the potential is the 'not yet' made actual. We look forward not to what is merely 'not yet' actual, but to what God makes possible.[10]

Following Mary Bryden, who notes that Beckett's writing 'exhibits much less readiness to exclude the possibility of a God than it does to dismiss some of God's rumoured properties', Fiddes argues that *Endgame* and *Waiting for God* reject a concept of God rooted in Greek philosophy.[11] To illustrate his point, Fiddes observes how, under the influence of thinkers such as Plato, Christian theologians have sometimes assigned God qualities such as impassibility. Qualities like impassibility, says Fiddes, threaten to distance God from the suffering of the world. They distract us from Scripture's revelation of Yahweh as a character who is deeply concerned with the plight of humanity. The problem with constructing God along the lines of Greek philosophy is, as Fiddes explains, that it risks consigning the divine to the philosophical scrapheap articulated by Lucky in his famous 'think' monologue.[12]

If Beckett's plays invite us to question conceptions of God that are part of the 'poverty of philosophy', then we might also question the sort of eschatological framework that Beckett is responding to when he stages his own endgame. When twentieth-century philosophers including Martin Heidegger and Jacques Derrida critiqued the fixed metaphysical claims of classical theology, they highlighted a weakness in Christian thought that theologians became increasingly aware of over the course of the twentieth century. The weakness revolved around the widespread failure of classical theology to take seriously the relationship between God and time, a relationship that has subsequently been explored at length by theologians such as Robert Jenson and Jeremy Begbie, and one that has informed the work of narrative theologians and those who have sought to understand theology dramatically.[13] Accompanying the twentieth-century's renewed theological appreciation of time has been a rediscovery of the importance of eschatology. David Fergusson tells us that: 'One of the hallmarks of twentieth-century theology has been its insistence that eschatology is a central Christian doctrine and conditions every other article of faith.'[14] Through the work of theologians such as Jürgen Moltmann, eschatology came to be seen as a wide-ranging theological perspective rather than just a discrete, marginal study of the four last things – death, judgement, heaven and hell.[15] It is a way of thinking about the end towards which creation moves, the incompleteness of theological understanding, and the narrative orientation of the biblical story. Understood in this way, eschatology becomes a wide-ranging and resourceful idea rather than a constrained and limited account of death, judgement, heaven and hell. Highlighting the faults of a more limited definition of the last things, Colin Gunton complains that: 'it supposes a merely otherworldly account of eschatology'; 'it supposes a merely linear account of the way things are'; and, 'the most astonishing omission of all', the traditional conception of the last things makes no reference to resurrection.[16]

As will have been evident in the preceding chapters of this book, theological reflections on eschatology do not just inform our thinking about the last things. They do, however, become more prominent in ideas and texts that are overtly concerned with the future. In the discussion that follows, I will draw on recent eschatological thinking to help interpret two twentieth-century novels that imagine the future in contrasting ways: George Orwell's *Nineteen Eighty-Four* (1949) and Douglas Coupland's *Girlfriend in a Coma* (1998). Neither text is religious by design, but each offers a vision of the future that is heavily influenced by Christian thought. In different ways, the novels recognize that an adequate intervention into the problems of sin and suffering must originate from outside the systems that dominate our current situation.[17] This is especially evident in *Nineteen Eighty-Four*, a dystopian novel that imagines a totalitarian vision of the future from which there is no escape. The pessimistic vision of the future in *Nineteen Eighty-Four* has caused consternation among some critics, who struggle to reconcile the novel's perspective with both their own commitment to the possibility of socio-political transformation and

Orwell's socialism.[18] Such consternation often forgets the fictional nature of Orwell's novel, hence the importance of Elaine Scarry's essay 'A Defense of Poesy', which uses an imagined treatise from Julia to Winston to make the case for the importance of fiction in the world of *Nineteen Eighty-Four*: 'To think even simple thoughts about what is happening, you need the counterfactual, and to think in a sustained way requires that your mind acquire not only an expansive acquaintance with the world as it is, and has in the past been, but, equally, expansive tracts of fiction where you loan your mind to what never was the case.'[19] *Nineteen Eighty-Four* is a fictional work about the future rather than a pseudo-scientific prediction. It borrows a religious metaphor – hell – and imagines the contours of a world without love and without hope.[20] The hopelessness of hell is expressed most powerfully through the tragic failure of Winston and Julia's love. Although the novel locates the moment of their mutual betrayal in the ironically named Ministry of Love, the world that Orwell describes throughout the novel renders love impossible at every stage. Rather than defining the moment in which love is lost, Winston's cry – 'Do it to Julia! Do it to Julia!' – evokes and inverts the work of Jesus on the Cross, reminding readers that we have been transported to another world in which there is no hope in hell that love might bring about joy or transformation.[21]

A different vision of the future is presented in *Girlfriend in a Coma*, the most eschatological of what Andrew Tate terms 'Coupland's ambiguous, experimental and theologically-charged fiction'.[22] Beginning with the ghostly and prophetic figure of Jared, the novel employs several eschatological motifs to imagine another view of the world. Tate explains: 'Jared, like Benjamin's angel [the Angel of History], watches the woeful spectacle of a decadent "progress"-focused humanity, but he is able to revive and transform the self-satisfied lives of his peers . . . Jared becomes an unlikely angel – one who is able to impart a renewed *eschaton* to a lethargic and complacent culture – and embodies an irreverent, postmodern whisper of divine judgement.'[23] Jared's witness to 'news from elsewhere' parallels the role of the biblical prophets and the people of God in the Book of Revelation, and it is the focus of the second section of this chapter.[24] The hopefulness of the references to witnessing and judgement in *Girlfriend in a Coma*, though far from utopian, offer a stark contrast to the betrayal and lack of critique in the witness of *Nineteen Eighty-Four*. It is a hopefulness implicit throughout the eschatological resources of Christian theology; perhaps most explicitly in the idea of resurrection. Tate alerts us to the way in which '[t]he Christian hope of bodily resurrection is played out in the extraordinary, miraculous conclusion to *Girlfriend in a Coma*', and it is this, along with the novel's profound interest in the Christian tropes of a new creation, that are the subject of this chapter's final section.[25]

The ministry of love and the hopelessness of hell

Nineteen Eighty-Four imagines the same sort of bleak dystopian future that we encounter in *Endgame*, though it contains none of the latter's black humour. Like Beckett, Orwell describes the life that his protagonists are caught up in as a game of chess. Towards the end of the novel Winston sits in the Chestnut Tree Café, where a 'chessboard was always waiting for him', and tries to solve a 'tricky ending'.[26] The endgame that Winston is presented with – involving knights as well as two kings – offers more possibilities of a meaningful out-come than the one played out by Beckett in *Endgame*, but it still signifies a world with limited alternatives. Earlier on in the novel, Orwell opts for a related analogy to describe the futility of Winston's attempts to contact Julia and inau-gurate a relationship free from the control of Big Brother: 'It was like trying to make a move at chess when you were already mated. Whichever way you turned, the telescreen faced you.'[27] Chess is the not the only analogy that Beckett and Orwell use to convey the hopelessness of their worlds. In addition to the lack of windows through which the Sun's light might enter – compare the two small windows in the stage directions of *Endgame* with the windowless Ministry of Love – Beckett and Orwell symbolize the state of their worlds through rubbish heaps and trash cans. *Endgame* houses two of its characters in ashbins, while *Nineteen Eighty-Four* is set in 'London, vast and ruinous, city of a million dustbins', a physical image of decay reinforced by Winston's meeting with an old man whose 'memory was nothing but a rubbish-heap of details'.[28]

The dark, decaying settings chosen by Beckett and Orwell owe a great deal to Dante's account of the Inferno in the first part of *The Divine Comedy*.[29] In an illuminating article on the proliferation of references to hell and the demonic in Orwell's novel, Malcolm Pittock tell us that: '*Nineteen Eighty-Four* has successfully recreated the idea of hell and endowed it with an immediacy and significance which Milton and Dante (whose *Divine Comedy* Orwell was reading in the last year of his life) can no longer command.'[30] While much of the immediacy comes from the fusion of an imagined future with contempo-rary political trends, the influence of Dante and other parts of the Christian tradition make a significant contribution to the novel's overall effect. Pittock details the multiplicity of references to hell in *Nineteen Eighty-Four*, paying special attention to the pseudo-demonic powers of O'Brien and the Thought Police (who are able, mysteriously, to get inside Winston's private thoughts, fears and dreams). O'Brien's satanic origins are hinted at throughout the novel, from the suggestion that he ministers a black mass to Winston and Julia when they visit his flat, to the description of him as the 'tormentor' who 'directed everything'.[31] But the pain and humiliation that O'Brien orchestrates in the Ministry of Love make explicit the hell that Winston and others find themselves in. Containing hellish nightmares on many levels, literal and figurative, the Ministry of Love is a microcosm of the world that Oceania aspires towards. O'Brien explains: 'Do you begin to see, then, what kind of world we are creating? It is the exact opposite of the stupid hedonistic Utopias that the old reformers imagined. A world of fear and treachery and torment . . .'[32]

The word 'hell' possesses a complex etymology that is worth exploring further, albeit briefly. Since Dante, hell has most commonly been understood along the lines outlined by O'Brien, 'a place of fear, treachery and torment', but there are other, less-penitential, ways of thinking about it.[33] Orwell's willingness to depart from Dante's vision is evident in the absence of Purgatory or Paradise, and Pittock alerts us to Orwell's engagement with a source that predates Dante: '*Nineteen-Eighty Four* is a hell without a countervailing heaven: the reign of Antichrist for ever, not as a preliminary to the New Jerusalem. There are no angels, only devils.'[34] Orwell draws on biblical sources to imagine a world that is stalked by death at every turn. When Winston sees Jones, Aaronson and Rutherford at the Chestnut Tree Café he describes them as 'corpses waiting to be sent back to the grave', and O'Brien's first words to Winston leave him with 'a chilly shuddering feeling [that] had taken possession of his body. He had the sensation of stepping into the dampness of a grave . . .'[35] O'Brien's later insistence that 'we do not allow the dead to rise up against us' perpetuates the novel's preoccupation with death and echoes the '[w]e are the dead' mantra that is used on several occasions.[36] Death marks the cessation of life as we know it, and hell, rather than being the place where the unregenerate go after death, is seen as the place of death itself. The antecedent for this idea is the Hebrew concept of 'Sheol, Abaddon, the Pit, the grave. The dark, deep regions, the land of forgetfulness.' As the New Testament scholar N. T. Wright goes on to explain: 'These almost interchangeable terms denote a place of gloom and despair, a place where one can no longer enjoy life, and where the presence of YHWH himself is withdrawn. It is a wilderness: a place of dust to which creatures made of dust have returned. Those who have gone there are "the dead" . . . '[37] Wright points out that Sheol has a complex textual history and it is not the only term that the Bible uses to describe hell. It is, however, a word that imagines death in stasis and without end. Sheol epitomizes a dystopian nightmare, a place without hope or a future, at least in so far as it is unaccompanied by the Jewish or Christian hope of a resurrection from the dead.[38] The deadening nature of life in such a world is encapsulated by Winston's growing relationship with gin in the final pages of the novel: 'He took up his glass and sniffed at it. The stuff grew not less but more horrible with every mouthful he drank. But it had become the element he swam in. It was his life, his death and his resurrection.'[39]

Orwell uses religious language elsewhere in *Nineteen Eighty-Four* to augment his dystopian vision of death. The deathly, totalitarian system of government, in which every alternative (including Emmanuel Goldstein's *The Theory and Practice of Oligarchical Collectivism*) is shown to be a product of the dominant regime, takes us back to the all-encompassing reach of Original Sin discussed in the previous chapter. Sin also informs the description of Winston's experiences in Room 101, although, in this case, it is an inversion of the Christian solution to sin that helps convey the sense of hopelessness. Faced with the prospect of enduring his worst nightmare, Winston redeploys the language associated with Christ's death on the Cross to turn the possibility of hope on its head: 'he came out of the blackness clutching an idea. There was one and only one way to save himself. He must interpose another human being, the *body* of another human being, between himself and the rats.' The narrative continues: 'he had suddenly understood that in the whole world there was just *one* person to whom he could transfer his punishment – *one* body that he could thrust between himself and the rats.'[40] In place of Christ's substitutionary atonement for the sake of the world, Winston sacrifices the very person he claims to love, for the sake of himself.

Winston's willingness to sacrifice Julia brings the hopelessness of Oceania to a theologically-inflected climax – '[h]e was falling backwards . . . he had fallen . . . through the earth' – but evidence of betrayal and hopelessness can be found earlier in the text.[41] Despite several narrative protestations to the contrary, Room 101 is not the place where Winston betrays and stops loving Julia: it is the place where he realizes that a world of death offers no possibility of love. As Winston acknowledges earlier in the novel, 'the tragic and sorrowful' nature of his mother's death belonged 'to a time when there was still privacy, love, and friendship'.[42] Genuine love requires that we give ourselves to someone else and put their interests first; in contrast, Winston and Julia's relationship is a 'hopeless fancy', manufactured by the state and motivated by self-interest.[43] Winston is pleased to hear Julia's boasts of sexual promiscuity because they benefit his own agenda – '[t]hat was above all what he wanted to hear . . . the animal instinct, the simple undifferentiated desire: that was the force that would tear the Party to pieces' – and Julia's actions are motivated by the same sort of personal concern: 'Except where it touched upon her own life she had no interest in Party doctrine.'[44] It may well be the case that Winston and Julia are conditioned to act in the way that they do but this insight does not make their love for one another any more real. Although the relationship between Winston and Julia shows signs of an increasing tenderness as the novel progresses, neither of them proves capable of acting in the interests of the other, of embodying the 'I love you' that Julia's first note to Winston announces. The absence of love in *Nineteen Eighty-Four* testifies to Oceania as hell on earth, a place where O'Brien's demonic Thought Police are the only active agents. It is, in short, a place where death reigns over everything.

Witnessing news from elsewhere

Winston's attempt to bear witness in his diary to the totalitarian world of *Nineteen Eighty-Four* epitomizes the hopeless situation in which he finds himself. Writing for the first time (in a diary bought from Mr Charrington's junk shop and thus tainted by the Thought Police from the very start), Winston is overwhelmed by the difficulty of keeping an accurate record: 'A sense of complete helplessness had descended upon him. To begin with he did not know with any certainty that this *was* 1984.'[45] The impediments to recording history accurately are familiar to Winston through his work in the Records Department, but as soon as he starts to write in the diary he realizes that historical accuracy is far from being his only problem: 'For the first time the magnitude of what he had undertaken came home to him. How could you communicate with the future? It was of its nature impossible. Either the future would resemble the present, in which case it would not listen to him: or it would be different from it, and his predicament would be meaningless.'[46] While the stark choices articulated here reflect Winston's pessimistic mode of reasoning, the problem he identifies, of how one might bear witness to and in a totalitarian world, is hard to answer. Witnessing requires distance (with the space that it opens up for evaluation and critique) and proximity (which enables understanding and empathy). The suffocating control of Big Brother leaves Winston with too much distance from those who might hear his witness and too much proximity to the things he is witnessing about. Readers of the novel are able to hear Winston's witness, admittedly, but only because of the mediating influence of Orwell. Winston lacks the independence necessary to bear meaningful witness to the events that take place. Aware of this, he despairs: 'The diary would be reduced to ashes and himself to vapour. Only the Thought Police would read what he had written, before they wiped it out of existence and out of memory. How could you make appeal to the future when not a trace of you, not even an anonymous word scribbled on a piece of paper, could physically survive?'[47]

Winston's attempts to bear witness are made more difficult by the introduction of Newspeak. As the appendix to the novel explains, '[t]he purpose of Newspeak was not only to provide a medium of expression for the world-view and mental habits proper to the devotees of Ingsoc, but to make all other modes of thought impossible'.[48] Conscious of the way that language accumulates meaning over time, Big Brother introduces Newspeak in an effort to prevent access to equivocating words and the alternate modes of thought they bring. Newspeak is a systematic attempt to annihilate the imaginative freedom of grammar, and its progress is marked by successive editions of the Newspeak Dictionary.[49] One of the compilers of the latest Newspeak Dictionary, Syme, upbraids Winston for his failure to embrace the eleventh edition with sufficient enthusiasm: 'In your heart you'd prefer to stick to Oldspeak, with all its vagueness and its useless shades of meaning. You don't grasp the beauty of the destruction of words.'[50] The irony of Syme's admonishment is that the dictionaries he works on are an inherently conservative form, interested less in the experimental use of language and more in the standardization of meaning. New thinking is more likely to be found in other forms of writing, forms that express what Paul Ricoeur has termed 'limit expressions'. Summarizing Ricoeur's work, Walter Brueggemann tells us that: 'Limit experiences are those in which all conventional descriptions and explanations are inadequate. When one is pushed experientially to such extremity, one cannot continue to mouth commonplaces but is required to utter something "odd". The odd limit expression is in language that effectively *redescribes* reality away from and apart from all usual assumptions about reality.'[51] Whereas 'Limit expressions' helps us articulate another view of the universe, Newspeak actively prevents the citizens of Oceania from talking about the world in other ways.

Arguing that the 'odd' language of the biblical prophets exemplifies the 'limit expressions' spoken by Ricoeur, Brueggemann makes a claim for the transformative power of what he terms the 'prophetic imagination':

> The task of prophetic imagination and ministry is *to bring to public expression those very hopes and yearnings* that have been denied so long and suppressed so deeply that we no longer know they are there. Hope, on the one hand, is an absurdity too embarrassing to speak about, for it flies in the face of all those claims we have been told are facts. Hope is the refusal to accept the reading of reality which is the majority opinion; and one does that only at great political and existential risk. On the other hand, hope is subversive, for it limits the grandiose pretension of the present, daring to announce that the present to which we have all made commitments is now called into question.[52]

Brueggemann's account of the 'prophetic imagination' is rooted in the biblical prophets of the Old Testament: controversial figures who spoke in strange and unusual ways to remind people of Yahweh's promises. The 'prophetic imagination' of the Old Testament also has an eschatological orientation, and it is this that manifests itself in the contemporary, non-religious group of prophets who speak about the future in *Girlfriend in a Coma*. In the novel, a group of friends reject a bleak vision of a meaningless future in favour of another, more hopeful vision, one that is committed to asking questions and trying to help others appreciate all that existence has to offer: 'Every day for the rest of your lives, all of your living moments are to be spent making others aware of this need – the need to probe and drill and examine and locate the words that take us beyond ourselves.'[53] Words that re-describe the world are not another form of utopianism and they are not predicated on a belief that the world will inevitably get better. Jared spells this out to his friends when he tells them of the costly consequences of embodying the 'prophetic imagination': 'You're going to be forever homesick, walking through a cold railway station until the end, whispering strange ideas about existence into the ears of children. Your lives will be tinged with urgency, as though rescuing buried men . . . You'll be mistaken for crazies . . . There aren't enough words for "transform." You'll invent more.'[54]

The character of Jared personifies transformation and invention, even though he is already dead when the narrative begins. His jarring introduction – 'I'm Jared, a ghost' – makes it clear that the novel is interested in exploring news from elsewhere, and his questionable behaviour over the course of the novel, which includes impregnating Wendy and '[r]eading a bit of porn', casts him as an unlikely angel.[55] Jared's unconventionality may suggest awareness on the part of Coupland that a fictional portrayal of angelic messengers and prophets needs rescuing from traditional modes of thought if it is to bear witness to something different. Whether or not Coupland's novel involves an implied critique of tired expressions of religious revelation in North America, the association it makes between witnessing and judgement is difficult to ignore. Those who witness to other ways of being defy established norms and critique the status quo: they judge the world in its current state and envision a time when things might be different. Judgements of this sort are unsettling, as John Caputo acknowledges: 'The prophets use their stories to make impossible, mad demands on everyone, especially themselves. The voice of the prophet interrupts the self-assured voices of the powerful, of the *archē*, the princes of this world, bringing them up short, calling them to account for themselves.'[56] But such judgements are also hopeful. Rather than having to choose between hope and judgement, prophetic witness finds hope in judgement. When Jared calls his friends to account for the way in which they have wasted their second chances, he becomes the subject of abuse. Yet, as he explains, his witness judges things that needs to change. Prophetic hope cannot be imagined without some level of violence to the world as it is: 'Go clear the land for a new culture – bring your axes, scythes and guns . . . If you're not spending every waking moment of your life radically rethinking the nature of the world – if you're not plotting every moment boiling the carcass of the old order – then you're wasting your day.'[57]

Recognizing that all revolutions threaten to reinstate a new version of the oppressive regimes they overthrow, *Girlfriend in a Coma* imagines a world that is perpetually open to new possibilities: 'We *will* be kneeling in front of the Safeway, atop out-of-date textbooks whose pages we have chewed out. We'll be begging passers by to see the need to question and question and question and never stop questioning until the world stops spinning.'[58] Commenting on these final lines of *Girlfriend in a Coma*, with their strong preference for ongoing inquiry rather than pre-formed answers, Tate writes: 'Far from closure, the ecstatic vision suggests an eternal messianic openness – a welcome to what is unknown and a rejection of undemanding acquiescence in banal certainty.'[59] The openness is consistent with the recent eschatological perspective of Christian theologians, which sees the 'not-yet' of the Christian story as a means of avoiding collusion in the totalizing narratives that have produced such destructive results in the history of the church and the history of other secular institutions. Bauckham and Hart point out that Christian eschatology's 'resistance to premature closure' is in keeping with 'the postmodernist suspicion of all metanarratives as oppressive and potentially violent, suppressing what is different and other in the name of what they falsely claim to be universal'.[60] The need for a 'resistance to premature closure' might also explain the interest of many continental philosophers in the messianic beliefs of Judaism. As Caputo reminds us, these messianic beliefs share (and predate) the anticipatory expectation of Christian eschatology: 'The call of "come," . . . belongs to another time, other than philosophy's time, to a more Jewish and biblical time, a time organized around the promise not the present. The Bible does not think of time in terms of the enduring permanence of *ousia* but in terms of fidelity to the promise of something that is to come, even something a little impossible.'[61]

Can these bones live? Revelation, resurrection and the new creation

In contrast to Caputo, who avoids detailing explicitly 'the promise of something that is to come', Moltmann has little hesitation in locating the 'eschatological surplus of promise in Christ's resurrection'.[62] The resurrection of Jesus Christ is a belief unique to the Christian faith but it is rooted in the eschatological hope of early Judaism. N. T. Wright explains that 'by the time of Jesus . . . most Jews either believed in some form of resurrection or at least knew that it was standard teaching,' and the Hebrew Bible makes repeated reference to resurrection as a source of hope.[63] One of the most famous biblical accounts of resurrection is chapter 37 of the Book of Ezekiel, a passage that sees Ezekiel glimpsing something 'impossible' when he is taken to the valley of dry bones and told to prophesy life. The valley of dry, lifeless bones offers a precursor to the vision of hell imagined by *Nineteen Eighty-Four*. Winston's desire that 'everyone . . . be corrupt to the bones' is part of the reason for his attraction to Julia – 'Well then, I ought to suit you, dear. I'm corrupt to the bones' – but corrupt bones offer little hope, as Winston realizes when he sees a hollow reflection of himself at the Ministry of Love: 'the truly frightening thing was the emaciation of his body. The barrel of the ribs was as narrow as that of a skeleton: the legs had shrunk so that the knees were thicker than the thighs.'[64] The bones and skeletons that stand out in the Book of Ezekiel and *Nineteen Eighty-Four* find a more recent expression in the contemporary events narrated in *Girlfriend in a Coma*. Richard recalls that '[a] strong memory of that early period of TV production was of bodies: bodies on gurneys, bodies in boxes, bits of bodies, bodies bleeding, dummy bodies, alien bodies, bodies embedded with artificial components, bodies slated to vanish, bodies popping out of bodies, bodies just returned from the beyond, and bodies set to explode'.[65] Similarly, Karen's awakening from a 17-year coma leads to her expressing concern at a body that seems to have wasted away: 'what happened to me – my body – I can't move. I can't see any of it. What the hell's happened?'[66] Although Coupland uses skeletons and decaying bodies to symbolize lifelessness, he follows Ezekiel rather than Orwell in choosing to combine talk of dry bones with talk of resurrection. The emergence of Karen from a coma heralds an awakening in the lives of her friends, with Richard concluding: 'the woman I love is *not* a papery husk of a woman, breathing shallow thimbles of air as her gray hair crackles and her body turns to leather and bone. My friends are *not* lonely and tired and dried-up and sad. And I'm not just fooling myself, either. That's all over – we made the trade.'[67]

Karen's coma foreshadows a worldwide apocalypse in which everyone falls asleep, leaving Karen and her friends alone in the world to contemplate the purpose of their lives. Throughout the novel, sleep is likened to death. Karen's prophetic dreams picture a world of 'atomization and amnesia and comas' and other characters inadvertently testify to the derelict state of the world by slipping into drunken and drug-induced states of unconsciousness.[68] When Jared calls Wendy to live differently, he insists 'no drugs, no sleeping, no booze, no overworking, no repetition or insulation or efforts to make time disappear'.[69] Tate observes that 'Coupland's warning is against the anaesthetic qualities of contemporary Western life'.[70] That warning, however, is accompanied by a hope that the world can be brought back to life and made new. The latter stages of Coupland's novel make it clear that the hope of resurrection involves a radical break (rather than an escape) from the current order of things, and N. T. Wright's account of the biblical language of resurrection offers a helpful means of reflecting on the nature of this 'impossible' awakening: 'It involves, not a *reconstrual* of life after death, but the *reversal* of death itself . . . The language of awakening is not a new, exciting way of talking about sleep. It is a way of saying that a time will come when sleepers will sleep no more. Creation itself, celebrated throughout the Hebrew scriptures, will be reaffirmed, remade.'[71]

The future that is remade in *Girlfriend in a Coma* is unashamedly physical. Eschewing the idea that souls depart from the physical world to enjoy new life in a disembodied region of the universe, Coupland's novel expresses its commitment to the transformation of the material world. Explaining the Plan B that he offers, Jared urges his friends:

> Grind questions onto the glass on photocopiers. Scrape challenges onto old auto parts and throw them off of bridges so that future people digging in the mud will question the world, too. Carve eyeballs into tire treads and onto shoe leathers so that your every trail speaks of thinking and questioning and awareness. Design molecules that crystallize into question marks. Make bar-codes print out fables, not prices. You can't even throw away a piece of litter unless it has a question stamped on it – a demand for people to reach a finer place.[72]

The physicality of these images is striking, with the references to grinding, scraping and carving indicating the considerable effort involved in remaking a world that proves resistant to change. Resurrection calls for a radical break from the world as it currently exists, but it also envisages a continuity of material existence, hence Jared's not-always-harmonious use of images of reproduction ('photocopiers') and recycling ('old auto parts' and 'litter' stamped with questions). Holding these ideas together is not easy, as Christian theologians writing about the resurrection have long been aware, but Gunton insists that 'whatever happens "after death" it is continuous both with what happened before – life in the body – and with the life of the whole material creation'.[73]

The insistence on continuity recognizes that if the future is to offer hope, it must take account of the world that is and the world that has been. To do otherwise, and rely on replacing the current world with a better alternative, would offer no hope for the experiences that we have had up until this point. Any eschatological account that ignores the pain and suffering of history is hopeless, for our experiences in the world are part of who we are and cannot be ignored. The point is taken seriously by Bauckham and Hart, who explain:

> In the resurrection all the dead of all history will rise to judgement and life in the new creation. There is no danger that people in the past or the present be considered means to the greater good of people in the future. The countless victims of history, those whose lives were torture and those who scarcely lived at all, are not to be forgotten, but remembered in hope of the resurrection.[74]

The resurrection of the dead explored in the closing stages of *Girlfriend in a Coma* involves a group of friends returning to their previous lives, albeit with a very different understanding of what their prior experiences mean.

Instead of thinking that resurrection leaves history behind, Coupland sees that eschatological hope requires a commitment to history: 'Richard thinks about being alive at this particular juncture in history and he can only marvel – to be alive at this wondrous point – this jumping-off point towards farther reaches.'[75]

As well as expressing a commitment to the physical world and the continuity of past, present and future, the bodily resurrection envisaged by the New Testament writers and evident in Coupland's novel says something about the sociality of Christian eschatology. Resurrection is not an individual experience: 'bodily resurrection is a decisively important feature of the orthodox hope for a further reason. Not only is the body integral to human personal identity; it is also the medium of human sociality and of human solidarity with the rest of the material creation.'[76] *Girlfriend in a Coma* links together Karen's emergence from a coma, the decision of her friends to go back to the world as eschatological prophets, and a worldwide awakening; the novel follows the Book of Revelation in connecting the sociality of resurrection to the emergence of a new creation. This is most apparent when Coupland's book borrows vocabulary from the biblical text to describe the new world that the group of friends seek after: 'We'll crawl and chew and dig our way into a radical new world. We will change minds and souls from stone and plastic into linen and gold – that's what I believe. That's what I know.'[77] The reference to a world made up of transformed commodities points us in the direction of the new eternal city spoken of at the end of the Book of Revelation. Noting the way in which the Book of Revelation draws on the architectural imagery of the New Testament, with its reference to Christ and the people of God as parts of a new living Temple, Janet Martin Soskice describes 'the story of the stones and of the Temple as an image of the Resurrection: Christ's risen body, the new Temple, is a New Jerusalem built of living stones'.[78] If the friends that return to the world in Coupland's novel convey something of the ecclesial community described in the New Testament, then it is crucial that they see themselves as a community whose purpose is to build and invite others into the New Jerusalem of the eschaton.

Following a major paradox of the New Testament, Coupland's vision of a new creation acknowledges the role played by everyone in transforming the world yet insists on a central figure that makes this transforming work possible. The necessity of Karen's sacrifice for her friends recalls the redemptive work of Christ, particularly as it serves no other discernable narrative purpose in the novel. Karen's sacrifice derails an idea that runs throughout *Girlfriend in a Coma* – that transformation might be possible through good intentions alone. When Richard articulates this possibility by insisting that '[w]e *could* build a new society', Karen corrects him: 'Sacrifices need to be made. This is mine.'[79] The parallel with the New Testament is clear, yet Coupland's novel is significantly less certain about the nature and the outcome of the sacrifice. Karen's return to a coma enables the possibility of a new creation but because her resurrection is only temporary, one cannot be sure what will happen when her friends return to the world. Despite the strong message of hope on which the novel ends, there is always the possibility that Plan B will fail. In contrast, Revelation ends with the firmer hope of an eternally risen saviour, whose resurrection 'provides not only a promise but also, as enacted promise, the paradigm case of what the future general resurrection and the new creation of all things must involve'.[80]

The decision to end the final chapter of this book by noting one of the differences between *Girlfriend in a Coma* and the Book of Revelation runs the risk of suggesting that, in the final instance, religious and literary texts are different. To reach this conclusion would be a mistake, however; partly because the differences between religion and literature are often no greater than the internal differences within religion and literature, and partly because the possibility of other readings are a vital component of our interpretive activity, as this book has sought to make clear. The Book of Revelation may finish with the firm hope of a new creation inaugurated by the resurrection of Christ, but that new creation does not close reading down. Bauckham offers a helpful analogy when he likens the eschatological hope of Christian theology to the sense of an ending that we encounter in fairy tales:

> In speaking of the end of the story we are, of course, speaking of an end that also constitutes a new beginning, because it is the new creation of all things. The Creed's 'his kingdom shall have no end' is like the 'they live happily ever after' of the classic fairy tale. It is as that definitive result that the story's end completes and concludes the meaning of the whole story. Every such fairy-tale ending, like every seemingly satisfactory end of a fictional or historical story, is implicitly eschatological.[81]

The analogy is far from perfect, not least because it leaves itself open to those who want to attack religious stories for being too detached from the world's so-called reality, but it does witness the sort of hopeful future that Christian theology envisages. Eschatology articulates something other than a violent and deadly endgame in which, to quote Adorno's commentary on Beckett's play, '[h]ope skulks out of the world'.[82] Aware of the extent of our past suffering and the material needs that continue to surround us, eschatology commits itself to imagining a future in which the whole of creation might be resurrected and made new.

Notes

Introduction

1 John Milton, *Paradise Lost*, eds., Stephen Orgel and Jonathan Goldberg (Oxford: Oxford World's Classics, 2004), I. 16, 25.

2 Ibid., I. 13.

3 William Blake famously suggested that Milton was of the 'Devils party without knowing it', see William Blake, *The Marriage of Heaven and Hell* (1790), plate 6. Other influential contributors to the debate about Satan in *Paradise Lost* include C. S. Lewis, *A Preface to Paradise Lost* (London: Oxford University Press, 1942) and Stanley Fish, *Surprised by Sin: The Reader in Paradise Lost* (London: Macmillan, 1967). For a more recent discussion of the critical responses to Milton's characterisation of Satan, see John Carey, 'Milton's Satan' in Dennis Danielson, ed., *The Cambridge Companion to Milton*, 2nd ed. (Cambridge: Cambridge University Press, 1999).

4 See, for example, T. R. Wright, *Theology and Literature* (Oxford: Blackwell, 1988), Paul S. Fiddes *Freedom and Limit: A Dialogue Between Literature and Christian Doctrine* (New York: St Martin's Press, 1991), David Jasper, *The Study of Religion and Literature: An Introduction*, 2nd ed. (Basingstoke: Macmillan, 1992), Robert Detweiler and David Jasper, eds., *Religion and Literature: A Reader* (Louisville: John Knox Press, 2000), Mark Knight and Thomas Woodman, eds., *Biblical Religion and the Novel, 1700–2000* (Aldershot: Ashgate, 2006), and Andrew Haas, David Jasper and Elisabeth Jay, eds., *The Oxford Handbook of English Literature and Theology* (Oxford: Oxford University Press, 2007). It goes without saying that this list is not even close to being exhaustive. A wide-ranging selection of work in the area can be found in journals such as *Literature and Theology*, *Religion and Literature*, *Christianity and Literature* and *Religion and the Arts*.

5 For further discussion of narrative theology, see Hans Frei, *The Eclipse of Biblical Narrative* (New Haven: Yale University Press, 1974), George Lindbeck, *The Nature of Doctrine: Religion and Theology in a Postliberal Age* (London: SPCK, 1984), Stanley Hauerwas and L. Gregory Jones, eds., *Why Narrative? Readings in Narrative Theology* (Grand Rapids: Eerdmans, 1989), Brian Horne, 'Theology in the Narrative Mode', in Leslie Houlden and Peter Byrne, eds., *Companion Encyclopedia of Theology* (London: Routledge, 1995), and Gerard Loughlin, *Telling God's Story: Bible, Church and Narrative Theology* (Cambridge: Cambridge University Press, 1996). Perhaps the most useful

starting point for thinking about what a reception history of the Bible might entail is the Blackwell Bible Commentaries series.

6 Paul Ricoeur, *From Text to Action: Essays in Hermeneutics II*, trans. Kathleen Blamey and John B. Thompson (Evanston: Northwestern University Press, 1991), p. 83; see also Roland Barthes, 'The Death of the Author', *Image, Music, Text* (1977; repr. London: Fontana Press, 1987).

7 Much of the historic work on hermeneutics, from Friedrich Schleiermacher to important twentieth-century thinkers such as Hans-Georg Gadamer and Paul Ricoeur, emerges out of, or at least engages with, questions about how the Bible might be read. For a selection of more recent work on questions of biblical hermeneutics, see John Barton, ed., *The Cambridge Companion to Biblical Interpretation* (Cambridge: Cambridge University Press, 1998), Francis Watson, *Text, Church and Truth: Redefining Biblical Theology* (Edinburgh: T & T Clark, 1998), Luke Ferretter, *Towards A Christian Literary Theory* (Basingstoke: Palgrave, 2002) and Yvonne Sherwood, ed., *Derrida's Bible: Reading a Page of Scripture with a Little Help from Derrida* (New York: Palgrave, 2004).

8 G. K. Chesterton, *Heretics* (1905; repr. London: The Bodley Head Ltd, 1928), p. 303.

Chapter 1

1 John Milton, *Paradise Lost*, eds., Stephen Orgel and Jonathan Goldberg (Oxford: Oxford World's Classics, 2004) I. 19–22.

2 Colin Gunton, *The Christian Faith: An Introduction to Christian Doctrine* (Oxford: Blackwell, 2002), p. 7.

3 Milton, *Paradise Lost*, XII. 469–73.

4 J. Hillis Miller, *On Literature* (London: Routledge, 2002), p. 18.

5 Kevin J. Vanhoozer, 'Philosophical Antecedents to Ricoeur's *Time and Narrative*' in David Wood, ed., *On Paul Ricoeur: Narrative and Interpretation* (London: Routledge, 1991), p. 48.

6 Paul Ricoeur, 'On Interpretation', in *From Text to Action: Essays in Hermeneutics II*, trans. Kathleen Blamey and John B. Thompson (Evanston: Northwestern University Press, 1991), p. 6.

7 Gunton, *The Christian Faith*, p. 5.

8 Milton, *Paradise Lost*, XI. 17. Mary Fenton's argument about the relationship between prayer and place can be found in *Milton's Places of Hope: Spiritual and Political Connections of Hope with Land* (Aldershot: Ashgate, 2006), chapter 4.

9 Milton, *Paradise Lost*, XII. 646–9.

10 For a thoughtful, provocative account of the influence of Greek philosophy on the development of the Christian understanding of creation, see the chapter by Colin Gunton on the doctrine of creation in Colin Gunton, ed., *The Cambridge Companion to Christian Doctrine* (Cambridge: Cambridge University Press, 1997).

11 Stanley Fish, *How Milton Works* (Cambridge, MA: Harvard University Press, 2001), pp. 491–2.

12 I discuss some of the implications of the Christian doctrine of the Trinity further in Chapter 2.

13 Geoffrey Hartman, 'Milton's Counterplot', *A Critic's Journey: Literary Reflections, 1958–1998* (New Haven: Yale University Press, 1999), p. 111; Harold Fisch, *The Biblical Presence in Shakespeare, Milton and Blake* (Oxford: Clarendon Press, 1999), chapter 6.

14 Oliver Davies, *The Creativity of God: World, Eucharist, Reason* (Cambridge: Cambridge University Press, 2004), p. 104.

15 Regina Schwartz, *Remembering and Repeating: Biblical Creation in Paradise Lost* (Cambridge: Cambridge University Press, 1988), p. 1. The understanding of creation that Schwartz identifies in *Paradise Lost* parallels the multivocality of the poem's composition. Afflicted by blindness, Milton dictated the poem and then had it read back to him.

16 Ibid., pp. 91, 92.

17 Fish, *How Milton Works*, p. 287; Milton, *Paradise Lost*, VII. 217; Fish, *How Milton Works*, p. 299.

18 Jeremy S. Begbie, *Theology, Music and Time* (Cambridge: Cambridge University Press, 2000), p. 6.

19 See chapter 7 and chapter 8 of Begbie's work.

20 Milton, *Paradise Lost*, IX. 736–7; II. 379–80.

21 Ibid., X. 508.

22 Ibid., III. 368; V. 196.

23 Fish, *How Milton Works*, p. 284.

24 Milton, *Paradise Lost*, V. 146–50. It is worth noting that Fish reads the variety described in this quotation as 'only a surface phenomenon'. See Fish, *How Milton Works*, p. 286.

25 For a rich, imaginative exploration of Milton's 'dark materials' trope, see the Philip Pullman trilogy, *His Dark Materials* (*Northern Lights*, 1995; *The Subtle Knife*, 1997; *The Amber Spyglass*, 2001).

26 Milton, *Paradise Lost*, VI. 408.

27 Gunton, *The Christian Faith*, p. 14. For a more extended treatment of the theological resources that might be brought to bear on the challenge of holding together the interests of unity and diversity, see Colin Gunton, *The One, The Three and the Many* (Cambridge: Cambridge University Press, 1993).

28 Gunton, *The Christian Faith*, p. 5.

29 Milton, *Paradise Lost*, II. 916.

30 C. A. Patrides, *Milton and the Christian Tradition* (Oxford: Clarendon Press, 1966), pp. 32–3.

31 Milton, *Paradise Lost*, XII. 285–6.

32 Mary Shelley, *Frankenstein*, ed. M. K. Joseph (Oxford: Oxford World's Classics, 1998), pp. 54–5.

33 Alan Rauch, *Useful Knowledge: The Victorians, Morality, and the March of Intellect* (Durham: Duke University Press, 2001), p. 98.

34 Ibid., p. 100.

35 Shelley, *Frankenstein*, pp. 209, 27.

36 Maureen McLane, *Romanticism and the Human Sciences* (Cambridge: Cambridge University Press, 2000), pp. 15–16.

37 The importance of the opening chapters of Genesis to the narrative of *Paradise Lost* means that the monster's reflections on Milton's poem implicitly involve the biblical account of creation.

38 Ana Acosta, *Reading Genesis in the Long Eighteenth Century: From Milton to Mary Shelley* (Aldershot: Ashgate, 2006), p. 169.

39 Ibid., p. 171.

40 Shelley, *Frankenstein*, p. 202.

41 Peter K. Garrett, *Gothic Reflections: Narrative Force in Nineteenth-Century Fiction* (Ithaca: Cornell University Press, 2003), pp. 99, 100.

42 For another perspective on the (mis)reading common to all literary interpretation, see Paul de Man, *Blindness and Insight: Essays in the Rhetoric of Contemporary Criticism* (Minneapolis: University of Minnesota Press, 1971).

43 Gunton, *The Christian Faith*, p. 61. For a more extended discussion of the way in which sin shapes our reading practices, see Chapter 5 of this volume, 'The Stain of Sin: Tales of Transgression in the Modern World'.

44 Garrett, *Gothic Reflections*, p. 93.

45 Davies, *The Creativity of God*, p. 191.

46 Paul Ricoeur, 'Life in Quest of Narrative', in Wood, ed., *On Paul Ricoeur*, pp. 20–1.

47 Ibid., p. 27. For a more detailed outline of Ricoeur's understanding of emplotment, see part 1, chapter 2 of the first volume of Paul Ricoeur, *Time and Narrative*, 3 vols. (1983–5; trans. Kathleen McLaughlin and David Pellauer, Chicago: The University of Chicago Press, 1984–8).

48 For an important set of essays on midrash, see Geoffrey Hartman and Sanford Budick, eds., *Midrash and Literature* (New Haven: Yale University Press, 1986).

49 Harold Fisch, *New Stories for Old: Biblical Patterns in the Novel* (Basingstoke: Macmillan Press, 1998), p. 4.

50 Angela Carter, 'Notes from the Front Line', in Michelene Wandor, ed., *On Gender and Writing* (London: Pandora Press, 1983), p. 71.

51 Angela Carter, *The Sadeian Woman* (London: Virago, 1979), p. 5.

52 Sarah M. Henstra, 'The Pressure of New Wine: Performative Reading in Angela Carter's *The Sadeian Woman*', *Textual Practice* 13.1 (1999), p. 101. Butler's notion of performativity is developed in *Gender Trouble* (1990) and *Bodies that Matter* (1993).

53 Carter, 'Notes from the Front Line', p. 71.

54 Angela Carter, *The Passion of New Eve* (1977; repr. London: Virago, 1982), p. 174.

55 Roland Barthes, *Mythologies* (1957; trans. Annette Lavers, London: Vintage, 1993), p. 129.

56 Carter, *The Passion of New Eve*, p. 99.

57 Paul Ricoeur, 'Myth as the Bearer of Possible Worlds', in Richard Kearney, *On Paul Ricoeur: The Owl of Minerva* (Aldershot: Ashgate, 2004), p. 120.

58 Richard Kearney, 'Between Tradition and Utopia: The Hermeneutical Problem of Myth', in Wood, ed., *On Paul Ricoeur*, p. 67.

59 Ricoeur, 'Myth as the Bearer of Possible Worlds', p. 124.

60 Carter, *The Passion of New Eve*, p. 128.

61 Sarah Gamble, *Angela Carter: Writing from the Front Line* (Edinburgh: Edinburgh University Press, 1997), p. 123. In her discussion, Gamble helpfully draws attention to the interest in America and the desert that Carter shares with Jean Baudrillard. For a theological exploration of the symbol of the desert in art and literature, see David Jasper, *The Sacred Desert: Religion, Literature, Art, and Culture* (Oxford: Blackwell, 2004).

62 Gamble, *Angela Carter*, p. 128.

63 Carter, *The Passion of New Eve*, p. 191.

64 Ibid., p. 145.

65 Ibid., p. 145.

66 Ibid., p. 146.

67 I discuss Douglas Coupland's use of Ezekiel 37 in Chapter 6 of this volume, 'Suffering and Redemption in Eschatological Perspective'.

68 Carter, *The Passion of New Eve*, p. 146.

69 Ricoeur, 'Myth as the Bearer of Possible Worlds', p. 125.

70 Carter, *The Passion of New Eve*, p. 148.

71 Shelley, *Frankenstein*, p. 112.

Chapter 2

1 See, for example, Northrop Frye, *The Great Code: The Bible and Literature* (London: Routledge and Kegan Paul, 1982), Stephen Prickett, *Words and the Word: Language, Poetics and Biblical Interpretation* (Cambridge: Cambridge University Press, 1986), Harold Fisch, *New Stories for Old: Biblical Patterns in the Novel* (Basingstoke: Macmillan Press, 1998), and Yvonne Sherwood, *A Biblical Text and Its Afterlives: The Survival of Jonah in Western Culture* (Cambridge: Cambridge University Press, 2000).

2 All references in this chapter to Emily Dickinson's poetry are from Emily Dickinson, *The Complete Poems*, ed. Thomas H. Johnson (London: Faber & Faber, 1975).

3 Quoted in Hélène Cixous, *Three Steps on the Ladder of Writing* (New York: Columbia University Press, 1993), p. 17.

4 John Donne, *John Donne: The Complete English Poems*, ed. A. J. Smith (Harmondsworth: Penguin, 1986), pp. 314–15. All Donne quotations in this chapter are from this edition.

5 Ilona Bell tells us: 'Donne rarely lingers over the woman's physical appearance. For this and other more theoretical or ideological reasons, twentieth-century critics generally assume that the woman in Donne's poems is a shadowy figure, the object or reflection of male desire, a pretext for self-fashioning, a metaphor for the poet's professional aspirations, a sex object to be circulated for the titillation and amusement of Donne's male coterie.' See Ilona Bell, 'Gender matters: the women in Donne's poems', in Achsah Guibbory, ed., *The Cambridge Companion to John Donne* (Cambridge: Cambridge University Press, 2006), p. 201. It is worth noting that Bell's essay goes on to make it clear that contemporary feminist criticism reads Donne in a variety of (sometimes conflicting) ways. And it should also be noted that not every critic presumes the speaker of 'Batter My Heart' to be female – for a useful introduction to homoerotic readings of Donne, see Paula Blank, 'Comparing Sappho to Philaenis: John Donne's "Homepoetics"', *PMLA* 110. 3 (1995): 358–68.

6 See Gerald O'Collins, 'John Donne on the Trinity' in Miroslav Volf and Michael Welker, eds., *God's Life in the Trinity* (Minneapolis: Fortress, 2006) and Sarah Coakley, '"Batter my Heart . . ."? On Sexuality, Spirituality, and the Christian Doctrine of the Trinity', *Graven Images* II (1995): 74–83.

7 Coakley, '"Batter my Heart . . ."? On Sexuality, Spirituality, and the Christian Doctrine of the Trinity', p. 74.

8 For a thoughtful counter-reading of the Book of Hosea, see Yvonne Sherwood, *The Prophet and the Prostitute: Hosea's Marriage in Literary-Theological Perspective* (Sheffield: Sheffield Academic Press, 1996).

9 Coakley, '"Batter my Heart..."? On Sexuality, Spirituality, and the Christian Doctrine of the Trinity', p. 74.

10 Ibid., p. 75. In this article and in some of her other writing, Coakley argues, persuasively, that the renewal of interest in the Trinity among contemporary theologians does not provide as easy an answer to feminist concerns as some (male) trinitarian theologians have implied.

11 In grouping these theologians together, it is important to remember that there are considerable differences between them, both in terms of how they think about the Trinity and in terms of how that trinitarianism affects the rest of their theology.

12 Immanuel Kant, *The Conflict of the Faculties* (1798; trans. Mary J. Gregor, Lincoln: University of Nebraska Press, 1979), p. 65; Christoph Schwöbel, 'Introduction', in Christoph Schwöbel and Colin E. Gunton, eds., *Persons, Divine and Human: King's College Essays in Theological Anthropology* (Edinburgh: T & T Clark, 1991), p. 10.

13 While references to the Other proliferate in postcolonial literary theory, the most extensive treatment of the ethical significance of the Other can be found in the work of Emmanuel Levinas. A useful selection of material by Levinas can be found in Emmanuel Levinas, *The Levinas Reader*, edited by Sean Hand (Oxford: Blackwell, 1989).

14 There is, of course, much more complexity and nuance to the doctrine of the Trinity than I can hope to convey here, including detailed theories as to how the relation between Father, Son and Spirit might be understood. For a useful introduction to the doctrine, see Colin Gunton, *The Promise of Trinitarian Theology*, 2nd ed. (Edinburgh: T & T Clark, 1997).

15 Donne, 'Divine Litany IV: The Trinity', *The Complete English Poems*, p. 318.

16 John D. Zizioulas, *Being as Communion: Studies in Personhood and the Church* (London: Darton, Longman and Todd, 1985), p. 44.

17 Ibid., p. 44.

18 Alan J. Torrance, 'What is a Person?' in Malcolm Jeeves, ed., *From Cells to Souls – And Beyond: Changing Portraits of Human Nature* (Grand Rapids: Eerdmans, 2004), pp. 199, 202.

19 Ibid., p. 202.

20 Ibid., p. 203.

21 Alan J. Torrance, *Persons in Communion: An Essay on Trinitarian Description and Human Participation* (Edinburgh: T & T Clark, 1996), p. 283.

22 Gunton, 'Trinity, Ontology and Anthropology: Towards a Renewal of the Doctrine of the *Imago Dei*' in Schwöbel and Gunton, eds., *Persons, Divine and Human*, p. 56.

23 For a helpful reflection on movement and dance within the triune relationship, see Paul Fiddes, *Participating in God: A Pastoral Doctrine of the Trinity* (London: Darton, Longman and Todd, 2000).

24 Contrasting the 'classificatory systems' of modernity with the theological emphasis encouraged by postmodernism, David Cunningham writes: 'In contrast to the modernist penchant for division, isolation, and classification, postmodernism posits a much more interdependent approach. Individual instances are not so much sorted into discrete categories as they are *set in relation* to other instances. In the modern era, the grand metaphor for the organization of knowledge had been the tree (with a single trunk, major branches, and minor branches all related . . .). In postmodern

perspective, a more appropriate metaphor is a complex *network* of relationships, in which hierarchies are much more difficult to identify . . .' See David S. Cunningham, 'The Trinity', in Kevin J. Vanhoozer, ed., *The Cambridge Companion to Postmodern Theology* (Cambridge: Cambridge University Press, 2003), pp. 188, 189.

25 Ben Saunders, *Desiring Donne: Poetry, Sexuality, Interpretation* (Cambridge, MA: Harvard University Press, 2006), p. 1; Theresa M. DisPaquale, *Literature and Sacrament; The Sacred and the Secular in John Donne* (1999; repr. Cambridge: James Clarke & Co., 2001), p. 16. Similarly, in Guibbory, ed., *The Cambridge Companion to John Donne*, Guibbory tell us in his essay on 'Erotic poetry' that 'Donne brings politics and religion in to his erotic poems' (p. 139), while the essay on 'Devotional writing' by Helen Wilcox insists on 'the profound interconnection of secular and sacred experience in Donne's work' (p. 150).

26 Andrew Mousley, 'Transubstantiating Love: John Donne and Cultural Criticism', in Douglas Burnham and Enrico Giaccherini, eds., *The Poetics of Transubstantiation: From Theology to Metaphor* (Aldershot: Ashgate, 2005), p. 62.

27 Saunders, *Desiring Donne*, p. 14.

28 For an informative account of Donne's understanding of the Trinity, see Jeffrey Johnson, *The Theology of John Donne* (Cambridge: D. S. Brewer, 1999).

29 For a helpful account of Levinas' objection to Buber, see Michael Purcell, *Levinas and Theology* (Cambridge: Cambridge University Press, 2006), pp. 136–7.

30 Robert Jenson, *Systematic Theology, Volume 2: The Works of God* (New York: Oxford University Press, 1999), pp. 25–6.

31 In an eloquent and engaging essay on the persuasive power of Donne's poetry, Fish writes: 'the God Donne imagines is remarkably like the protagonist he presents (and I would say *is*) in the elegies, a jealous and overbearing master who brooks no rivals . . . It is as if Donne could only imagine a God in his own image, and therefore a God who acts in relation to him as he acts in relations to others, as a self-aggrandizing bully.' See Fish, 'Masculine Persuasive Force: Donne and Verbal and Power', in Elizabeth D. Harvey and Katharine Eisaman Maus, eds., *Soliciting Interpretation: Literary Theory and Seventeenth-Century English Poetry* (Chicago: The University of Chicago Press, 1990), p. 241.

32 Judith Banzer, 'Compound Manner: Emily Dickinson and the Metaphysical Poets', *American Literature* 32. 4 (1961), p. 421; see also Louis L. Martz, *The Poetry of Meditation* (New Haven: Yale University Press, 1954).

33 Janet Martin Soskice, 'Trinity and feminism' in Susan Parsons, ed., *The Cambridge Companion to Feminist Theology* (Cambridge: Cambridge University Press, 2002), p. 136.

34 See Jacques Derrida, *Of Grammatology* (1967; trans. Gayatri Chakravorty Spivak, Baltimore: Johns Hopkins University Press, 1997), p. 158.

35 See the essays on cultural context by David S. Reynolds, Domnhall Mitchell and Paula Bernat Bennett in the final section of Wendy Martin, ed., *The Cambridge Companion to Emily Dickinson* (Cambridge: Cambridge University Press, 2002); and Martin Orzeck and Robert Wesibuch, eds., *Dickinson and Audience* (Ann Arbor: The University of Michigan Press, 1996). In the latter we read: 'The poems of Emily Dickinson stand as the strongest testimony to her desire to be known by language. Though she wrote many poems that rank silence, instead of speaking, as supreme virtue,

it does not seem that she believed "True poems flee" all of the time.' Charlotte Nekola, '"Red in my Mind": Dickinson, Gender and Audience', in *Dickinson and Audience*, p. 31. In a similar vein, Beth Maclay Doriani draws on Dickinson's poem #441 ('This is my letter to the World') and writes: 'Dickinson's impulse to write was greater than a passing desire to send an elegy or a flower. Her letters and poems were created out of the need for communication; she was a transmitter of a "message" addressed to her "Sweet – countrymen –"'. See *Emily Dickinson, Daughter of Prophecy* (Amherst: University of Massachusetts Press, 1996), p. 40.

36 Margot K. Louis, 'Emily Dickinson's Sacrament of Starvation', *Nineteenth-Century Literature* 43. 4 (1988), p. 360.

37 Emily Dickinson, poem #1212.

38 See the first chapter of the Gospel of John.

39 Janet Martin Soskice, *Metaphor and Religious Language* (Oxford: Clarendon Press, 1985), p. 49.

40 Gerard Loughlin, *Telling God's Story: Bible, Church and Narrative Theology* (Cambridge: Cambridge University Press, 1996), p. 192. For further theological engagements with the insights and challenges of post-structuralism, see Graham Ward, *Barth, Derrida and the Language of Theology* (Cambridge: Cambridge University Press, 1995); Kevin Hart, *The Trespass of the Sign: Deconstruction, Theology and Philosophy*, rev. ed. (New York: Fordham University Press, 2000), and Kevin Hart and Yvonne Sherwood, eds., *Derrida and Religion: Other Testaments* (London: Routledge, 2005).

41 A good discussion of the linguistic difficulties involved in speaking of God, particularly a triune God, can be found in Torrance, *Persons in Communion*. There is extensive literature on the problems of religious language and it is impossible to detail it properly here. For a good introduction to Thomas Aquinas's doctrine of analogy, see 'Chapter Four: Talking about God' in Brian Davies, *The Thought of Thomas Aquinas* (Oxford: Clarendon Press, 1992). On the subject of negative theology, see John D. Caputo, *The Prayers and Tears of Jacques Derrida: Religion without Religion* (Bloomington: Indiana University Press, 1997); Oliver Davies and Denys Turner, eds., *Silence and the Word: Negative Theology and Incarnation* (Cambridge: Cambridge University Press, 2002); and Arthur Bradley, *Negative Theology and Modern French Philosophy* (London: Routledge, 2004).

42 Dickinson, poem #568

43 Regina M. Schwartz, 'Communion and Conversation' in Graham Ward, ed., *The Blackwell Companion to Postmodern Theology* (Oxford: Blackwell, 2001), p. 49.

44 Ibid., pp. 49–50.

45 Ibid., pp. 50–51.

46 Ibid., p. 66.

47 Dickinson, poem #437.

48 Ibid.

49 Dickinson, poem #626.

50 Graham Ward, '"In the daylight forever?": language and silence', in Davies and Turner, eds., *Silence and the Word*, p. 179. Further discussion of the relationship between poetry and silence can be found in George Steiner, *Language and Silence* (London: Faber, 1967), pp. 55–74.

51 Oliver Davies, 'Towards a Theological Poetics of Silence', in Davies and Turner, eds., *Silence and the Word*, p. 211.

52 Diane D'Amico has also discussed the importance of the Eucharist in 'Goblin Market', although the emphasis she places on a distinction between the soul and the body differs from the reading I pursue here. See Diane D'Amico, *Christina Rossetti: Faith, Gender and Time* (Baton Rouge: Louisiana State University Press, 1999), pp. 76–81.

53 Loughlin, *Telling God's Story*, p. 236. See also, Herbert McCabe, *God Matters* (London: Geoffrey Chapman, 1987).

54 Robert Jenson, 'The Church and the Sacraments', in Gunton, *The Cambridge Companion to Christian Doctrine*, p. 212.

55 Ibid., pp. 212–13.

56 Christina Rossetti, 'Goblin Market' in Christina Rossetti, *Poems*, ed. Jan Marsh (London: Everyman, 1996), lines 465–74. All references to 'Goblin Market' are from this edition.

57 See Marilyn McCord Adams, *Christ and Horrors: The Coherence of Christology* (Cambridge: Cambridge University Press, 2006), chapter 10; Jenson, *Systematic Theology Volume 2*, chapter 26; and Jenson, 'The Church and the Sacraments', in Gunton, ed., *The Cambridge Companion to Christian Doctrine*.

58 Adams, *Christ and Horrors*, p. 294.

59 Ibid., p. 295.

60 Rossetti, 'Goblin Market', lines 370–1.

61 Ibid., lines 3, 233–4.

62 Ibid., lines 93–5.

63 See Terrence Holt, '"Men Sell Not Such in Any Town": Exchange in Goblin Market', *Victorian Poetry* 28. 1 (1990): 51–67; Elizabeth K. Helsinger, 'Consumer Power and the Utopia of Desire: Christina Rossetti's "Goblin Market"', *ELH* 58. 4 (1991): 903–33; and Herbert F. Tucker, 'Rossetti's Goblin Marketing: Sweet to Tongue and Sound to Eye', *Representations* 82 (2003): 117–33.

64 Alison Chapman, *The Afterlife of Christina Rossetti* (Basingstoke: Macmillan, 2000), pp. 140–1.

65 Kathryn Tanner, *The Economy of Grace* (Minneapolis: Fortress Press, 2005), p. 1. The idea of theology involving a contestatory relationship with other systems of thought is taken from Tanner's earlier work, *Theories of Culture* (1997). Tanner does not propose a complete divide between Christian theology and other systems of thought; she merely notes that some level of critique is present.

66 The social and political consequences of these ideas are developed further in the next chapter.

67 Revelation 21. 6. All biblical quotations are from the King James Version.

68 Isaiah 55. 1.

69 Rossetti, 'Goblin Market', lines 525–9.

70 M. Douglas Meeks, 'The Social Trinity and Property', in Volf and Welker, eds., *God's Life in Trinity*, p. 20.

Chapter 3

1 See Exodus 19 and 20.

2 Paul Ricoeur, *The Just* (1995; trans. David Pellauer, Chicago: The University of Chicago Press, 2000), p. xiii.

3 Charles Dickens, *Bleak House*, ed. Norman Page (1852–3; Harmondsworth: Penguin Books, 1971), p. 145.

4 Ibid., pp. 145–6.

5 Gordon Bigelow, *Fiction, Famine, and the Rise of Economics in Victorian Britain and Ireland* (Cambridge: Cambridge University Press, 2003), p. 107.

6 For a more detailed discussion of the parallels between *The Trial* and *Bleak House*, see Mark Spilka, *Dickens and Kafka: A Mutual Interpretation* (London: Dennis Dobson, 1963), chapters 10–12.

7 Franz Kafka, *The Trial* (1925; trans. Idris Parry, Harmondsworth: Penguin Books, 1994), pp. 35–6.

8 Jacques Derrida, 'Before the Law', in *Acts of Literature*, ed. Derek Attridge (New York: Routledge, 1992), p. 220.

9 Matthew 5.17.

10 2 Corinthians 3. 6.

11 Dickens, *Bleak House*, p. 256.

12 Ibid., p. 307.

13 Jacques Derrida, *Given Time: I. Counterfeit Money* (1991; trans. Peggy Kamuf, Chicago: University of Chicago Press, 1994), p. 7.

14 Alan Schrift, 'Introduction' to Alan Schrift, ed., *The Logic of the Gift: Toward an Ethic of Generosity* (New York: Routledge, 1997), p. 19.

15 For an important introduction to the theology of Radical Orthodoxy, see John Milbank, Catherine Pickstock, and Graham Ward, eds., *Radical Orthodoxy* (London: Routledge, 1999).

16 John Milbank, 'Can a Gift be Given? Prolegomena to a Future Trinitarian Metaphysic', *Modern Theology* 11. 1 (1995), p. 131.

17 Dickens, *Bleak House*, p. 915.

18 Kathryn Tanner, *Economy of Grace* (Minneapolis: Fortress Press, 2005), p. 52.

19 Ibid., pp. 52–3.

20 See Mark M. Anderson, *Kafka's Clothes: Ornament and Aestheticism in the Habsburg Fin de Siècle* (Oxford: Clarendon Press, 1992), chapter 6.

21 Kafka, *The Trial*, p. 66.

22 Ibid., p. 66.

23 Ibid., p. 66.

24 Ibid., pp. 69–70.

25 Tanner, *Economy of Grace*, p. 62.

26 Ibid., p. 63.

27 Kafka, *The Trial*, p. 71.

28 Tanner, *Economy of Grace*, p. 67.

29 Alain Badiou, *Saint Paul: The Foundation of Universalism* (1997; trans. Ray Brassier, Stanford: Stanford University Press, 2003), p. 77.

30 For a contemporary theological attempt to explain how Christian theology might accommodate the Law without slipping into supersessionism, see Bruce D. Marshall, 'Christ and the cultures: the Jewish people and Christian theology' in Colin Gunton, ed., *The Cambridge Companion to Christian Doctrine* (Cambridge: Cambridge University Press, 1997), pp. 91–4.

31 2 Corinthians 3.6.

32 Geoffrey Hartman, *Scars of the Spirit: The Struggle Against Inauthenticity* (New York: Palgrave Macmillan, 2002), p. 112.

33 Janet L. Larson, 'The Battle of Biblical Books in Esther's Narrative', *Nineteenth-Century Fiction* 38.2 (1983), p. 131. For a discussion of how biblical sources inform other novels by Dickens, see Janet L. Larson, *Dickens and the Broken Scripture* (Athens: University of Georgia Press, 1985).

34 Theodore W. Jennings, *Reading Derrida/Thinking Paul: On Justice* (Stanford: Stanford University Press, 2006), p. 182.

35 Dickens, *Bleak House*, p. 50.

36 Ibid., p. 50.

37 Ibid., p. 50.

38 Ibid., p. 145.

39 Ibid., p. 773.

40 Ibid., p. 589.

41 Ibid., pp. 876, 605.

42 Ibid., p. 567.

43 Ibid., pp. 715–16.

44 Ibid., pp. 567, 631/7, 637.

45 Ibid., p, 646.

46 J. Hillis Miller, 'Introduction' to Dickens, *Bleak House*, p. 28.

47 Ibid., pp. 30–1.

48 Dickens, *Bleak House*, p. 888.

49 See, for example, the argument by Timothy Peltason that 'the counter-drama of Esther's growing self assertion' is a means by which the novel 'stresses the importance not of transcending but of discovering the personal will'. Timothy Peltason, 'Esther's Will', *ELH* 59. 3 (1992), p. 672.

50 Alexander Welsh, *Dickens Redressed: The Art of Bleak House and Hard Times* (New Haven: Yale University Press, 2000), p. 145.

51 It was Gottfried Wilhelm Leibniz who described creation as the best of all possible worlds in his important work, *Theodicy* (1710). The notion that our sufferings in the world are 'all for the best' was criticized by Voltaire in *Candide* (1759).

52 Dickens, *Bleak House*, p. 66.

53 Ibid., p. 106.

54 Larson, 'The Battle of Biblical Books in Esther's Narrative', p. 151

55 Hartman, *Scars of the Spirit*, p. 106.

56 Dickens, *Bleak House*, pp. 162–3.

57 Ibid., p. 887.

58 Miller, 'Introduction', p. 30.

59 Matthew 6.10.

60 See, for example, Kieran Dolin, *Fiction and the Law: Legal Discourse in Victorian and Modernist Literature* (Cambridge: Cambridge University Press, 1999), and Jan-Melissa Schramm, *Testimony and Advocacy in Victorian Law, Literature and Culture* (Cambridge: Cambridge University Press, 2000).

61 Paul Ricoeur, 'The Act of Judging,' *The Just*, pp. 127–8.

62 Dickens, *Bleak House*, pp. 60–1.

63 Welsh refers to the linguistic acrobatics of Skimpole and Chadband in *Dickens Redressed*, p. 100.

64 Miller, 'Introduction', p. 11.

65 Dickens, *Bleak House*, p. 61.

66 Kafka, *The Trial*, pp. 114–15.

67 Ibid., p. 167.

68 Ibid., p. 41.

69 Ibid., p. 41.

70 Northrop Frye, *The Great Code: The Bible and Literature* (London: Routledge and Kegan Paul, 1982), p. 195.

71 Jill Robbins notes: 'A number of critics, among them Benjamin, Blanchot, Buber, and Politzer, have suggested, in different ways, that Kafka be returned to the Jewish tradition'. See Jill Robbins, 'Kafka's Parables', in Geoffrey H. Hartman and Sanford Budick, eds., *Midrash and Literature* (New Haven: Yale University Press, 1986), p. 272.

72 James L. Kugel, 'Two Introductions to Midrash,' in Hartman and Budick, eds., *Midrash and Literature*, p. 91.

73 Kafka, *The Trial*, p. 172.

74 Harold Fisch, *New Stories for Old: Biblical Patterns in the Novel* (Basingstoke: Macmillan Press, 1998), p. 96.

75 Beth Hawkins, *Reluctant Theologians: Franz Kafka, Paul Celan, Edmond Jabès* (New York: Fordham University Press, 2003), p. xv.

76 Kafka, *The Trial*, p. 178.

77 Robbins, 'Kafka's Parables', p. 272.

78 Hartman, 'The Struggle for the Text', in Hartman and Budick, eds., *Midrash and Literature*, p. 17.

Chapter 4

1 See Gerard Loughlin, *Telling God's Story: Bible, Church and Narrative Theology* (Cambridge: Cambridge University Press, 1996).

2 See Terry R. Wright, The *Genesis of Fiction: Modern Novelists as Biblical Interpreters* (Aldershot: Ashgate, 2007).

3 Emmanuel Levinas, *Beyond the Verse*, trans. Garry D. Mole (London: Athlone, 1994), p. 109.

4 Margaret Atwood, *The Handmaid's Tale* (1985; repr. London: Vintage, 1996), pp. 204–5.

5 Ibid., p. 175.

6 Ibid., p. 98.

7 I am indebted to Louise Lee for encouraging me to think further about the word 'incendiary'.

8 Jeanette Winterson, *Oranges Are Not the Only Fruit* (1985; repr. London: Vintage, 2001), p. 170.

9 Ibid., p. 134. A helpful discussion of some of the specific influences at work in Winterson's intertextual reworking of the Bible can be found in Anita Gnagnatti, 'Discarding God's Handbook: Winterson's Oranges Are Not the Only Fruit and the Tension of Intertextuality', in Mark Knight

and Thomas Woodman, eds., *Biblical Religion and the Novel, 1700–2000* (Aldershot: Ashgate, 2006). Gnagnatti concludes that although 'Winterson emphatically begins by engaging with biblical myth . . . she has to move away from it, both to express adequately her character's, and to some degree her own, experiences, and to enable the reader of her work to engage with another way of seeing and thinking' (p. 134). For further discussion of the intertextual relationship between Winterson's novel and the Bible, see Tess Cosslett, 'Intertextuality in Oranges Are Not the Only Fruit: The Bible, Malory, and Jane Eyre', in Helena Grice and Tim Woods, eds., *'I'm telling you stories': Jeanette Winterson and the Politics of Reading* (Amsterdam: Rodopi, 1998).

10 Hans-Georg Gadamer, *Truth and Method* (1960; 2nd rev. ed., trans. Joel Weinsheimer and Donald G. Marshall, London: Continuum, 2004), p. 385.

11 Ibid., p. 389.

12 Rushdie's reflections are more complex than my brief summary suggests. See the essays in the final section of Salman Rushdie, *Imaginary Homelands: Essays and Criticism 1981–91* (1991; rev. ed. London: Granta Books, 1992).

13 Tracing the history of theoretical trends always involves questionable narratives and generaliza- tions, and I certainly do not want to imply that close reading is incompatible with the literary the- ory that emerged in the second half of the twentieth century. A number of major theorists are well known for their ability to read texts closely, and their work retains and reinvents certain aspects of an earlier formalist methodology. See, for example, Geoffrey Hartman, *Saving the Text* (Baltimore: Johns Hopkins University Press, 1981), and Frank Lentricchia and Andrew DuBois, ed., *Close Reading: The Reader* (Durham: Duke University Press, 2002). For an informative review essay on the recent movement that has been described as New Formalism, see Marjorie Levinson, 'What is New Formalism?', *PMLA* 122. 2 (2007): 558–69.

14 Stanley Fish, *Is There a Text in This Class?: The Authority of Interpretive Communities* (Cambridge, MA: Harvard University Press, 1980), p. 322.

15 Ibid., p. 322.

16 Ibid., p. 323.

17 Loughlin, *Telling God's Story*, p. 69.

18 Ibid., p. 79.

19 Stanley Hauerwas, *Unleashing the Scripture: Freeing the Bible from Captivity to America* (Nashville: Abingdon Press, 1993), pp. 32; 25. A key influence on the argument that Hauerwas develops is Stephen D. Moore, *Literary Criticism and the Gospels: The Theoretical Challenge* (New Haven: Yale University Press, 1989).

20 Hauerwas, *Unleashing the Scripture*, p. 26.

21 Ibid., p. 21. The insistence on locating reading within interpretive communities does not mean that individuals are to be seen as incapable of reading against the grain or exploring new lines of thought. Fish discusses this at length in *Is There a Text in This Class?*, explaining both that readers typically inhabit multiple interpretive communities and that the perspective of an interpretive community is never static.

22 For a more extended reflection on the relation between George Eliot's theological outlook and the use of a secularization narrative to account for the development of nineteenth-century literature,

see chapter 5 of Mark Knight and Emma Mason, *Nineteenth-Century Religion and Literature* (Oxford: Oxford University Press, 2006).

23 George Eliot, *Silas Marner*, ed. David Carroll (Harmondsworth: Penguin, 1996), p. 13.

24 Ibid., p. 14.

25 For further discussion of the ideas that influence Eliot's writing, see T. R. Wright, *The Religion of Humanity: The Impact of Comtean Positivism on Victorian Britain* (Cambridge: Cambridge University Press, 1986); Gillian Beer, *Darwin's Plots: Evolutionary Narrative in Darwin, George Eliot, and Nineteenth-Century Fiction*, 2nd ed. (Cambridge: Cambridge University Press, 2000); and David Carroll, *George Eliot and the Conflict of Interpretations: A Reading of the Novels* (Cambridge: Cambridge University Press, 1992).

26 Eliot, *Silas Marner*, p. 82.

27 Ibid., p. 143.

28 Ibid., p. 157.

29 Loughlin, *Telling God's Story*, p. 46.

30 Ibid., pp. 47, 95.

31 For further material on the controversy surrounding the publication of *The Satanic Verses*, see Ruvani Ranasinha, 'The *fatwa* and its aftermath', in Abdulrazak Gurnah, ed., *The Cambridge Companion to Salman Rushdie* (Cambridge: Cambridge University Press, 2007); Joel Kuortti, *Place of the Sacred: The Rhetoric of the Satanic Verses Affair* (Frankfurt: Peter Lang, 1997); and Dan Cohn-Sherbok, ed., *The Salman Rushdie Controversy in Interreligious Perspective* (Lampeter: Edwin Mellon Press, 1990).

32 Ranasinha, 'The *fatwa* and its aftermath', pp. 45, 46.

33 Rushdie, 'In Good Faith', in *Imaginary Homelands*, p. 397.

34 Ranasinha, 'The *fatwa* and its aftermath', p. 46.

35 Steve Bruce, *Fundamentalism* (Cambridge: Polity Press, 2000), p. 117.

36 Klaus Stierstorfer, 'Tariq Ali and Recent Negotiations of Fundamentalism', in Catherine Pesso-Miquel and Klaus Stierstorfer, eds., *Fundamentalism and Literature* (Basingstoke: Palgrave, 2007), pp. 147–8.

37 Bruce, *Fundamentalism*, p. 2.

38 For a thoughtful set of essays examining some of the Western ideological assumptions evident in the aftermath of the Rushdie Affair, see the special issue ('Beyond the Rushdie Affair') of *Third Text: Third World Perspectives on Contemporary Art & Culture* 11 (Summer 1990), ed. Don F. Miller.

39 Ranasinha, 'The *fatwa* and its aftermath', p. 49.

40 Homi K. Bhabha, 'Unpacking My Library . . . Again', in Iain Chambers and Lidia Curti, eds., *The Post-Colonial Question: Common Skies, Divided Horizons* (London and New York: Routledge, 1996), pp. 209, 211.

41 Stierstorfer, 'Tariq Ali and Recent Negotiations of Fundamentalism', p. 148.

42 Joel Kuortti, 'The Satanic Verses: "To be born again, first you have to die"', in Gurnah, ed., *The Cambridge Companion to Salman Rushdie*, p. 133.

43 Salman Rushdie, 'In Good Faith', *Imaginary Homelands*, p. 394.

44 Salman Rushdie, *The Satanic Verses* (1988; repr. London: Vintage Books, 2006), p. 192.

45 Rushdie, 'In Good Faith', *Imaginary Homelands*, p. 404.

46 Rushdie, *The Satanic Verses*, p. 367.

47 Homi K. Bhabha, 'How Newness Enters the World', *The Location of Culture* (New York: Routledge, 1994), p. 226.

48 Rushdie, *The Satanic Verses*, p. 79.

49 Ibid., p. 123.

50 Ibid., p. 123.

51 Ibid., p. 103.

52 Ibid., p. 10.

53 Ibid., p. 97.

54 Salman Rushdie, 'Is Nothing Sacred', *Imaginary Homelands*, p. 418.

55 Ibid., p. 418.

56 Ibid., p. 427.

57 Luke Bretherton, *Hospitality as Holiness: Christian Witness Amid Moral Diversity* (Aldershot: Ashgate, 2006), p. 122.

58 Winterson, *Oranges Are Not the Only Fruit*, p. 165.

59 Ibid., p. 164.

60 Bretherton, *Hospitality as Holiness*, p. 122.

61 Ibid., p. 5. For a different perspective, involving a theological defence of tolerance, see Ian S. Markham, *A Theology of Engagement* (Oxford: Blackwell, 2003), chapter 8.

62 Bretherton, *Hospitality as Holiness*, p. 128.

63 For a stimulating set of essays exploring the crossover between Christian ecclesiology and the range of ideas that literature entertains, see John Schad, ed., *Writing the Bodies of Christ: The Church from Carlyle to Derrida* (Aldershot: Ashgate, 2001).

64 See Mikhail Bakhtin, *The Dialogic Imagination: Four Essays* (trans. Caryl Emerson and Michael Holquist, Austin: University of Texas Press, 1981).

65 Winterson, *Oranges Are Not the Only Fruit*, p. 91.

66 J. Hillis Miller, 'The Critic as Host', in Harold Bloom et al., *Deconstruction and Criticism* (1979; repr. London: Continuum, 2004), p. 177.

67 Ibid., p. 182.

68 Noting a tendency for some deconstructionists to lock themselves into a prison house of language, Valentine Cunningham offers a corrective to what he sees as Miller's emphasis on words rather than things: 'You can't, to put it bluntly, discuss the emblematic force, the deep linguistic logics of parasites and hosts, without also pondering some of the actual social, historical, biological relations of those real parasites and hosts who share each others' tables, salt, bodies, life.' See Valentine Cunningham, *In the Reading Gaol: Postmodernity, Texts, and History* (Oxford: Blackwell, 1994), p. 341.

69 Atwood, *The Handmaid's Tale*, p. 153.

70 A similar idea permeates Atwood's later dystopian text, *Oryx and Crake* (2003).

71 Atwood, *The Handmaid's Tale*, p. 182.

72 Miller, 'The Critic as Host', p. 180.

73 Atwood, *The Handmaid's Tale*, p. 149.

74 For a more detailed discussion of the theological significance of the Eucharist, see Chapter2 of this book.

75 Loughlin, *Telling God's Story*, p. 225.

Chapter 5

1 See, for example, Robert Penn Warren, 'A Poem of Pure Imagination: An Experiment in Reading' in *Selected Essays* (New York: Random House, 1958); Jerome McGann, 'The Ancient Mariner: The Meaning of the Meanings', in *The Beauty of Inflections: Literary Investigations in Historical Method and Theory* (Oxford: Clarendon Press, 1985); and Peter Larkin 'Repetition, Difference and Liturgical Participation in Coleridge's "The Ancient Mariner"', *Literature and Theology* 21. 2 (2007): 146–59.

2 Larkin, 'Repetition, Difference and Liturgical Participation', p. 149.

3 Gerard Loughlin, *Telling God's Story: Bible, Church and Narrative Theology* (Cambridge: Cambridge University Press, 1996), pp. 87–8.

4 Ronald Paulson, *Sin and Evil: Moral Values in Literature* (New Haven: Yale University Press, 2007), p. 346.

5 Ibid., p. xii.

6 Charles Mathewes, *Evil and the Augustinian Tradition* (Cambridge: Cambridge University Press, 2001), p. 3.

7 Ibid., p. 28.

8 Charles Mathewes finds considerable continuity between Arendt's account of evil and the account offered by St Augustine. Arendt is one of the two major twentieth-century conversation partners that Mathewes engages with in his book.

9 Hannah Arendt, *Eichmann in Jerusalem: A Report on the Banality of Evil* (Harmondsworth: Penguin, 1994), p. 252.

10 Philip Roth, *The Human Stain* (London: Vintage, 2001), pp. 153–4.

11 Ibid., p. 290.

12 Ibid., p. 213.

13 See, for example, the review of Roth's novel by Lorrie Moore, 'The Wrath of Athena', *The New York Times*, 7 May 2000.

14 Geoffrey Hartman, *Saving the Text* (Baltimore: Johns Hopkins University Press, 1981), p. 129.

15 Robert Jenson, *Systematic Theology Volume 2: The Works of God* (New York: Oxford University Press, 1999), p. 150.

16 Roth, *The Human Stain*, p. 303.

17 Ibid., p. 92.

18 Rebecca Lemon, *Treason by Words: Literature, Law, and Rebellion in Shakespeare's England* (Ithaca: Cornell University Press, 2006), p. 86.

19 Macbeth describes Duncan as 'so meek', so 'clear', 'that his virtues / Will plead like angels, trumpet-tongu'd, against / The deep damnation of his taking-off'. William Shakespeare, *Macbeth*, ed. Kenneth Muir (Arden Shakespeare; repr. London: Routledge, 1994), I. VII. 17–20.

20 Ibid., IV. III. 12.

21 Lemon, *Treason by Words*, p. 12.

22 Janette Dillon, *The Cambridge Introduction to Shakespearean Tragedies* (Cambridge: Cambridge University Press, 2007), p. 116.

23 Shakespeare, *Macbeth*, IV. I. 49.

24 Alexander Leggatt, *Shakespeare's Tragedies: Violation and Identity* (Cambridge: Cambridge University Press, 2005), p. 179. John D. Cox finds less ambiguity when it comes to the question of Macbeth's agency. Pursuing a different reading to the one that I am proposing here, he writes: 'Macbeth's suffering would seem to be the least enigmatic of all the suffering in the tragedies, because he so clearly brings it on himself.' See John D. Cox, *Seeming Knowledge: Shakespeare and Skeptical Faith* (Waco: Baylor University Press, 2007), p. 84.

25 Cox, *Seeming Knowledge*, p. 29.

26 See Thomas Aquinas, *Summa Theologica* part 2, question 49, article 1. The most comprehensive treatment of Augustine's understanding of evil is G. R. Evans, *Augustine on Evil* (Cambridge: Cambridge University Press, 1982). For a further discussion of the literary implications of understanding evil as a privation, see Mark Knight, *Chesterton and Evil* (New York: Fordham University Press, 2004).

27 Leggatt, *Shakespeare's Tragedies*, p. 204.

28 Further discussion of this point can be found in Brian Horne, *Imagining Evil* (London: Darton, Longman and Todd, 1996).

29 Shakespeare, *Macbeth*, I. I. 11–12.

30 Macbeth sees the dagger in act II.I; Banquo's ghost appears in act III. IV; Lady Macbeth's tells her husband that he is seeing things in act III. IV. 60; and Lady Macbeth imagines blood on her hands in act V. I.

31 The quotation is from Geoffrey Hartman, *Scars of the Spirit: The Struggle Against Inauthenticity* (New York: Palgrave, 2002), p. 106.

32 Roth, *The Human Stain*, p. 6.

33 Ibid., p. 343.

34 Ibid., p. 84.

35 For a thoughtful discussion of the representation of sin in the work of John Updike, see chapter 3 of Andrew Tate, *Contemporary Fiction and Christianity* (London: Continuum, 2008).

36 Roth, *The Human Stain*, pp. 310–11.

37 Nathaniel Hawthorne, *The Scarlet Letter*, ed. Brian Harding (Oxford: Oxford World's Classics, 2007), pp. 28–9.

38 Erika M. Kreger, '"Depravity Dressed Up in a Fascinating Garb": Sentimental Motifs and the Seduced Hero(ine) in The Scarlet Letter', *Nineteenth-Century Literature* 54. 3 (1999): p. 308.

39 Ibid., p. 309.

40 Hawthorne, *The Scarlet Letter*, p. 51.

41 Roth, *The Human Stain*, p. 242.

42 David Brauner, *Philip Roth* (Manchester: Manchester University Press, 2007), p. 179.

43 Hawthorne, *The Scarlet Letter*, p. 39.

44 Roth, *The Human Stain*, p. 161.

45 Ibid., p. 291.

46 Ibid., p. 293.

47 Ibid., p. 291.

48 For an illuminating discussion of the deceptive narrative strategies employed by Zuckerman, see Derek Parker Royal, 'Plotting the Frames of Subjectivity: Identity, Death, and Narrative in Philip Roth's *The Human Stain*', *Contemporary Literature* 47. 1 (2006): 114–40.

49 Roth, *The Human Stain*, p. 282.

50 Brauner, *Philip Roth*, p. 176. Zuckerman writes: 'I'd intruded upon – no, trespassed upon; it was almost an unlawful sense . . . I'd trespassed upon a setting as pristine, I would think, as unviolated . . .' (Roth, *The Human Stain*, p. 345).

51 Brauner, *Philip Roth*, p. 177.

52 Roth, *The Human Stain*, p. 361.

53 Hawthorne, *The Scarlet Letter*, pp. 126–7.

54 Roth, *The Human Stain*, p. 242.

55 Ibid., p. 170.

56 Ibid., p. 242.

57 Ibid., p. 100.

58 Brian Finney, 'Briony's Stand Against Oblivion: The Making of Fiction in Ian McEwan's *Atonement*', *The Journal of Modern Literature* 27. 3 (2004): p. 69.

59 Ian McEwan, *Atonement* (London: Jonathan Cape, 2001), p. 371.

60 Colin Gunton, *The Actuality of Atonement: A Study of Metaphor, Rationality and the Christian Tradition* (Edinburgh: T & T Clark, 1988), p. 5.

61 Roth, *The Human Stain*, p. 315.

62 Gunton, *The Actuality of Atonement*, p. 43.

63 Paul Fiddes, 'The Passion Story in Literature', in Andrew Haas, David Jasper and Elisabeth Jay, eds., *The Oxford Handbook to English Literature and Theology* (Oxford: Oxford University Press, 2007), pp. 742–3.

64 McEwan, *Atonement*, p. 349.

65 Marilyn McCord Adams, *Horrendous Evils and the Goodness of God* (Ithaca: Cornell University Press, 1999), p. 156.

66 For a more detailed account of how such resources might be employed, see Marilyn McCord Adams, *Christ and Horrors: The Coherence of Christology* (Cambridge: Cambridge University Press, 2006).

67 Samuel Taylor Coleridge, 'The Rime of the Ancient Mariner', in *The Major Works*, ed. H. L. Jackson (Oxford: Oxford World's Classics, 2000), line 584.

68 Larkin, 'Repetition, Difference and Liturgical Participation', p. 147.

69 Ibid., p. 157.

70 Paulson, *Sin and Evil*, p. 258.

71 Gunton, *The Actuality of Atonement*, p. 105.

Chapter 6

1 The allusion is to Frank Kermode's influential work on narrative closure, *The Sense of an Ending* (Oxford: Oxford University Press, 1967).

2 See Ben Quash, *Theology and the Drama of History* (Cambridge: Cambridge University Press, 2005).

3 Although Clov goes off-stage on a number of occasions, he does not go far and the set seen by the audience remains within the confines of the one room.

4 Richard Bauckham and Trevor Hart, *Hope Against Hope: Christian Eschatology at the Turn of the Millenium* (Grand Rapids: Eerdmans, 1999), pp. 35–6.

5 Paul Fiddes, *The Promised End: Eschatology in Theology and Literature* (Oxford: Blackwell, 2000), p. 157.

6 For a helpful discussion of the complexity and ambiguity of Beckett's engagement with the idea of God, see Mary Bryden, *Samuel Beckett and the Idea of God* (Basingstoke: Macmillan, 1998).

7 Theodor Adorno, 'Trying to Understand *Endgame*', *Notes to Literature* Vol. 1, trans. Shierry Weber Nicholsen (New York: Columbia University Press, 1991), p. 244.

8 Ibid., p. 244.

9 Fiddes, *The Promised End*, p. 164.

10 Ibid., pp. 167–8.

11 Bryden, *Samuel Beckett and the Idea of God*, p. 125.

12 Fiddes, *The Promised End*, pp. 175–9. Lucky's think monologue can be found in Samuel Beckett's *Waiting for Godot* (New York: Grove Press, 1954).

13 The work of Jenson, Begbie and narrative theologians such as Gerard Loughlin has been detailed in previous chapters. For the classic study on the relationship between theology and drama, see Hans Urs von Balthasar, *Theo-Drama: Theological Dramatic Theory*, 5 vols. (trans. Graham Harrison; San Francisco: Ignatius Press, 1988–98). See also Kevin J. Vanhoozer, *The Drama of Doctrine: A Canonical-Linguistic Approach to Christian Theology* (Louisville: Westminster John Knox Press, 2005), and Quash, *Theology and the Drama of History*.

14 David Fergusson, 'Eschatology', in Colin Gunton, ed., *The Cambridge Companion to Christian Doctrine* (Cambridge: Cambridge University Press, 1997), p. 226.

15 Jürgen Moltmann's work includes *Theology of Hope: On the Ground and the Implications of a Christian Eschatology* (1964; trans. J. W. Leitch, London: SCM Press, 1967) and *The Coming of God: Christian Eschatology* (1995; trans. M. Kohl, London: SCM Press, 1996).

16 Colin Gunton, *The Christian Faith: An Introduction to Christian Doctrine* (Oxford: Blackwell, 2001), pp. 157–8.

17 See Bauckham and Hart, *Hope Against Hope*, pp. 42–3.

18 Raymond Williams exemplifies the consternation felt by a certain school of political literary criticism when he complains about the political analysis offered by Orwell in *Nineteen*

Eighty-Four. 'By assigning all modern forms of repression and authoritarian control to a single political tendency, he not only misrepresented it, but cut short the kind of analysis that would recognise these inhuman and destructive forces wherever they appeared, under whatever names and masked by whatever ideology . . . In projecting a world that is all too recognisable, Orwell confused us about its structures, its ideologies, and the possibilities of resisting it.' See Raymond Williams, *Orwell* (London: Fontana, 1984), p. 77.

19 Elaine Scarry, 'A Defense of Poesy', in Abbott Gleason, Jack Goldsmith, and Martha C. Nussbaum, eds., *On Nineteen Eighty-Four: Orwell and our Future* (Princeton: Princeton University Press, 2005), p. 27.

20 Orwell is far from being the only writer to draw on the resources of hell: 'Any work of literature that deals with conflict, pain, suffering, grief, misery, and disaster . . . bears an analogy to hell, where life lacks love, bliss, and harmony.' See Elena Volkova, 'Visions of Heaven and Hell', in Andrew Haas, David Jasper and Elizabeth Jay, eds., *The Oxford Handbook of English Literature and Theology* (Oxford: Oxford University Press, 2007), p. 795.

21 George Orwell, *Nineteen Eighty-Four* (1949; repr. Harmondsworth: Penguin Books, 1987), p. 227.

22 Andrew Tate, *Contemporary Fiction and Christianity* (London: Continuum 2008), p. 108.

23 Ibid., p. 123.

24 The quotation is from Kevin Vanhoozer, who makes an interesting distinction between the utopian 'news from nowhere' and the eschatological 'news from elsewhere'. See Vanhoozer, *The Drama of Doctrine*, p. 357.

25 Tate, *Contemporary Fiction and Christianity*, p. 123.

26 Orwell, *Nineteen Eighty-Four*, p. 229.

27 Ibid., p. 90.

28 Ibid., pp. 61, 75.

29 The influence of Dante on Beckett is explored at length by Daniela Caselli in *Beckett's Dantes: Intertextuality in the Fiction and Criticism* (Manchester: Manchester University Press, 2005).

30 Malcolm Pittock, 'The Hell of Nineteen Eighty-Four', *Essays in Criticism* 47. 2 (1997), p. 145.

31 Orwell, *Nineteen Eighty-Four*, p. 193.

32 Ibid., pp. 211–12.

33 For a useful and suggestive exploration of references to hell in contemporary western literature, see Rachel Falconer, *Hell in Contemporary Literature: Western Descent Narratives since 1945* (Edinburgh: Edinburgh University Press, 2005).

34 Pittock, 'The Hell of Nineteen Eighty-Four', p. 147.

35 Orwell, *Nineteen Eighty-Four*, pp. 63, 130.

36 Ibid., p. 202. The phrase 'We are the dead' can be found on pp. 111, 143 and 174.

37 N. T. Wright, *The Resurrection of the Son of God* (London: SPCK, 2003), pp. 88–9.

38 There are considerable differences between and within Jewish and Christian understandings of resurrection. See Wright, *The Resurrection of the Son of God*.

39 Orwell, *Nineteen Eighty-Four*, p. 233.

40 Ibid., p. 227.

41 Ibid., p. 227.

42 Ibid., p. 27.

43 The quotation is from the first line of the song sung by the women hanging out washing: 'It was only an 'opeless fancy'. Ibid., p. 113.

44 Ibid., pp. 103, 107.

45 Ibid., p. 9.

46 Ibid., p. 10.

47 Ibid., p. 25.

48 Ibid., p. 237.

49 On the imaginative possibilities of grammar, see George Steiner, *After Babel: Aspects of Language and Translation*, 3rd ed. (Oxford: Oxford University Press, 1998). For an informative engagement with Steiner, see Trevor Hart, 'Imagination for the Kingdom of God?: Hope, Promise, and the Transformative Power of an Imagined Future', in Richard Bauckham, ed., *God Will Be All In All: The Eschatology of Jürgen Moltmann* (Edinburgh: T & T Clark, 1999).

50 Orwell, *Nineteen Eighty-Four*, p. 44.

51 Walter Brueggemann, *Cadences of Home: Preaching among Exiles* (Louisville: Westminster John Knox Press, 1997), p. 15. Ricoeur talks about 'limit experiences' and 'limit expressions' in his essay, 'Biblical Hermeneutics', *Semeia* 4 (1975): 107–45.

52 Walter Brueggemann, *The Prophetic Imagination*, 2nd ed. (Minneapolis: Fortress Press, 2001), p. 65.

53 Douglas Coupland, *Girlfriend in a Coma* (1998; repr. London: Harper Perennial, 2004), p. 269.

54 Ibid., p. 270.

55 Ibid., pp. 3, 277.

56 John D. Caputo, *Demythologizing Heidegger* (Bloomington: Indiana University Press, 1993), p. 201. Brueggemann praises Caputo's 'stunning' opposition between the 'prophetic imagination' of 'Emmanuel Levinas, Jacques Derrida, and Jean-Francois Lyotard', and the 'totalizing universalism' of Martin Heidegger. See *Texts that Linger, Words that Explode: Listening to Prophetic Voices* (Minneapolis: Fortress Press, 2000), pp. 18–19.

57 Coupland, *Girlfriend in a Coma*, pp. 270–1.

58 Ibid., p. 281.

59 Andrew Tate, *Douglas Coupland* (Manchester: Manchester University Press, 2007), p. 156.

60 Bauckham and Hart, *Hope Against Hope*, p. 42.

61 John Caputo, *The Prayers and Tears of Jacques Derrida: Religion without Religion* (Bloomington: Indiana University Press, 1997), p. 70.

62 Jürgen Moltmann, *The Way of Jesus Christ: Christology in Messianic Dimensions* (1989; trans. M. Kohl, London: SCM Press 1990), p. 215.

63 Wright, *The Resurrection of the Son of God*, p. 129.

64 Orwell, *Nineteen Eighty-Four*, pp. 103, 215.

65 Coupland, *Girlfriend in a Coma*, p. 88.

66 Ibid., p. 116.

67 Ibid., p. 280.

68 Ibid., p. 60.

69 Ibid., p. 271.

70 Tate, *Douglas Coupland*, p. 154.

71 Wright, *The Resurrection of the Son of God*, pp. 127–8.

72 Coupland, *Girlfriend in a Coma*, p. 269.

73 Gunton, *The Christian Faith*, p. 152.

74 Bauckham and Hart, *Hope Against Hope*, pp. 39–40.

75 Coupland, *Girlfriend in a Coma*, pp. 280–1.

76 Bauckham and Hart, *Hope Against Hope*, pp. 126–7. For a thoughtful discussion of the implications of bodily resurrection for questions of personal identity in the science fiction of Doris Lessing, see chapter 4 of Fiddes, *The Promised End*.

77 Coupland, *Girlfriend in a Coma*, p. 281.

78 Janet Martin Soskice, 'Resurrection and the New Jerusalem', in Stephen Davis, Daniel Kendall and Gerald O'Collins, eds., *The Resurrection* (Oxford University Press, 1997), p. 45.

79 Coupland, *Girlfriend in a Coma*, p. 274.

80 Richard Bauckham, 'Eschatology' in John Webster, Kathryn Tanner and Iain Torrance, eds., *The Oxford Handbook of Systematic Theology* (Oxford: Oxford University Press, 2007), p. 310.

81 Richard Bauckham, 'The Future of Jesus Christ', in Markus Bockmuehl, ed., *The Cambridge Companion to Jesus* (Cambridge: Cambridge University Press, 2001), p. 271.

82 Adorno, 'Trying to Understand *Endgame*', p. 275.

Bibliography

Acosta, Ana, *Reading Genesis in the Long Eighteenth Century: From Milton to Mary Shelley* (Aldershot: Ashgate, 2006)

Adams, Marilyn McCord, *Horrendous Evils and the Goodness of God* (Ithaca: Cornell University Press, 1999)

—, *Christ and Horrors: The Coherence of Christology* (Cambridge: Cambridge University Press, 2006)

Adorno, Theodor, *Notes to Literature* Vol. 1, trans. Shierry Weber Nicholsen (New York: Columbia University Press, 1991)

Anderson, Mark M., *Kafka's Clothes: Ornament and Aestheticism in the Habsburg Fin de Siècle* (Oxford: Clarendon Press, 1992)

Aquinas, Thomas, *Summa Theologica*, 3 vols. (trans. English Dominican Fathers, London: Burns & Oates, 1947–8)

Arendt, Hannah, *Eichmann in Jerusalem: A Report on the Banality of Evil* (Harmondsworth: Penguin, 1994)

Atwood, Margaret, *The Handmaid's Tale* (1985; repr. London: Vintage, 1996)

—, *Oryx and Crake* (London: Bloomsbury, 2003)

Badiou, Alain, *Saint Paul: The Foundation of Universalism* (1997; trans. Ray Brassier, Stanford: Stanford University Press, 2003)

Bakhtin, Mikhail, *The Dialogic Imagination: Four Essays*, trans. Caryl Emerson and Michael Holquist (Austin: University of Texas Press, 1981)

Balthasar, Hans Urs von, *Theo-Drama: Theological Dramatic Theory*, 5 vols. (trans. Graham Harrison, San Francisco: Ignatius Press, 1988–98)

Banzer, Judith, 'Compound Manner: Emily Dickinson and the Metaphysical Poets', *American Literature* 32. 4 (1961): 417–33

Barthes, Roland, *Image, Music, Text* (1977; repr. London: Fontana Press, 1987)

—, *Mythologies* (1957; trans. Annette Lavers, London: Vintage, 1993)

Barton, John, ed., *The Cambridge Companion to Biblical Interpretation* (Cambridge: Cambridge University Press, 1998)

Bauckham, Richard, 'The Future of Jesus Christ', in Markus Bockmuehl, ed., *The Cambridge Companion to Jesus* (Cambridge: Cambridge University Press, 2001)

—, 'Eschatology', in John Webster, Kathryn Tanner and Iain Torrance, eds., *The Oxford Handbook of Systematic Theology* (Oxford: Oxford University Press, 2007)

Bauckham, Richard, ed., *God Will Be All in All: The Eschatology of Jürgen Moltmann* (Edinburgh: T & T Clark, 1999)

Bauckham, Richard and Trevor Hart, *Hope Against Hope: Christian Eschatology at the Turn of the Millennium* (Grand Rapids, Eerdmans, 1999)

Beckett, Samuel, *Waiting for Godot* (New York: Grove Press, 1954)

—, *Endgame* (London: Faber, 1958)

Beer, Gillian, *Darwin's Plots: Evolutionary Narrative in Darwin, George Eliot, and Nineteenth-Century Fiction* 2nd ed. (Cambridge: Cambridge University Press, 2000)

Begbie, Jeremy S., *Theology, Music and Time* (Cambridge: Cambridge University Press, 2000)

Bell, Ilona, 'Gender Matters: The Women in Donne's Poems', in Achsah Guibbory, ed., *The Cambridge Companion to John Donne* (Cambridge: Cambridge University Press, 2006)

Bhabha, Homi K., *The Location of Culture* (New York: Routledge, 1994)

—, 'Unpacking My Library . . . Again', in Iain Chambers and Lidia Curti, eds., *The Post-Colonial Question: Common Skies, Divided Horizons* (London and New York: Routledge, 1996)

Bigelow, Gordon, *Fiction, Famine and the Rise of Economics in Victorian Britain and Ireland* (Cambridge: Cambridge University Press, 2003)

Blake, William, *Blake's Poetry and Designs*, eds. Mary Lynn Johnson and John E. Grant (New York: Norton, 1980)

Blank, Paula, 'Comparing Sappho to Philaenis: John Donne's "Homepoetics"', *PMLA* 110. 3 (1995): 358–68.

Bloom, Harold, Paul De Man, Jacques Derrida, Geoffrey H. Hartman and J. Hillis Miller, *Deconstruction and Criticism* (1979; repr. London: Continuum, 2004)

Bockmuehl, Markus, ed., *The Cambridge Companion to Jesus* (Cambridge: Cambridge University Press, 2001)

Bradley, Arthur, *Negative Theology and Modern French Philosophy* (London: Routledge, 2004)

Brauner, David, *Philip Roth* (Manchester: Manchester University Press, 2007)

Bretherton, Luke, *Hospitality as Holiness: Christian Witness Amid Moral Diversity* (Aldershot: Ashgate, 2006)

Bruce, Steve, *Fundamentalism* (Cambridge: Polity Press, 2000)

Brueggemann, Walter, *Cadences of Home: Preaching among Exiles* (Louisville: Westminster John Knox Press, 1997)

—, *Texts That Linger, Words that Explode: Listening to Prophetic Voices* (Minneapolis: Fortress Press, 2000)

—, *The Prophetic Imagination* 2nd ed. (Minneapolis: Fortress Press, 2001)

Bryden, Mary, *Samuel Beckett and the Idea of God* (Basingstoke: Macmillan, 1998)

Burnham, Douglas and Enrico Giaccherini, eds., *The Poetics of Transubstantiation: From Theology to Metaphor* (Aldershot: Ashgate, 2005)

Butler, Judith, *Gender Trouble: Feminism and the Subversion of Identity* (New York: Routledge, 1990)

—, *Bodies that Matter: On the Discursive Limits of 'Sex'* (New York: Routledge, 1993).

Caputo, John D., *Demythologizing Heidegger* (Bloomington: Indiana University Press, 1993)

—, *The Prayers and Tears of Jacques Derrida: Religion without Religion* (Bloomington: Indiana University Press, 1997)

Carey, John, 'Milton's Satan', in Dennis Danielson, ed., *The Cambridge Companion to Milton* 2nd ed., (Cambridge: Cambridge University Press, 1999)

Carroll, David, *George Eliot and the Conflict of Interpretations: A Reading of the Novels* (Cambridge: Cambridge University Press, 1992)

Carter, Angela, *The Passion of New Eve* (1977; repr. London: Virago, 1982)

—, *The Sadeian Woman* (London: Virago, 1979)

—, 'Notes from the Front Line', in Michelene Wandor, ed., *On Gender and Writing* (London: Pandora Press, 1983).

Caselli, Daniela, *Beckett's Dantes: Intertextuality in the Fiction and Criticism* (Manchester: Manchester University Press, 2005)

Chambers, Iain and Lidia Curti, eds., *The Post-Colonial Question: Common Skies, Divided Horizons* (London: Routledge, 1998)

Chapman, Alison, *The Afterlife of Christina Rossetti* (Basingstoke: Macmillan, 2000)

Chesterton, G. K., *Heretics* (1905; repr. London: The Bodley Head Ltd, 1928)

Cixous, Hélène, *Three Steps on the Ladder of Writing* (New York: Columbia University Press, 1993)

Coakley, Sarah, '"Batter my Heart…?" On Sexuality, Spirituality, and the Christian Doctrine of the Trinity', *Graven Images* II (1995): 74–83

Coleridge, Samuel Taylor, *The Major Works*, ed. H. L. Jackson (Oxford: Oxford World's Classics, 2000)

Con-Sherbok, Dan, ed., *The Salman Rushdie Controversy in Interreligious Dialogue* (Lampeter: Edwin Mellon Press, 1990)

Cosslett, Tess, 'Intertextuality in Oranges Are Not the Only Fruit: The Bible, Malory, and Jane Eyre', in Helena Grice and Tim Woods, eds., *'I'm telling you stories': Jeanette Winterson and the Politics of Reading* (Amsterdam: Rodopi, 1998)

Coupland, Douglas, *Girlfriend in a Coma* (1998; repr. London: Harper Perennial, 2004)

Cox, John D., *Seeming Knowledge: Shakespeare and Skeptical Faith* (Waco: Baylor University Press, 2007)

Cunningham, David S. 'The Trinity', in Kevin J. Vanhoozer, ed., *The Cambridge Companion to Postmodern Theology* (Cambridge: Cambridge University Press, 2003)

Cunningham, Valentine, *In the Reading Gaol: Postmodernity, Texts and History* (Oxford: Blackwell, 1994)

D'Amico, Diane, *Christina Rossetti: Faith, Gender and Time* (Baton Rouge: Louisiana State University Press, 1999)

Danielson, Dennis, ed. *The Cambridge Companion to Milton* 2nd ed. (Cambridge: Cambridge University Press, 1999)

Davies, Brian, *The Thought of Thomas Aquinas* (Oxford: Clarendon Press, 1992)

Davies, Oliver, *The Creativity of God: Word, Eucharist, Reason* (Cambridge: Cambridge University Press, 2004)

Davies, Oliver and Denys Turner, eds., *Silence and the Word: Negative Theology and Incarnation* (Cambridge: Cambridge University Press, 2002)

Davis, Stephen, Daniel Kendall and Gerald O'Collins, eds., *The Resurrection* (Oxford: Oxford University Press, 1997)

De Man, Paul, *Blindness and Insight: Essays in the Rhetoric of Contemporary Criticism* (Minneapolis: University of Minnesota Press, 1971)

Derrida, Jacques, *Acts of Literature*, ed. Derek Attridge (New York: Routledge, 1992)

—, *Given Time: I. Counterfeit Money* (1991; trans. Peggy Kamuf, Chicago: The University of Chicago Press, 1994)

—, *Of Grammatology* (1967; trans. Gayatri Chakravorty Spivak, Baltimore: Johns Hopkins University Press, 1997)

Detweiler, Robert and David Jasper, eds., *Religion and Literature: A Reader* (Louisville: John Knox Press, 2000)

Dickens, Charles, *Bleak House*, ed. Norman Page (Harmondsworth: Penguin Books, 1971)

Dickinson, Emily, *The Complete Poems*, ed. Thomas H. Johnson (London: Faber & Faber, 1975)

Dillon, Janette, *The Cambridge Introduction to Shakespearean Tragedies* (Cambridge: Cambridge University Press, 2007)

DisPaquale, Theresa M., *Literature and Sacrament: The Sacred and the Secular in John Donne* (1999; repr. Cambridge: James Clarke & Co., 2001)

Dolin, Kieran, *Fiction and the Law: Legal Discourse in Victorian and Modernist Literature* (Cambridge: Cambridge University Press, 1999)

Donne, John, *John Donne: The Complete English Poems*, ed. A. J. Smith (Harmondsworth: Penguin, 1986)

Doriani, Beth Maclay, *Emily Dickinson, Daughter of a Prophecy* (Amherst: University of Massachusetts Press, 1996)

Eliot, George, *Silas Marner*, ed. David Carroll (Harmondsworth: Penguin, 1996)

Evans, G. R., *Augustine on Evil* (Cambridge: Cambridge University Press, 1982)

Falconer, Rachel, *Hell in Contemporary Literature: Western Descent Narratives since 1945* (Edinburgh: Edinburgh University Press, 2005)

Fenton, Mary, *Milton's Places of Hope: Spiritual and Spiritual Connections of Hope with Land* (Aldershot: Ashgate, 2006)

Fergusson, David, 'Eschatology', in Colin Gunton, ed., *The Cambridge Companion to Christian Doctrine* (Cambridge: Cambridge University Press, 1997)

Ferretter, Luke, *Towards A Christian Literary Theory* (Basingstoke: Palgrave, 2002)

Fiddes, Paul S., *Freedom and Limit: A Dialogue Between Literature and Christian Doctrine* (New York: St Martin's Press, 1991)

—, *Participating in God: A Pastoral Doctrine of the Trinity* (London: Darton, Longman and Todd, 2000)

—, *The Promised End: Eschatology in Theology and Literature* (Oxford: Blackwell, 2000)

—, 'The Passion Story in Literature', in Andrew Haas, David Jasper and Elisabeth Jay, eds., *The Oxford Handbook to English Literature and Theology* (Oxford: Oxford University Press, 2007)

Finney, Brian, 'Briony's Stand Against Oblivion: The Making of Fiction in Ian McEwan's Atonement', *The Journal of Modern Literature* 27. 3 (2004): 66–82

Fisch, Harold, *New Stories for Old: Biblical Patterns in the Novel* (Basingstoke: Macmillan, 1998)

—, *The Biblical Presence in Shakespeare, Milton and Blake* (Oxford: Clarendon Press, 1999)

Fish, Stanley, *Surprised by Sin: The Reader in Paradise Lost* (London: Macmillan, 1967)

—, *Is There A Text in This Class?: The Authority of Interpretive Communities* (Cambridge, MA: Harvard University Press, 1980)

—, 'Masculine Persuasive Force: Donne and Verbal and Power', in Elizabeth D. Harvey and Katharine Eisaman Maus, eds., *Soliciting Interpretation: Literary Theory and Seventeenth-Century English Poetry* (Chicago: The University of Chicago Press, 1990)

—, *How Milton Works* (Cambridge, MA: Harvard University Press, 2001)

Frei, Hans, *The Eclipse of Biblical Narrative* (New Haven: Yale University Press, 1974)

Frye, Northrop, *The Great Code: The Bible and Literature* (London: Routledge and Kegan Paul, 1982)

Gadamer, Hans-Georg, *Truth and Method* (1960; 2nd rev. ed., trans. Joel Weinsheimer and Donald G. Marshall, London: Continuum, 2004)

Gamble, Sarah, *Angela Carter: Writing from the Front Line* (Edinburgh: Edinburgh University Press, 1997)

Garrett, Peter K., *Gothic Reflections: Narrative Force in Nineteenth-Century Fiction* (Ithaca: Cornell University Press, 2003)

Gleason, Abbott, Jack Goldsmith and Martha C. Nussbaum, eds., *On Nineteen Eighty-Four: Orwell and our Future* (Princeton: Princeton University Press, 2005)

Gnagnatti, Anita, 'Discarding God's Handbook: Winterson's Oranges Are Not the Only Fruit and the Tension of Intertextuality', in Mark Knight and Thomas Woodman, eds., *Biblical Religion and the Novel, 1700–2000* (Aldershot: Ashgate, 2006)

Grice, Helena and Tim Woods, eds., *'I'm telling you stories': Jeanette Winterson and the Politics of Reading* (Amsterdam: Rodopi, 1998)

Guibbory, Achsah, ed., *The Cambridge Companion to John Donne* (Cambridge: Cambridge University Press, 2006)

Gunton, Colin, *The Actuality of Atonement: A Study of Metaphor, Relationality and the Christian Tradition* (Edinburgh: T & T Clark, 1988)

—, 'Trinity, Ontology and Anthropology: Towards a Renewal of the Doctrine of the *Imago Dei*', in Christoph Schwöbel and Colin E. Gunton, eds., *Persons, Divine and Human: King's College Essays in Theological Anthropology* (Edinburgh: T & T Clark, 1991)

—, *The One, the Three and the Many* (Cambridge: Cambridge University Press, 1993)

—, *The Promise of Trinitarian Theology* 2nd ed., (Edinburgh: T & T Clark, 1997)

—, *The Christian Faith: An Introduction to Christian Doctrine* (Oxford: Blackwell, 2002)

Gunton, Colin, ed., *The Cambridge Companion to Christian Doctrine* (Cambridge: Cambridge University Press, 1997)

Gurnah, Abdulrazak, ed., *The Cambridge Companion to Salman Rushdie* (Cambridge: Cambridge University Press, 2007)

Haas, Andrew, David Jasper and Elisabeth Jay, eds., *The Oxford Handbook of English Literature and Theology* (Oxford: Oxford University Press, 2007)

Hart, Kevin, *The Trespass of the Sign: Deconstruction, Theology and Philosophy* rev. ed. (New York: Fordham University Press, 2007)

Hart, Kevin and Yvonne Sherwood, eds., *Derrida and Religion: Other Testaments* (London: Routledge, 2005)

Hart, Trevor, 'Imagination for the Kingdom of God?: Hope, Promise, and the Transformative Power of an Imagined Future', in Richard Bauckham, ed., *God Will Be All In All: The Eschatology of Jürgen Moltmann* (Edinburgh: T & T Clark, 1999)

Hartman, Geoffrey, *Saving the Text* (Baltimore: Johns Hopkins University Press, 1981)

—, *A Critic's Journey: Literary Reflections 1958–1998* (New Haven: Yale University Press, 1999)

—, *Scars of the Spirit: The Struggle Against Inauthenticity* (New York: Palgrave Macmillan, 2002)

Hartman, Geoffrey and Sanford Budick, eds., *Midrash and Literature* (New Haven: Yale University Press, 1986)

Harvey, Elizabeth D. and Katherine Eisaman Maus, eds., *Soliciting Interpretation: Literary Theory and Seventeenth-Century English Poetry* (Chicago: The University of Chicago Press, 1990)

Hauerwas, Stanley, *Unleashing the Scripture: Freeing the Bible from Captivity to America* (Nashville: Abingdon Press, 1993)

Hauerwas, Stanley and L. Gregory Jones, eds., *Why Narrative? Readings in Narrative Theology* (Grand Rapids: Eerdmans, 1989)

Hawkins, Beth, *Reluctant Theologians: Franz Kafka, Paul Celan, Edmond Jabès* (New York: Fordham University Press, 2003)

Hawthorne, Nathaniel, *The Scarlet Letter*, ed. Brian Harding (Oxford: Oxford World's Classics, 2007)

Helsinger, Elizabeth K., 'Consumer Power and the Utopia of Desire: Christina Rossetti's "Goblin Market"', *ELH* 58.4 (1991): 903–33

Henstra, Sarah M., 'The Pressure of New Wine: Performative Reading in Angela Carter's *The Sadeian Woman*', *Textual Practice*. 13. 1 (1999): 97–117

Holt, Terence, '"Men Sell Not Such in Any Town': Exchange in Goblin Market', *Victorian Poetry* 28. 1 (1990): 51–67

Horne, Brian, 'Theology in the Narrative Mode', in Leslie Houlden and Peter Byrne, eds., *Companion Encyclopedia of Theology* (London: Routledge, 1995)

—, *Imagining Evil* (London: Darton, Longman and Todd, 1996)

Houldon, Leslie and Peter Byrne, eds., *Companion Encyclopedia of Theology* (London: Routledge, 1995)

Jasper, David, *The Study of Religion and Literature: An Introduction* 2nd ed. (Basingstoke: Macmillan, 1992)

—, *The Sacred Desert: Religion, Literature, Art, and Culture* (Oxford: Blackwell, 2004)

Jeeves, Malcolm, ed., *From Cells to Souls – And Beyond: Changing Portraits of Human Nature* (Grand Rapids: Eerdmans, 2004)

Jennings, Theodore W., *Reading Derrida/Thinking Paul: On Justice* (Stanford: Stanford University Press, 2006)

Jenson, Robert, 'The Church and the Sacraments', in Colin Gunton, ed., *The Cambridge Companion to Christian Doctrine* (Cambridge: Cambridge University Press, 1997)

—, *Systematic Theology*, 2 vols.. (New York: Oxford University Press, 1997–9)

Johnson, Jeffrey, *The Theology of John Donne* (Cambridge: D. S. Brewer, 1999)

Kafka, Franz, *The Trial* (1925; trans. Idris Parry, Harmondsworth: Penguin Books, 1994)

Kant, Immanuel, *The Conflict of the Faculties* (1798; trans. Mary J. Gregor, Lincoln: University of Nebraska Press, 1979)

Kearney, Richard, 'Between Tradition and Utopia: The Hermeneutical Problem of Myth', in David Wood, ed., *On Paul Ricoeur: Narrative and Interpretation* (London: Routledge, 1991)

—, *On Paul Ricoeur: The Owl of Minerva* (Aldershot: Ashgate, 2004)

Kermode, Frank, *The Sense of an Ending* (Oxford: Oxford University Press, 1967)

Knight, Mark, *Chesterton and Evil* (New York: Fordham University Press, 2004)

Knight, Mark and Emma Mason, *Nineteenth-Century Religion and Literature: An Introduction* (Oxford: Oxford University Press, 2006)

Knight, Mark and Thomas Woodman, eds., *Biblical Religion and the Novel, 1700–2000* (Aldershot: Ashgate, 2006)

Kreger, Erika M., '"Depravity Dressed Up in a Fascinating Garb": Sentimental Motifs and the Seduced Hero(ine) in The Scarlet Letter', *Nineteenth-Century Literature* 54. 3 (1999): 308–35.

Kugel, James L., 'Two Introductions to Midrash,' in Geoffrey H. Hartman and Sanford Budick, eds., *Midrash and Literature* (New Haven: Yale University Press, 1986)

Kuortti, Joel, *Place of the Sacred: The Rhetoric of the Satanic Verses Affair* (Frankfurt: Peter Lang, 1997)

—, 'The Satanic Verses: "To be born again, first you have to die"', in Abdulrazak Gurnah, ed., *The Cambridge Companion to Salman Rushdie* (Cambridge: Cambridge University Press, 2007)

Larkin, Peter, 'Repetition, Difference and Liturgical Participation in Coleridge's "The Ancient Mariner"', *Literature and Theology* 21. 2 (2007): 146–59.

Larson, Janet L., 'The Battle of Biblical Books in Esther's Narrative', *Nineteenth-Century Fiction* 38. 2 (1983): 131–60.

—, *Dickens and the Broken Scripture* (Athens: The University of Georgia Press, 1985)

Leggatt, Alexander, *Shakespeare's Tragedies: Violation and Identity* (Cambridge: Cambridge University Press, 2005)

Lemon, Rebecca, *Treason by Words: Literature, Law, and Rebellion in Shakespeare's England* (Ithaca: Cornell University Press, 2006)

Lentricchia, Frank and Andrew DuBois, eds., *Close Reading: The Reader* (Durham: Duke University Press, 2002)

Levinas, Emmanuel, *The Levinas Reader*, ed. Sean Hand (Oxford: Blackwell, 1989)

—, *Beyond the Verse*, trans. Garry D. Mole (London: Athlone, 1994)

Levinson, Marjorie, 'What is New Formalism?' *PMLA* 122. 2 (2007): 558–69

Lewis, C. S., *A Preface to Paradise Lost* (London: Oxford University Press, 1942)

Lindbeck, George, *The Nature of Doctrine: Religion and Theology in a Postliberal Age* (London: SPCK, 1984)

Loughlin, Gerard, *Telling God's Story: Bible, Church and Narrative Theology* (Cambridge: Cambridge University Press, 1996)

Louis, Margot K., 'Emily Dickinson's Sacrament of Starvation', *Nineteenth-Century Literature* 43. 4 (1988): 346–60.

Markham, Ian S., *A Theology of Engagement* (Oxford: Blackwell, 2003)

Marshall, Bruce D., 'Christ and the Cultures: the Jewish People and Christian Theology', in Colin Gunton, ed., *The Cambridge Companion to Christian Doctrine* (Cambridge: Cambridge University Press, 1997)

Martin, Wendy, ed., *The Cambridge Companion to Emily Dickinson* (Cambridge: Cambridge University Press, 2002)

Martz, Louis L., *The Poetry of Meditation* (New Haven: Yale University Press, 1954)

Mathewes, Charles, *Evil and the Augustinian Tradition* (Cambridge: Cambridge University Press, 2001)

McCabe, Herbert, *God Matters* (London: Geoffrey Chapman, 1987)

McEwan, Ian, *Atonement* (London: Jonathan Cape, 2001)

McGann, Jerome, *The Beauty of Inflections: Literary Investigations in Historical Method and Theory* (Oxford: Clarendon Press, 1985)

McLane, Maureen, *Romanticism and the Human Sciences* (Cambridge: Cambridge University Press, 2000)

Meeks, M. Douglas, 'The Social Trinity and Property', in Miroslav Volf and Michael Welker, eds., *God's Life in Trinity* (Minneapolis: Fortress, 2006)

Milbank, John, 'Can a Gift be Given? Prolegomena to a Future Trinitarian Metaphysic', *Modern Theology* 11. 1 (1995): 119–61.

Milbank, John, Catherine Pickstock and Graham Ward, eds., *Radical Orthodoxy* (London: Routledge, 1999)

Miller, Don F., ed., 'Beyond the Rushdie Affair', in special issue of *Third Text: Third World Perspectives on Contemporary Art & Culture* 11 (Summer 1990)

Miller, J. Hills, *On Literature* (London: Routledge, 2002)

—, 'The Critic as Host', in Harold Bloom, Paul De Man, Jacques Derrida, Geoffrey H. Hartman and J. Hillis Miller, *Deconstruction and Criticism* (1979; repr. London: Continuum, 2004)

Milton, John, *Paradise Lost*, eds., Stephen Orgel and Jonathan Goldberg (Oxford: Oxford World's Classics, 2004)

Moltmann, Jürgen, *Theology of Hope: On the Ground and the Implications of a Christian Eschatology* (1964; trans. J. W. Leitch, London: SCM Press, 1967)

—, *The Way of Jesus Christ: Christology in Messianic Dimensions* (1989; trans. M. Kohl, London: SCM Press, 1990)

—, *The Coming of God: Christian Eschatology* (1995; trans. M. Kohl, London: SCM Press, 1996)

Moore, Lorrie, 'The Wrath of Athena', *The New York Times*, 7 May 2000

Moore, Stephen D., *Literary Criticism and the Gospels: The Theoretical Challenge* (New Haven: Yale University Press, 1989)

Mousley, Andrew, 'Transubstantiating Love: John Donne and Cultural Criticism', in Douglas Burnham and Enrico Giaccherini, eds., *The Poetics of Transubstantiation: From Theology to Metaphor* (Aldershot: Ashgate, 2005)

O'Collins, Gerald, 'John Donne on the Trinity', in Miroslav Volf and Michael Welker, eds., *God's Life in Trinity* (Minneapolis: Fortress, 2006)

Orwell, George, *Nineteen Eighty-Four* (1949; repr. Harmondsworth: Penguin Books, 1987)

Orzeck, Martin and Robert Wesibuch, eds., *Dickinson and Audience* (Ann Arbor: The University of Michigan Press, 1996)

Quash, Ben, *Theology and the Drama of History* (Cambridge: Cambridge University Press, 2005)

Parsons, Susan, ed., *The Cambridge Companion to Feminist Theology* (Cambridge: Cambridge University Press, 2002)

Patrides, C. A., *Milton and the Christian Tradition* (Oxford: Clarendon Press, 1966)

Paulson, Ronald, *Sin and Evil: Moral Values in Literature* (New Haven: Yale University Press, 2007)

Peltason, Timothy, 'Esther's Will', *ELH* 59. 3 (1992): 671–91.

Pesso-Miquel, Catherine and Klaus Stierstorfer, eds., *Fundamentalism and Literature* (Basingstoke: Palgrave, 2007)

Pittock, Malcolm, 'The Hell of Nineteen Eighty-Four', *Essays in Criticism* 47. 2 (1997): 143–64

Prickett, Stephen, *Words and the Word: Language, Poetics and Biblical Interpretation* (Cambridge: Cambridge University Press, 1986)

Pullman, Philip, *His Dark Materials* (London: Scholastic, 2001)

Purcell, Michael, *Levinas and Theology* (Cambridge: Cambridge University Press, 2006)

Ranasinha, Ruvani 'The *fatwa* and its aftermath', in Abdulrazak Gurnah, ed., *The Cambridge Companion to Salman Rushdie* (Cambridge: Cambridge University Press, 2007)

Rauch, Alan, *Useful Knowledge: The Victorians, Morality, and the March of the Intellect* (Durham: Duke University Press, 2001)

Robbins, Jill, 'Kafka's Parables', in Geoffrey H. Hartman and Sanford Budick, eds., *Midrash and Literature* (New Haven: Yale University Press, 1986)

Ricoeur, Paul, 'Biblical Hermeneutics', *Semeia* 4 (1975): 107–45

—, *Time and Narrative*, 3 vols. (1983–5; trans. Kathleen McLaughlin and David Pellauer, Chicago: The University of Chicago Press, 1984–8)

—, *From Text to Action: Essays in Hermeneutics II*, trans. Kathleen Blamey and John B. Thompson, (Evanston: Northwestern University Press, 1991)

—, 'Life in Quest of Narrative', in David Wood, ed., *On Paul Ricoeur: Narrative and Interpretation* (London: Routledge, 1991)

—, *The Just* (1995; trans. David Pellauer, Chicago: The University of Chicago Press, 2000)

—, 'Myth as the Bearer of Possible Worlds', in Richard Kearney, *On Paul Ricoeur: The Owl of Minerva* (Aldershot: Ashgate, 2004)

Rossetti, Christina, *Poems*, ed. Jan Marsh (London: Everyman, 1996)

Roth, Philip, *The Human Stain* (London: Vintage, 2001)

Royal, Derek Parker, 'Plotting the Frames of Subjectivity: Identity, Death, and Narrative in Philip Roth's *The Human Stain*', *Contemporary Literature* 47. 1 (2006): 114–40.

Rushdie, Salman, *Imaginary Homelands: Essays and Criticism 1981–91* (1991; rev. ed., London: Granta Books, 1992)

—, *The Satanic Verses* (1988; repr. London: Vintage Books, 2006)

Saunders, Ben, *Desiring Donne: Poetry, Sexuality, Interpretation* (Cambridge, MA: Harvard University Press, 2006)

Scarry, Elaine, 'A Defense of Poesy', in Abbott Gleason, Jack Goldsmith, and Martha C. Nussbaum, eds., *On Nineteen Eighty-Four: Orwell and our Future* (Princeton: Princeton University Press, 2005)

Schad, John, *Queer Fish: Christian Unreason from Darwin to Derrida* (Brighton: Sussex Academic Press, 2004)

Schad, John, ed., *Writing the Bodies of Christ: The Church from Carlyle to Derrida* (Aldershot: Ashgate, 2001)

Schramm, Jan-Melissa, *Testimony and Advocacy in Victorian Law, Literature and Culture* (Cambridge: Cambridge University Press, 2000)

Schrift, Alan, ed., *The Logic of the Gift: Toward an Ethic of Generosity* (New York: Routledge, 1997)

Schwartz, Regina, *Remembering and Repeating: Biblical Creation in Paradise Lost* (Cambridge: Cambridge University Press, 1988)

—, 'Communion and Conversation', in Graham Ward, ed., *The Blackwell Companion to Postmodern Theology* (Oxford: Blackwell, 2001)

Schwöbel, Christoph and Colin E. Gunton, eds., *Persons, Divine and Human: King's College Essays in Theological Anthropology* (Edinburgh: T & T Clark, 1991)

Shakespeare, William, *Macbeth*, ed. Kenneth Muir (Arden Shakespeare: repr. London: Routledge, 1994)

Shelley, Mary, *Frankenstein*, ed. M. K. Joseph (Oxford: Oxford World's Classics, 1998)

Sherwood, Yvonne, *The Prophet and the Prostitute: Hosea's Marriage in Literary-Theological Perspective* (Sheffield: Sheffield Academic Press, 1996)

—, *A Biblical Text and Its Afterlives: The Survival of Jonah in Western Culture* (Cambridge: Cambridge University Press, 2000)

Sherwood, Yvonne, ed., *Derrida's Bible: Reading a Page of Scripture with a Little Help from Derrida* (New York: Palgrave, 2004)

Soskice, Janet Martin, *Metaphor and Religious Language* (Oxford: Clarendon Press, 1985)

—, 'Resurrection and the New Jerusalem', in Stephen Davis, Daniel Kendall and Gerald O'Collins, eds., *The Resurrection* (Oxford University Press, 1997)

—, 'Trinity and feminism', in Susan Parsons, ed., *The Cambridge Companion to Feminist Theology* (Cambridge: Cambridge University Press, 2002)

Spilka, Mark, *Dickens and Kafka: A Mutual Interpretation* (London: Dennis Dobson, 1963)

Steiner, George, *Language and Silence* (London: Faber, 1967)

—, *After Babel: Aspects of Language and Translation* 3rd ed. (Oxford: Oxford University Press, 1998)

Stierstorfer, Klaus, 'Tariq Ali and Recent Negotiations of Fundamentalism', in Catherine Pesso-Miquel and Klaus Stierstorfer, eds., *Fundamentalism and Literature* (Basingstoke: Palgrave, 2007)

Tanner, Kathryn, *Theories of Culture: A New Agenda for Theology* (Minneapolis: Fortress Press, 1997)

—, *The Economy of Grace* (Minneapolis: Fortress Press, 2005)

Tate, Andrew, *Douglas Coupland* (Manchester: Manchester University Press, 2007)

—, *Contemporary Fiction and Christianity* (London: Continuum, 2008)

Torrance, Alan J., *Persons in Communion: An Essay on Trinitarian Description and Human Participation* (Edinburgh: T & T Clark, 1996)

—, 'What is a Person?' in Malcolm Jeeves, ed., *From Cells to Souls – And Beyond: Changing Portraits of Human Nature* (Grand Rapids: Eerdmans, 2004)

Tucker, Herbert F., 'Rossetti's Goblin Marketing: Sweet to Tongue and Sound to Eye', *Representations* 82 (2003): 117–33

Vanhoozer, Kevin J., 'Philosophical Antecedents to Ricoeur's Time and Narrative', in David Wood, ed., *On Paul Ricoeur: Narrative and Interpretation* (London: Routledge, 1991)

Vanhoozer, Kevin J., *The Drama of Doctrine: A Canonical-Linguistic Approach to Christian Theology* (Louisville: Westminster John Knox Press, 2005)

Vanhoozer, Kevin J., ed., *The Cambridge Companion to Postmodern Theology* (Cambridge: Cambridge University Press, 2003)

Volf, Miroslav and Michael Welker, eds., *God's Life in Trinity* (Minneapolis: Augsburg Fortress, 2006)

Volkova, Elena, 'Visions of Heaven and Hell', in Andrew Haas, David Jasper and Elizabeth Jay, eds., *The Oxford Handbook of English Literature and Theology* (Oxford: Oxford University Press, 2007)

Wandor, Michelene, ed., *On Gender and Writing* (London: Pandora Press, 1983)

Ward, Graham, *Barth, Derrida and the Language of Theology* (Cambridge: Cambridge University Press, 1995)

—, ed., *The Blackwell Companion to Postmodern Theology* (Oxford: Blackwell, 2001)

—, '"In the daylight forever?": Language and Silence', in Oliver Davies and Denys Turner, eds., *Silence and the Word: Negative Theology and Incarnation* (Cambridge: Cambridge University Press, 2002)

Warren, Robert Penn, 'A Poem of Pure Imagination: An Experiment in Reading', in *Selected Essays* (New York: Random House, 1958)

—, *Selected Essays* (New York: Random House, 1958)

Watson, Francis, *Text, Church and Truth: Redefining Biblical Theology* (Edinburgh: T & T Clark, 1998)

Webster, John, Kathryn Tanner and Iain Torrance, eds., *The Oxford Handbook of Systematic Theology* (Oxford: Oxford University Press, 2007)

Welsh, Alexander, *Dickens Redressed: The Art of* Bleak House *and* Hard Times (New Haven: Yale University Press, 2000)

Williams, Raymond, *Orwell* (London: Fontana, 1984)

Winterson, Jeanette, *Oranges Are Not the Only Fruit* (1985; repr. London: Vintage, 2001)

Wood, David, ed., *On Paul Ricoeur: Narrative and Interpretation* (London: Routledge, 1991)

Wright, N. T., *The Resurrection of the Son of God* (London: SPCK, 2003)

Wright, Terry R. *The Religion of Humanity: The Impact of Comtean Positivism on Victorian Britain* (Cambridge: Cambridge University Press, 1986)

—, *Theology and Literature* (Oxford: Blackwell, 1988)

—, *The Genesis of Fiction: Modern Novelists as Biblical Interpreters* (Aldershot: Ashgate, 2007)

Zizioulas, John D., *Being as Communion: Studies in Personhood and the Church* (London: Darton, Longman and Todd, 1985)

Index